D0801549

IN THE CROSSHAIRS

Famous Assassinations and Attempts

from Julius Caesar to John Lennon

Stephen J. Spignesi

BARNES & NOBLE BOOKS

NEW YORK

This is for two splendid women,
Melissa Grosso
and
Colleen Payne,
who know why.

———

I was aided and abetted in the research and writing of *In the Crosshairs* and, as always, my attempt to thank everyone who helped will fall short of my true depth of appreciation. The quality of the assistance I received from many, many angels was extraordinary; any mistakes that made it into the final text are mine, and mine alone. Thank you all.

John White, Mike Lewis, Colleen Payne, Melissa Grosso, Dr. Bob McEachern, Southern Connecticut State University, Lee Mandato, Jim Cole, Ron Fry, Career Press, Martin Wolcott, University of New Haven, Stacey Farkas, Kevin Quigley, Anne Brooks, ABC News, BBC News, CNN, the *New York Times*, the *New Haven Register*, the *Los Angeles Times*, *USA Today*, Yale University Press, Gale Research, Yahoo News, *Time, Time Europe, Time Asia, Newsweek,* PBS, E!, *www.cia.gov, www.whitehouse.gov, www.fbi.gov, www.newsmax.com, www.arttoday.com, www.abe.com, www.ebay.com.*

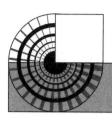

Contents

Introduction

Sic Semper Famous

Assassination is the extreme form of censorship.

—George Bernard Shaw[1]

Anybody can kill anybody.

—Lynette "Squeaky" Fromme[2]

When a famous person is attacked and mortally wounded, the medical personnel tending to him or her will often go to extreme (and obviously futile) lengths to resuscitate the victim.

When President Kennedy (page 123) was brought to Parkland Memorial Hospital in Dallas, part of his skull was missing and his brain was a bloody mess. Anyone else probably would have been declared DOA the moment he or she was wheeled in, but in Kennedy's case the doctors performed a tracheotomy; pumped in fluids, blood, and steroids; and worked 20 minutes to keep the President alive before giving up.

Indira Gandhi (page 76) was clinically dead when she was rushed to the hospital, but the doctors operated nonetheless, removing between 16 and 20 bullets from her body and even putting out a call for blood donations.

It must never be said that everything that could have been done, was not done; and, thus, the attempt to summon a miracle.

In the Crosshairs looks at assassinations and assassination attempts.

Assassination has been used for many reasons over the eons. It has been a political tool, and it has also been a manifestation of obsession, psychosis, and delusion.

Sometimes, when an assassination attempt succeeds, enormous political, cultural, and societal changes can result (as in the cases of John F. Kennedy

— 9 —

and Yitzhak Rabin, for instance). This is the exception, however, and, in most cases, the assassination has no effect whatsoever. Failed attempts become a footnote to history, usually consisting of no more than the details of where the assassin was incarcerated or when and where he (or, in the rare case, she) was executed. Arthur Bremer, who shot and wounded George Wallace (page 247), and who is currently in prison, has lamented his failure to achieve "Lee Harvey Oswald–type" assassin's fame. He has talked about the fact that not only is he unknown to most people, even his target, George Wallace, is unknown to most young people today.

Sometimes the reason for an assassination attempt is stunningly mundane. Ronald Reagan's (page 201) assassin wanted to impress an actress. Rebecca Schaeffer's (page 221) assassin was in love with her. Francisco Duran (see pages 35-37), who shot at the White House in an attempt to assassinate Bill Clinton, said that he was trying to destroy a mist connected by an umbilical cord to an alien being.

The most popular weapons for assassination among the assassins in *In The Crosshairs* are .38- and .44-caliber handguns. Among rifles, the .30-06 was preferred, followed by the AK-47 assault rifle. Knives were used less frequently, because stabbing requires close proximity to the target, as well as a personal mindset that accepts (and, in some cases, requires) physical contact with the victim.

There are creative killers here as well, assassins who turned to such exotic weapons as time bombs, butane bombs, hand grenades, an ice axe, poisoned mushrooms, a poisoned needle, swords, and even a camera tripod.

NOTE: Throughout *In the Crosshairs*, we use the term *assassin* (sometimes modified with "conspiring," "unsuccessful," and so on) when referring to the person who killed or attacked the subject— even if the person did not die from the assault. We are using the term in the spirit of the name of the secret order of Moslem fanatics who terrorized and killed Christian Crusaders and others, beginning in the 11th century A.D. Likewise, we use *assassination* in the dossier that leads off each section to describe both assassinations and attempts.

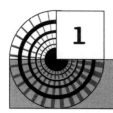

1

Thomas á Beckett

ASSASSINATED	✓
SURVIVED	—

To look upon he was slim of growth and pale of hue, with dark hair, a long nose, and a straightly featured face. Blithe of countenance was he, winning and loveable in his conversation, frank of speech in his discourses, but slightly stuttering in his talk, so keen of discernment and understanding that he could always make difficult questions plain after a wise manner.

—Robert of Cricklade[1]

Thomas á Beckett assassination

VICTIM: Thomas á Beckett

BORN: December 21, 1118

DIED: December 29, 1170

AGE When Attacked: 62

OCCUPATION: Chancellor of England, Archbishop of Canterbury, friend and enemy of King Henry II, English martyr now known as St. Thomas Beckett

ASSASSINS: Reginald FitzUrse,[2] William de Tracy, Hugh de Morville, and Richard le Breton: four over-ambitious knights in the service of corrupt King Henry II

DATE & TIME OF ATTACK: Tuesday, December 29, 1170, at dusk

LOCATION OF ATTACK: In front of the altar of St. Benedict in Canterbury Cathedral, Canterbury, England

WEAPONS: Swords

ASSASSINATION OUTCOME: After several blows from the knights' swords, including one that cracked open his skull and splattered his brains, Thomas died almost immediately.

JUDICIAL OUTCOME: The four knights, initially boastful and proud of their deed, were quickly excommunicated and had to flee to Scotland for refuge. They eventually gave themselves up to King Henry, who turned them over to the Pope for punishment. The Pontiff required them to fast, and they were then ordered to join the Crusades and spend 14 years in the Holy Land. King Henry later acknowledged his mistake in earlier accusing Thomas of theft by walking through Canterbury barefoot in a sackcloth as monks beat him with reeds.

Sometimes we have to watch what we say, especially if we happen to be the king of England.

King Henry II was traveling in France with one of his archbishops when he learned that Thomas Beckett, the highest cleric in the Church of England, had returned to England and had been met with crowds and great acclaim.

Thomas had been named Archbishop by his friend King Henry in an attempt to create an easy (but powerful) alliance between the monarchy and the church in England. Unfortunately for King Henry, things did not go as he had hoped. After the king implemented laws that would have given him control of all cases in England involving clergy, Thomas publicly denounced him and the new laws, greatly embarrassing the monarch and creating an untenable situation for King Henry.

Quick-thinking (and devious) King Henry summoned Thomas and accused him of stealing large sums of money from the Church when he was chancellor. King Henry hoped to distract the public from the Archbishop's contempt towards his authority, and there was such an uproar over the accusations that Thomas felt it wise to flee to France. He left England in October 1164 and stayed there six years in exile.

When King Henry heard that Thomas had been welcomed back to England with open arms, he was outraged. Archbishop Roger of York, who was with the king in France, stirred the monarch up even more by reminding him that he was going to have to contend with Thomas when he returned and that there would be no peace in his kingdom as long as Thomas was back in England.

It was then that King Henry angrily exclaimed (to anyone and everyone within earshot), "Who will rid me of this meddlesome priest?!"[3]

King Henry's words were heard by four of his knights who suddenly saw a great opportunity for "career advancement," so to speak. If they eliminated the "Thomas Problem" for King Henry, then they would immediately be elevated in the king's eye, and riches and privileges aplenty would soon come their way.

So what did these four ambitious knights do? They left without delay for England.

They arrived in England on December 29th and immediately set out for Canterbury. Their arrival in Canterbury was cause for great alarm, and the monks attending Thomas urged him to flee his residence and seek refuge in the cathedral, where a Vespers service was taking place at the time.

Thomas did as they asked, but the knights followed him into the cathedral and attacked him with swords. De Tracey struck first, and the others pierced him three additional times. Thomas fell to his knees, and then Breton struck Thomas on the top of the head with such force that his head actually split open and the tip of the sword broke off. Thomas's brains spilled out onto the floor of the cathedral, and the knights finished the job by spreading the archbishop's hacked-out brain matter all over the marble floor. By this time, the worshippers had fled the cathedral, and the knights followed soon thereafter, leaving Thomas's ravaged body and bloody, cracked-open head lying in a pool of his own blood and brains. Thomas's companion, Edward Grim, was wounded by one of the knight's swords, but he survived.

Three days after Thomas's murder, a series of miracles began to occur, all of which were believed to have been caused by Thomas's spirit. According to medieval texts, Thomas's spirit restored sight to the blind, gave speech to the dumb, brought hearing to the deaf, gave the ability to walk to the crippled, and reportedly even brought people back from the dead. Three years later, in 1173, Thomas was canonized St. Thomas Beckett by Pope Alexander III. His remains were initially buried behind one of the altars in the cathedral, but in 1220 they were moved to a shrine that had been specially constructed in his honor in the Trinity Chapel. Perhaps in vengeance for the disrespect shown to his namesake/ancestor by Thomas, King Henry VIII destroyed Thomas's Shrine in 1538. It is believed the martyr's remains were also destroyed at that time.

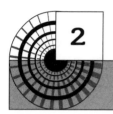

2

Alan Berg

ASSASSINATED   ✓

SURVIVED   ___

Alan Berg...is more famous in death than in life. His memory haunts many people...because his death could be read as a message: Be cautious, be prudent, be bland, never push anybody, never say what you really think, offer yourself as a hostage to the weirdos even before they make the first move. These days, a lot of people are opposed to the newfound popularity of "trash television," and no doubt they are right, and the hosts of these shows are shameless controversy-mongers. But at least they are not intimidated. Of what use is freedom of speech to those who fear to offend.
—Roger Ebert[1]

VICTIM: Alan Berg

BORN: 1934

DIED: June 18, 1984

AGE WHEN ATTACKED: 50

OCCUPATION: Controversial and confrontational radio talk-show host, self-proclaimed "Wildman of the Airwaves"

ASSASSINS: Bruce Carroll Pierce (b. 1954), 32, shooter; David Eden Lane (b. 1938), 46, driver of the getaway car; Robert Jay Mathews (1953–1984), leader/mastermind of the plot to assassinate Berg; all members of a Neo-Nazi, White Power/Aryan Resistance movement called The Order (a.k.a. Brüder Schweigen)

DATE & TIME OF ATTACK: Monday, June 18, 1984, shortly after 9 p.m.; the ambulance arrived at 9:39 p.m.; pronounced dead at 9:45 p.m.

LOCATION OF ATTACK: In the driveway of Berg's condominium in Denver, Colorado

WEAPON: A .45-caliber semi-automatic machine gun

ASSASSINATION OUTCOME: Berg died immediately from multiple gunshot wounds to the head and neck. Police found 10 spent .45-caliber shell casings in Berg's driveway; the police report showed close to 20 bullet holes in Berg. (Berg's feet were still in his car when his body was discovered.)

JUDICIAL OUTCOME: Bruce Carroll Pierce was arrested in 1985 and tried for Berg's murder. He was ultimately convicted of violating Berg's civil rights, violating the Hobbs Act, and counterfeiting. He was sentenced to 252 years in prison and is currently serving his time in Leavenworth, Kansas. David Eden Lane was arrested in March 1985 and went through three trials in three separate jurisdictions. In his first trial, in Seattle, Washington, in April 1985, he was charged with conspiracy, racketeering, and being in "The Order." He was convicted and received a 40-year sentence. At Lane's second trial, in October 1987, he was charged with violating Berg's civil rights and was convicted. He received a 150-year sentence. He appealed this sentence in 1989. Lane's third trial was in Fort Smith, Arkansas, in February 1987. He faced charges of sedition, conspiracy, and civil rights violations. Lane refused legal counsel and represented himself. The earliest Lane could be out of prison for his two prior convictions is March 29, 2035.

It was almost as though Alan Berg was daring someone to take a shot at him, and there were days on his radio show when the word almost could easily have been replaced with definitely.

From February 1984 until his death, Berg hosted a daily, four-hour clear-channel radio talk show on KOA-AM, reaching more than 200,000 listeners in 38 states. A former lawyer known for his in-your-face style, Berg manifested the same indignation-fueled rage on his radio program and gave new meaning to the word blunt. Berg talked about anything and everything, including his own personal problems, his alcoholism, and other hot-button topics that sometimes infuriated his listeners, but that always kept them listening.

Confrontation was Berg's forte, and it was not uncommon for him to hang up on callers—and sometimes for callers to hang up on him. Too many of his guests to count stormed out of his studio while the show was still on the air after they had had their fill of Berg's combative, insulting, interviewing "style."

All this considered, Berg's death is a dark irony. He never had a chance for his final confrontation.

A white supremacist who had been on the receiving end of some of Berg's taunting waited at Berg's condominium one Monday night. Berg had finished his show and, after stopping off for a can of dog food, pulled into his driveway. As soon as Berg opened his Volkswagen door, Bruce Pierce opened fire on him with a machine gun. Berg was struck so quickly with so many bullets that he fell to the ground immediately, his feet still inside the car. If he wasn't dead by the time he hit the ground, he was gone within seconds.

Nothing of Berg's was taken. His wallet was untouched; his condominium was locked and secure. The Order was not interested in robbing Berg; they simply wanted him dead.

Berg's murder was a hit, plain and simple, and it was because he was Jewish, and white, and anti-intolerance, and, of course, anti-Nazi. And he said so on the radio, often calling members of The Order and other white supremacist groups that worshipped Adolf Hitler "stupid."

Before his death, Berg had applied for a permit to carry a gun, but he was denied. He told the authorities that he regularly received death threats, but they did not take him seriously.

In 1987, the writer, comedian, actor, and monologist Eric Bogosian wrote and starred in a play, *Talk Radio*, which was based on Alan Berg but was not a literal biographical rendering of his story. Bogosian later starred in the 1989 acclaimed film adaptation of his play, directed by Oliver Stone.

3 Julius Caesar

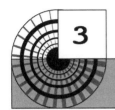

ASSASSINATED ✓

SURVIVED ___

Here was a Caesar!
when comes such another?

—William Shakespeare[1]

VICTIM: Caius Julius Caesar

BORN: July 12–13, 100? B.C.

DIED: March 15, 44 B.C., the "Ides of March"

AGE WHEN ATTACKED: 55

OCCUPATION: Roman dictator, general, and statesman; changed the Roman republic into a monarchy (although without ever taking on the title of emperor or king); returned to Rome and told the Senate, "Vini, vidi, vici"

Bust of Caesar

("I came, I saw, I conquered"), after a successful campaign in Asia; conquerer of Gaul (modern-day France); adopted Augustus (whose original name was Octavius Gaius), who became the first emperor of Rome; put Cleopatra on the throne of Egypt.

ASSASSINS: Plotted and initiated by Caesar's friends Marcus Brutus (85? B.C.– 42 B.C.) and Cassius. So many Roman senators were involved in the assassination that many of them were wounded by their fellow assassins' knives as they all stabbed wildly at Caesar. It is believed that between 23 and 60 senators participated in Caesar's murder.

— 17 —

DATE & TIME OF ATTACK: March 15, 44 B.C., shortly after noon

LOCATION OF ATTACK: The Roman Senate, in front of the statue of Pompey

WEAPONS: Daggers—many, many daggers

ASSASSINATION OUTCOME: Caesar was taken completely by surprise. After the first blade pierced him, he briefly fought back with a stylus used for writing on wax tablets, but then he surrendered when confronted with the great number of senators participating in the assassination. He covered his face and head with his robe and ultimately received 23 knife wounds, the combined effect of which were fatal. Caesar died on the floor of the Senate in front of the statue of Pompey.

JUDICIAL OUTCOME: Cassius and Brutus spoke to the Senate the day after Caesar was assassinated and explained that they plotted and carried out his murder because he was becoming a despot, because he had forbade the practice of taxing citizens for the Senators' personal gain, and because he was planning to dismantle the Roman capital of the empire and move it to Alexandria, Egypt, where he could be near Cleopatra, whom he had installed there as queen. The pro-Caesar senators did not debate these points, but welcomed Caesar's right-hand man, Marcus Antonius, as his successor. Marcus pardoned the assassins, but conflict soon began between the soldiers loyal to Brutus and those loyal to Caesar (and thus, Marcus). Marcus quickly suppressed the uprising and, shortly thereafter, Brutus and Cassius both committed suicide.

When Julius Caesar was being stabbed repeatedly by Roman senators, he did not say "Et tu, Brute." This phrase has been used in many literary accounts of the assassination in order to allow the character of Caesar to concisely express his shock when learning that his friend Brutus had so callously betrayed him.

The two earliest accounts of Caesar's death—by Plutarch and Suetonius—report that Caesar remained silent when attacked. He did not say a word. Suetonius does report, however, that "other people" recalled that Caesar's last words were addressed to Brutus and were, "And thou, son?" Many historians give some credence to this account, although Suetonius did not.

In the 16th century, William Shakespeare repeated the secondhand account from Suetonius, first in the First Quarto version of his play

The True Tragedie of Richard Duke of Yorke (which was not included in the revised *Richard II*) and then in Act 3 of his monumental *Julius Caesar* (as "Et tu, Brute, wilt thou stab Caesar, too?)"

It would have made sense for Caesar to say *something*, though, such was the enormity of Brutus's betrayal. Also, Caesar's reported use of the term *child* or *son* would likewise have been in character, because Caesar had been having a long-running affair with Brutus's mother and there was the widespread rumor that Caesar was Brutus's father. (Brutus stabbed Caesar in the genitals. This act would seem to have many interpretations, especially so when it is known that after Brutus stabbed him in the groin, Caesar gave up and accepted his death.)

Ancient Romans looked to omens, portents, dreams, and divination the way we moderns keep an eye on CNN and the Weather Channel.

The night before he was murdered, Caesar's wife Calpurnia dreamt that he would soon be killed. Caesar ignored her. Calpurnia then reminded him that a fortune-teller had warned him that the Ides of March (March 15th) would be deadly for him. This reminder, along with his wife's dream, convinced Caesar not to leave the house that day. One of his men arrived soon thereafter, however, and mocked him for being superstitious, and Caesar decided (albeit reluctantly) to go to Pompey's Theater at the Senate as he had originally planned.

The plot against Caesar, involving 60 senators, was scheduled to be carried out as soon as he arrived at the Senate. On the way there, someone (history does not tell us who, but it was clearly someone loyal to Caesar) handed him a parchment on which the assassination attempt was detailed. Caesar handed it to one of his slaves. He was always being handed "petitions," and he was apparently not in the mood to read one at that time.

As soon as he arrived and took a seat beneath the statue of Pompey, Tillius Cimber approached him and asked him to allow his brother, whom Caesar had banished from Rome, to return from exile. During this conversation, Casca stepped behind Caesar, pulled off the ruler's robe, and stabbed him in the upper back. This was the signal for the assassination to begin, and a free-for-all started immediately. In seconds, Julius Caesar was dead.

Caesar's assassination did nothing but put his adopted son, Augustus, into power and set the stage for the imperial Caesars who followed.

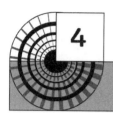

4

Jimmy Carter

ASSASSINATED   ___

SURVIVED   ✓

John W. Hinckley is every family's nightmare come to life. He is the child who drifts off into private hells of depression, despair and finally irrevocable disaster, leaving his parents only the bitterness of "perhaps," the futility of "if only."

—*Newsweek*[1]

VICTIM: James "Jimmy" Earl Carter

BORN: October 1, 1924

DIED: n/a

AGE WHEN ATTACKED: 56

OCCUPATION: 39th president of the United States (1977–1981)

IMPLICATED ASSASSIN: John W. Hinckley, Jr. (b. May 29, 1955), future attempted assassin of President Ronald Reagan

Carter

DATE & TIME OF ATTACK: The date for an attempt would probably have been sometime in October 1980, the period when Hinckley actively stalked Carter.

LOCATION OF ATTACK: The site of the attempt would probably have been at a campaign rally in Nashville, Tennessee.

WEAPON: The likely weapon would have been one of Hinckley's handguns.

ASSASSINATION OUTCOME: Hinckley stopped stalking President Carter and abandoned his plan to assassinate him. He, instead, decided to assassinate President Ronald Reagan (page 201).

JUDICIAL OUTCOME: Hinckley was on his way to one of Carter's campaign stops when he was arrested at an airport after security found guns in his possession when his luggage was X-rayed. This incident seems to have convinced Hinckley to abandon the idea of assassinating Carter, although the argument has also been made that Carter's very low standings in the polls at that time played a role in Hinckley's decision to wait for a more famous target. Hinckley's airport arrest was the only legal consequences of his plot against Jimmy Carter. His guns were confiscated, Hinckley paid a fine of $62.50, and he was released. Hinckley was not placed under surveillance by any law-enforcement agencies after this incident.

History is written after the fact, and all the history books would read quite differently today if John Hinckley had not been stopped at an airport when he was transporting guns. Jimmy Carter might have been the victim of presidential assassination, and Jim Brady would not be brain-damaged for life. But history is written after the fact, and that's not how it happened.

The Secret Service agent bent over the stacks of contact sheets and used a small magnifier to scan the images. Hundreds of faces flew by as he moved the lens over the crowd, looking for anyone who might be considered a threat to the president. The agent was scanning crowd scenes from a 1980 rally for President Carter in Nashville, Tennessee. As he slowly moved the magnifier over one of the sheets, he suddenly froze. Standing in the crowd watching President Carter was a young man he recognized. Stocky, unkempt, sandy-colored hair, glasses. The agent sat up. "Damn," he said softly, under his breath. He then placed the magnifier back on the contact sheet, bent down to it, and stared through the lens into the face of John W. Hinckley.

It was like the scene from *Taxi Driver* when Robert De Niro, wearing an army jacket and with a Mohawk haircut, attends a campaign rally for a presidential hopeful. Only this candidate was not a "hopeful"; he was, in fact, the president of the United States.

John W. Hinckley, Jr. stood on the outskirts of the crowd, his eyes hidden behind sunglasses, his hands thrust into his jacket pockets. His guns were back at his hotel. He would not shoot a president that day.

Jimmy Carter was one of John Hinckley's potential targets for assassination before he decided to shoot President Reagan. Hinckley was never recognized as a threat against the president, even though, as the Secret Service learned after he shot Reagan, he had been photographed in crowds watching Carter at public rallies.

As we know, Hinckley did not fire shots at President Carter, nor did he continue to stalk him from rally to rally. Instead, he whiled away the months between October 1980 and spring 1981, until a few days before the end of March of that year. Then he flew to Washington, this time managing to travel with two handguns undetected, checked into a hotel, and wrote Jodie Foster a letter.

He then walked to the Washington Hilton and waited on the sidewalk in a crowd, precisely the way he stood in a crowd in Nashville six months earlier. This time, his pockets were not empty, however, and the rest is history—as it is written in the books of today.

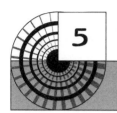

5

Fidel Castro

Assassinated	___
Survived	✓

If surviving assassination were an Olympic attempt, I would win the gold medal.

—Fidel Castro[1]

VICTIM: Fidel Castro

BORN: August 13, 1926

DIED: n/a

OCCUPATION: Lawyer, premier of Cuba (1959–1976), president of Cuba (1976–present)

ALLEGED ASSASSINS: The CIA (1960–?), the Mafia (1962–63), seven Cuban-Americans (1998)

DATE & TIME OF ATTACK: 1960–1998

LOCATION OF ATTACK: Somewhere in Cuba

WEAPONS: A bizarre melange of exotic, allegedly deadly assaults, including: putting fungus in Castro's diving suit to give him a chronic skin disease; putting tuberculosis spores on his diving tank's regulator; planting an exploding conch shell on the ocean floor where he often went scuba diving; rigging a pen with a hypodermic needle to inject a deadly insecticide into him; poisoning his cigars with a super-hallucinogen so that he would have an acid trip during a public appearance; poisoning his cigars with a viral toxin; booby-trapping his cigars with explosives (Exploding cigars? Yes. And no, this is not a joke.); planting thallium salts in his shoes so his beard, hair, eyebrows, and pubic hair would fall out; shooting him with a telescopic rifle; and setting off fireworks after propagandizing to the Cuban people that the Second Coming of Jesus Christ was imminent, with the hope that when they saw the explosions they would overthrow Castro in a rapturous revolution.

ASSASSINATION OUTCOME: Castro is alive and well.

JUDICIAL OUTCOME: None.

According to the BBC, Castro has "reputedly survived more than 600 CIA-sponsored attempts on his life."[2]

Six hundred *failed* attempts? Well, that explains the Bay of Pigs, eh?

To many in Cuba, Castro *is* Cuba. He is loved and he is hated, but there is no question that the identity of the island nation is defined by the dominating presence of Fidel Castro. French philosopher Jean-Paul Sartre once said, "Castro is at the same time the island, the men, the cattle and the earth. He is the whole island."[3]

He has survived through nine American presidencies. He is perceived by Americans and by the American government as the last Communist, and his proximity to the continental United States has long been a source of concern.

For decades, the U.S. government, as well as many American people, have believed the world would be a better place, a safer place, without Fidel Castro. We have imposed trade sanctions on Cuba for what seems like forever, and yet we put aside ideological differences and acted on behalf of the Cuban government when we returned Elian Gonzalez to his father in communist Cuba.

In the 1960s, the CIA concocted Operation Mongoose, which was a clandestine plot to assassinate Castro. The major stumbling block, however, was that the CIA had no way of successfully infiltrating Cuba and getting inside Castro's personal zone of access.

Their solution? Hire a Mafia hitman to do the job.

This is not as bizarre as it sounds upon first hearing. In the 50s, the Mafia had a huge gambling operation in Havana, Cuba, and the mob bosses in Chicago, New York, Florida, and elsewhere still had contacts in Cuba that could conceivably be utilized for Operation Mongoose.

The CIA began "working with" Chicago boss Sam Giancana, his associates Meyer Lansky, Johnny Rosselli, Santo Trafficante Jr. (in Florida), and other Mafia chieftains. However, the Mob being the Mob, they apparently took the CIA's money, and duped the organization into believing they were working diligently on the plan, when in reality they were doing absolutely nothing towards putting together a feasible assassination plot.

The CIA eventually pulled the plug on Operation Mongoose, but not before they had been bilked out of a lot of money and resources and embarrassed in the intelligence community for being "taken for a ride" by the Mafia.

In 1997, seven Cuban-Americans were arrested for trying to kill Castro at an international conference in Isla Margarita, Venezuela. The boat they were on started to sink and, when the Coast Guard came to their aid, they found weapons, ammunition, and military supplies on board. That was the end of the Cuban-American National Foundation's plot against Castro.

It is a certainty that plots continue to be hatched against Castro, and it is not known if he will be removed from office by resignation, death, or assassination. It is a given, though, that until he is gone, he will continue to be a thorn in the side of the American government.

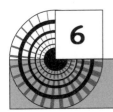

6

Jacques Chirac

ASSASSINATED   ___

SURVIVED   ✓

I don't think there was any plot because the shooter would have used a gun of a larger caliber. It looks like the act of a demented person.

—Nicolas Couteau[1]

VICTIM: Jacques Chirac

BORN: November 29, 1932

DIED: n/a

AGE WHEN ATTACKED: 69

OCCUPATION: President of France

UNSUCCESSFUL ASSASSIN: Maxime Brunerie (b. 1977), 25, Neo-Nazi with ties to the Union Defense Group (a rightist racist organization), student, part-time chauffeur, known to police for having emotional problems

DATE & TIME OF ATTACK: Sunday, July 14, 2002, Bastille Day, shortly before 10 a.m., during the annual Bastille Day parade

LOCATION OF ATTACK: On the Champs-Elysees near the Arc de Triomphe in Paris, France

WEAPON: A .22-caliber rifle

ASSASSINATION OUTCOME: Brunerie managed to fire one shot, which missed the president, who was standing and riding in an open military jeep.

As the assassin was attempting to fire a second shot, he was swarmed by people nearby watching the parade, and the gun was pointed upwards and then forcibly taken from him. Brunerie tried to turn the gun on himself after firing at the president but was taken into custody before he could do so.

JUDICIAL OUTCOME: Brunerie was held in psychiatric detention following the shooting. He was arraigned on Monday, July 15, 2002. His case is pending at this writing.

Another lone gunman, another open vehicle, another foiled assassination attempt, another citizen intervention, another security embarrassment.

The attempted assassination of French President Jacques Chirac is the most recent such incident chronicled here, and it occurred during France's annual celebration of Bastille Day, the day in 1789 when the Paris Bastille was stormed by citizens at the outset of the French Revolution.

Bastille Day is a national holiday in France, and its theme is Franco-American relations. Attending the enormous parade were 163 U.S. military cadets, plus 75 New York City firefighters and their relatives, led by a New York City fire engine.

There were a reported 2,500 uniformed and plainclothes police officers in the crowd, yet the assassin was able to carry a rifle concealed in a brown guitar case onto the parade route. His guitar case was not checked, and it is not known if there were security checkpoints on the parade route where people's bags were examined.

The gun was a .22-caliber hunting rifle and it had been bought legally one week earlier. It was fully loaded with five bullets.

After Chirac's Jeep passed the Arc de Triomphe, it headed down the Champs-Elysees with the president standing and waving at the crowd. When

Chirac's vehicle was about 450 feet from where Brunerie was standing, he opened his guitar case, pulled out the rifle, took aim, and fired. His aim was terrible, however, and the bullet went nowhere near the president. Jacques Weber, a tourist from Alsace, France, saw the gunman take aim. "I looked to my left and I saw a barrel pointed towards the procession. I looked behind me and I saw a man aiming at the procession. I heard a bang and

I said to myself, "That's it, he's shooting." I grabbed his rifle and pointed it upwards so that he wouldn't injure anyone, then I tried to overpower him. He was trying to kill himself. I snatched his weapon and other people overpowered him."[2]

People then began shouting for the police, and officers arrived two or three minutes later. Some witnesses expressed concern about the length of time it took for officers to get to where Brunerie was being restrained. The gunman was handcuffed and taken into custody. Chirac was unaware of the attempt on his life, and the parade continued uninterrupted.

Some French newspapers reported that Brunerie had been a candidate for the extreme-right National Republican Movement (NRM), an offshoot of Jean-Marie Le Pen's National Front and that he had run in the 2001 municipal elections. Le Pen, who had been defeated by Chirac in 2001, denied any connection with the gunman. He issued a statement in which he condemned "all assassination attempts aimed at the representative of the state. I was sure that if a madman one day fired at the president, then it would be said in one way or another that he was from the extreme right."[3]

The attempt on Chirac was the first known assassination attempt on the life of a French president since the many attempts against Charles De Gaulle (page 50) in the early 1960s.

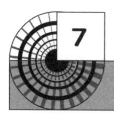

7

Winston Churchill

ASSASSINATED ___

SURVIVED ✓

We shall go on to the end, we shall fight in France, we shall fight on the seas and oceans, we shall fight with growing confidence and growing strength in the air, we shall defend our island, whatever the cost may be, we shall fight on the beaches, we shall fight on the landing grounds, we shall fight in the fields and in the streets, we shall fight in the hills; we shall never surrender.

—Winston Churchill[1]

VICTIM: Sir Winston Leonard Spenser Churchill

BORN: November 30, 1874

DIED: January 24, 1965

AGE WHEN ATTACKED: 68

OCCUPATION: Prime minister of England during World War II; Lord of the Admiralty of the British fleet; originator of the phrases "the Iron Curtain," "blood, toil, tears, and sweat," and "riddle wrapped in a mystery inside an enigma"; acclaimed journalist and author; winner of the Nobel Prize for Literature; honorary citizen of the United States.

Churchill

– 29 –

UNSUCCESSFUL ASSASSINS: The German Luftwaffe

DATE & TIME OF ATTACK: Tuesday, June 1, 1943, 12:54 p.m.

LOCATION OF ATTACK: In a British Overseas Airway Corporation (BOAC) DC-3 commercial airliner named *Ibis*, flying over the Bay of Biscayne, north of Spain and west of France

WEAPONS: Aircraft-mounted artillery

ASSASSINATION OUTCOME: Churchill did not board the doomed flight and was, thus, unharmed during this failed assassination attempt. Seventeen people on board the flight, however—13 passengers and four crews members—perished when the plane was shot down.

JUDICIAL OUTCOME: None. The Allies did win the war, however.

What do the movie *Gone With the Wind* and Winston Churchill have in common?

Actor Leslie Howard, who played Ashley Wilkes in the beloved adaptation of Margaret Mitchell's Civil War novel, was aboard the plane that was shot down by the German Luftwaffe in an attempt to assassinate Winston Churchill, thought to be on the plane.

After the war, it was revealed that Leslie Howard, who was fiercely patriotic, had deliberately taken the flight, knowing it was intended to be a decoy flight to divert attention away from Churchill's actual plane.

However (playing the devil's advocate here), could the story of Howard's willingness to martyr himself for the cause be apocryphal?

Three passengers who were supposed to fly on the *Ibis* on June 1, 1943, were removed so that Howard and his manager, Alfred Chenhalls, could take the flight. This sounds like it was a last-minute decision to board that particular plane. If Leslie Howard was confident that the DC-3 was going to be shot down, would he have waited until the plane was full to decide to board? Also, if he didn't think anyone on board would survive the flight, would he have also doomed his manager to death?

Interestingly, there is another theory about the plane being targeted that involves Leslie Howard's aforementioned business manager, Alfred Tregear Chenhalls. It suggests that Germans may have been scoping out the people boarding the plane and mistaken Chenhalls for Churchill. Chenhalls was small and portly, smoked cigars, and bore a striking resemblance to the British prime minister. If this is true, then it deflates the theory that Howard was a willing sacrificial lamb.

Neither the DC-3, nor any of the bodies of the people onboard, were ever found.

Churchill retired after the war and lived into his golden years. He died in 1965 at the ripe old age of 90.

Winston Churchill Bibliography	
1898 *The Story of the Malakand Field Force* 1899 *River War* 1900 *Savrola* 1908 *My African Journey* 1923 *The World Crisis* 1930 *My Early Life*	1931 *The Eastern Front* 1932 *Thoughts and Adventures* 1948 *Painting as a Pastime* 1948 *The Second World War* 1956 *A History of the English Speaking Peoples*

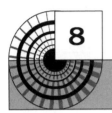

8

Claudius

ASSASSINATED   ✓

SURVIVED   ___

Ita feri ut se mori sentiat.
Strike him so that he can feel that he is dying.

—Suetonius[1]

VICTIM: Tiberius Claudius Caesar Augustus Germanicus

BORN: August 1, 10 B.C.

DIED: October 13, 54 A.D.

AGE When Attacked: 64

OCCUPATION: Emperor of Rome (41–54 A.D.), physically disabled, historian, writer, initiator of the annexation of Britain as a province of the Roman Empire, ascended to the throne by the assassination (which he may have had a hand in plotting) of his nephew, Caligula (Gaius Caesar)

Claudius–Rome, Vatican

ASSASSIN: His wife (and niece), Agrippina the Younger (15–59 A.D.), 39[2]

DATE & TIME OF ATTACK: October 13, 54 A.D., over a 24-hour span

LOCATION OF ATTACK: In his palace on the Palatine, the most important of the seven hills of ancient Rome

WEAPONS: Poisoned mushrooms: *Amanita Caesarea and Amanita phalloides*[3]

ASSASSINATION OUTCOME: Claudius ate poisoned mushrooms in a stew and, within a few hours began to feel sick. He summoned a physician who may or may not have been in on the assassination plot and may or may not have given the emperor a poison enema. Claudius began to deteriorate quickly, suffering horribly for close to a day before expiring the evening after he ate the mushroom-garnished stew. The symptoms of *Amanita* poisoning are extreme stomach pains, nausea, violent vomiting, intense thirst, cyanosis (turning blue) of the extremities, and bloody diarrhea, followed by fatal dehydration and lethal damage to the liver, kidneys, and heart. The victim remains conscious throughout the entire ordeal.

JUDICIAL OUTCOME: Agrippina's treachery succeeded in elevating her son Nero to the throne. Although Nero probably knew that his mother had killed her husband, no legal action was taken against Agrippina. Nero began to "indulge" himself (in food, women, drink, and gambling) as emperor, and the mother/son relationship quickly deteriorated. Nero decided to get rid of his mother by having a ship she was traveling on sunk. She survived the sinking, so he sent troops to execute her. She reportedly accepted her death sentence but asked that she be killed by being stabbed in the womb. She wanted her last act to be a defilement of the birthplace of her traitorous son. The soldiers did as she requested.

Before being elevated to emperor, Claudius was a unique character around Rome and its environs. He suffered from diplegia (the paralysis of certain body parts on both sides of the body, such as both arms, both legs, and so on), he stuttered, had a club foot, and drooled in public. Not a pretty picture. He would also fall asleep at banquets and the other guests would throw food at him as he slept. They would also put slippers on his hands and then wake him up and laugh uproariously as he wiped his face with shoes.

Claudius was believed to be an idiot, but, after he became emperor, he claimed that he faked stupidity to lull people into being unguarded around him. He was actually an intelligent, erudite man. He wrote well-received histories of the Etruscans and Carthaginians and was made consul by Caligula when he was 47, three years before Caligula's assassination and Claudius's elevation to the throne.

Claudius married four times: Plautia, Aelia, Messalina, and Agrippina. He divorced the first two; the third, the licentious Messalina, was executed; the fourth, Agrippina, killed *him*.

Messalina was executed on Claudius's orders. She had orgies right under his nose, and then married another man while she was married to him. He sentenced her to death, and then gave her time to commit suicide. When she did not, he had a guard stick a sword through her.

Once he was made emperor, Claudius proved to be a capable, if megalomaniacal and intolerant, leader. He appointed freed slaves to public office, he banned the Druids and expelled the Jews, and he put great resources into public works projects such as bridges and aqueducts.

Agrippina already had a son, Nero, when she married Claudius. From the beginning of their marriage, she had wanted Nero to take the throne when Claudius died or stepped down. Claudius, however, intended for his and Messalina's son, Britannicus, to succeed him. Agrippina thus decided to get rid of Claudius and then push Nero into the throne—which is precisely what she did. Not surprisingly, Claudius's son Britannicus died from poisoning four months after his father's death.

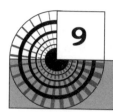

Bill Clinton

ASSASSINATED ___

SURVIVED ✓

It's great to be back in the safety and security of the White House.

—President Clinton[1]

VICTIM: William "Bill" Jefferson Clinton

BORN: August 19, 1946

DIED: n/a

AGE WHEN ATTACKED: 48

OCCUPATION: 42nd president of the United States (1993–2001)

CONVICTED ASSASSIN: Francisco Martin Duran (b. 1968), 26, upholsterer from Security, Colorado; born in Albuquerque, New Mexico; recipient of a dishonorable discharge from the U.S. Army after driving into a group of pedestrians while drunk (1981); Fort Leavenworth military prisoner for three and a half years.

DATE & TIME OF ATTACK: Saturday, October 29, 1994, at approximately 3 p.m.

LOCATION OF ATTACK: Shots were fired from outside the White House fence while Clinton was in the residence quarters.

WEAPONS: A Norinco semi-automatic rifle and a Mossberg pump-action shotgun.

ASSASSINATION OUTCOME: President Clinton was uninjured; the White House and some trees on the grounds were damaged by the 27 bullets fired by Duran.

JUDICIAL OUTCOME: Duran was charged with 11 felony counts, including attempted assassination of the president, and was found guilty of 10 of the 11 counts. He faced a maximum sentence of life imprisonment without parole. On October 8, 1996, Duran was sentenced to 40 years in prison.

Psychiatrists testifying in Francisco Duran's defense said that when Duran shot up the White House, he was trying to destroy a mist connected by an umbilical cord to an alien being. Apparently, Duran thought he had to destroy the mist in order to save the world and that he could do so by shooting at the White House. Insane? The purported motive certainly is, but a jury did not believe that *Duran* was, and he ended up in prison, supposedly still believing that the alien mist was bent on destroying the world.

Before the bombing of Pearl Harbor, the White House "security perimeter" began at the actual front doors of the building. After Japan's attack, the perimeter was moved outward to the high cast-iron fence at the edge of the property. Think about it: Before December 7, 1941, citizens could wander around on the grounds of the White House at will, even to the point of walking right up to the building and looking in the windows if they chose to. Nowadays, anyone setting foot on the grounds inside the fence sets off all manner of alarms and risks getting shot if he or she does not immediately freeze and obey every single command given by the Park Police or the Secret Service. (See Marcelino Corniel's story on page 38.)

The First Family's residence is on the second floor of the White House in the rear. The windows of the residence are made of bulletproof glass. The walls are four feet thick. A contingent of Secret Service agents are stationed nearby.

On Saturday, October 29, 1994, President Clinton was in the residence watching a college football game on TV. The president had just returned from a four-day trip to the Middle East, so this Saturday afternoon was probably a free period for him with no scheduled events so he could rest and recover from the trip. The afternoon turned out to be anything but relaxing, however, beginning at around 3 o'clock.

It was then that Secret Service agents burst into the room where the president was watching TV and immediately hustled him off to...well, we don't really know, because the specifics of the president's security are never discussed. But it is a certainty that whatever bunker/room/refuge he was removed to was probably the safest place he could be in at that time.

Francisco Duran had been lingering on the sidewalk outside the White House for close to an hour when he suddenly withdrew a semi-automatic rifle (specially modified by Duran so it would hold more bullets and so he could hide it easily) from his coat, poked the barrel through bars of the iron fence, and began firing. He then stepped back and began moving down the sidewalk towards the Treasury Building, continuing to spray bullets at the White House. When Duran stopped and began fumbling with the weapon in an attempt to reload it, two bystanders jumped him and overpowered him, restraining him until the Secret Service took him into custody.

Duran's bullets shattered a window in the pressroom, pockmarked the White House walls in several places, and lodged in trees on the grounds. The Secret Service's urgency aside, the president was never actually in any real danger, although at the time, it was not known precisely the amount of firepower that Duran may have been able to wield against the White House. What if he had been carrying explosives strapped to his body or had pocketfuls of live hand grenades? Another weapon was found in Duran's vehicle, but his shooting spree was the extent of his assault.

Duran never made a formal statement explaining his motives in trying to shoot the president, but it is believed the shooting was in protest of Clinton's increased restrictions of the sales and possession of assault weapons. That must have been in addition to saving the world from the killer alien mist.

Also, in August 1998, it was reported that Osama bin Laden had twice conspired to assassinate President Clinton, once in the Philippines, and another time in Pakistan.

9 recent security breaches at the White House

▶ September 12, 1994. *Frank Eugene Corder* stole a Cessna airplane, took off, breached White House airspace, and crashed the plane onto the lawn south of the Executive Mansion. The Cessna struck a tree near the South Portico steps and hit a corner of the White House below President Clinton's bedroom. Corder died in the crash.

▶ December 1994. *Joseph Maggio*, 36, parked his car by the White House fence and announced to anyone within earshot that he had a bomb in the vehicle. He then got out of his car and started running. He was chased and quickly apprehended by the Park Police and Secret Service officers. No bomb was found in Maggio's car.

▶ December 1994. *Franklin Ruff*, 27, of Las Vegas, was arrested on the Ellipse, an open park between the south grounds of the White House and the Washington Monument. Ruff was allegedly carrying a gun, but nothing further is known about this incident.

▶ December 1994. *Richard Green*, 44, of Washington, was arrested and charged with unlawful entry after he snuck onto the White House grounds when the southwest gate opened to allow a vehicle to leave.

▶ December 1994. *Marcelino Corniel*, 33, a homeless man, was shot and killed by police as he stood on the sidewalk outside the White House. Corniel had charged across Pennsylvania Avenue brandishing a knife.

▶ December 1994. An *unidentified man* fired a gun at the White House. Four bullets were found on the grounds, but nothing further is known about this incident.

▶ December 25, 1994. *Lolando Bello*, 19, was arrested and charged with unlawful entry and making threats after he was found hanging on a fence outside the White House on Christmas Day. Bello told police that he only wanted to see the president.

▶ May 23, 1995. *Leland W. Modjeski*, who had a history of mental illness, climbed over the security fence and began to run towards the White House. Secret Service agents shot him, but he survived. Modjeski was carrying an unloaded handgun and may have been trying to commit "blue suicide" (suicide by cop).

▶ December 1995. *Melvin Doyle Glover*, 63, of Texas, was arrested near the White House with a rifle in his car.

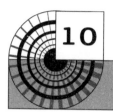

10

John Connally

ASSASSINATED _____

SURVIVED ✓

[I]n a matter of a few seconds, this incident occurred that changed all of our lives, changed the course of history for many people in what ways you never know, and it makes you reflect, ponder, and wonder if you do all that you ought to do day by day in trying to make whatever contribution you can to society in which you live because you never know when your day will come.

—Governor John Connally[1]

VICTIM: John Connally

BORN: February 27, 1917

DIED: June 15, 1993

AGE WHEN ATTACKED: 46

OCCUPATION: Governor of Texas, former Secretary of the Navy

ACKNOWLEDGED ASSASSIN: Lee Harvey Oswald (1939–1963), 24, assassin of President John F. Kennedy

DATE & TIME OF ATTACK: Friday, November 22, 1963, 12:30 p.m.

LOCATION OF ATTACK: In a motorcade in front of the Book Depository in Dallas, Texas

WEAPON: A 6.5-mm Mannlicher-Carcano bolt-action carbine rifle

— 39 —

ASSASSINATION OUTCOME: Following is the official description of the Governor's shooting from the Warren Commission Report,[2] followed by a description of the surgeries and treatment of the governor:

The Shooting

Before the shooting started, Governor Connally had been facing toward the crowd on the right. He started to turn toward the left and suddenly felt a blow on his back. The Governor had been hit by a bullet which entered at the extreme right side of his back at a point below his right armpit. The bullet traveled through his chest in a downward and forward direction, exited below his right nipple, passed through his right wrist which had been in his lap, and then caused a wound to his left thigh. The force of the bullet's impact appeared to spin the Governor to his right, and Mrs. Connally pulled him down into her lap.

Medical Treatment of John Connally

Governor Connally had a large sucking wound in the front of the right chest which caused extreme pain and difficulty in breathing. Rubber tubes were inserted between the second and third ribs to re-expand the right lung, which had collapsed because of the opening in the chest wall. At 1:35 p.m., after Governor Connally had been moved to the operating room, Dr. Shaw started the first operation by cutting away the edges of the wound on the front of the Governor's chest and suturing the damaged lung and lacerated muscles. The elliptical wound in the Governor's back, located slightly to the left of the Governor's right armpit was approximately 5/8ths-inch (a centimeter and a half) at its greatest diameter and was treated by cutting away the damaged skin and suturing the back muscle and skin. This operation was concluded at 3:20 p.m.

Two additional operations were performed on Governor Connally for wounds which he had not realized he had sustained until he regained consciousness the following day. From approximately 4 p.m. to 4:50 p.m. on November 22, Dr. Charles F. Gregory, chief of orthopedic surgery, operated on the wounds of Governor Connally's right wrist, assisted by Drs. William Osborne and John Parker. The wound on the back of the wrist was left partially open for draining, and the wound on the palm side was enlarged, cleansed, and closed. The fracture was set, and a cast was applied with some traction utilized. While the second operation was in progress, Dr. George T. Shires, assisted by Drs. Robert McClelland, Charles Baxter, and Ralph Don Patman, treated the gunshot wound in the left thigh. This punctuate missile wound, about 2/5ths-inch in diameter (1 centimeter) and located approximately 5 inches above the left knee, was cleansed and closed with sutures. A small metallic fragment remained in the Governor's leg.

JUDICIAL OUTCOME: Lee Harvey Oswald (Chapter 55) was shot and killed by Jack Ruby two days after President Kennedy was killed and Governor Connally was shot, so he never stood trial for his crimes.

Was Texas Governor John Connally simply in the line of fire in Dallas when Oswald started shooting and, thus, a collateral victim? Or was John Connally Oswald's intended target, and he missed?

It is known that Oswald had written a letter to Connally on January 30, 1962, when the Governor was Secretary of the Navy, complaining about having his Honorable Marine Corps Discharge changed to Dishonorable when it was learned he had sworn allegiance to the Soviet Union. In the letter Oswald told Connally that he would "employ all means to right this gross mistake or injustice to a bona-fide U.S. citizen" perpetrated against him by the Marine Corps and the U.S. Government.

Secretary Connally responded to Oswald, telling him that he had just resigned to run for governor of Texas and that he had forwarded Oswald's letter to his successor. Oswald accepted this but continued to pursue reversal of the Dishonorable Discharge, ultimately to no avail. The Navy Discharge Review Board notified Oswald in a letter dated July 25, 1963, that they would not be reversing the discharge decision.

So, did Oswald blame John Connally for the "gross injustice" against him? In testimony before the Warren Commission on September 6, 1964, Oswald's wife Marina stated that she thought her husband "was shooting at Connally rather than President Kennedy."[3]

But the answer is apparently no, Oswald did not blame Connally and, thus, the Governor was *not* his target on November 22, 1963, in Dallas. If Oswald had wanted to shoot Connally, he could have done it much simpler and with surer results than trying to pick him off in a presidential motorcade. And even during the motorcade, there were several instances when

Connally would have been a clearer target than after the car turned onto Elm Street and President Kennedy blocked Oswald's view of the governor. The Warren Commission conclusions on this theory are:

It would appear, therefore, that to the extent Oswald's undesirable discharge affected his motivation, it was more in terms of a general hostility against the government and its representatives rather than a grudge against any particular person.[4]

It seems that the preponderance of evidence tells us that Governor John Connally was in the wrong place at the wrong time and got caught in a presidential assassination.

The governor recovered fully from his gunshot wounds. He died in 1993 from pulmonary fibrosis at the age of 75.

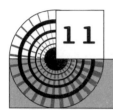

11

Bob Crane

ASSASSINATED   ✓

SURVIVED   ___

What was the speck? Nobody knows what it was, not even the doctor.

—Jury Foreman Marine Sgt. Michael Lake[1]

I feel like a 10,000-pound weight has been lifted off my head.

—John Carpenter[2]

VICTIM: Robert "Bob" Crane

BORN: July 13, 1928

DIED: June 29, 1978

AGE WHEN ATTACKED: 49

OCCUPATION: Actor, best known for starring as "Colonel Hogan" in the enormously popular TV sitcom *Hogan's Heroes* (1965–1971)

ASSASSIN: Unknown

DATE & TIME OF ATTACK: June 29, 1978, sometime during the night, probably around 3:00 or 3:30 a.m.

LOCATION OF ATTACK: In the bedroom of his rented apartment in the Winfield Apartments in Scottsdale, Arizona

WEAPON: A camera tripod

ASSASSINATION OUTCOME: Crane was beaten to death by at least two savage blows to the back of his head, behind his left ear.

JUDICIAL OUTCOME: In 1994, 16 years after Crane's murder, his friend, John Carpenter, was charged with the murder. After an eight-week trial and two and a half days of jury deliberation, Carpenter was acquitted. The crime remains unsolved.

Did John Carpenter—Bob Crane's best friend and his "costar" in homemade porn videos—bludgeon his friend Bob Crane to death and then drive away with a piece of Crane's brain on his car door? A jury of his peers said no. There are some who disagree with that verdict to this day.

Fourteen years after Bob Crane's murder, John Henry Carpenter was arrested and charged with first-degree murder. Carpenter, a video equipment salesman, had been out with Crane earlier that evening with two women, but Crane had gone home alone at approximately 2:30 a.m. His dead body was found the following afternoon at 2 p.m. by Victoria Berry, one of his costars in the regional production of *Beginner's Luck*, in which Crane had been starring. Crane had been beaten to death with what police described as a "blunt linear instrument," now believed to have been a camera tripod.

In Crane's case, there is a dark irony in the use of a camera tripod as a murder weapon.

Bob Crane liked to videotape himself having sex with women. His friend, John Carpenter, Sony's first American salesman, taught him how to use video cameras, and, over a period of years, Crane taped many of his sexual encounters and compiled quite a collection of homemade porn tapes. In exchange for the knowledge and training, it is believed that Carpenter shared in the sexual favors of Crane's many "girlfriends" and even appeared in one video with Crane, in which they both received oral sex from the same young woman.

The theory implicating Carpenter put forth at the trial was that Bob Crane had gotten tired of Carpenter hanging around with him and that he had either severed their friendship at the time of the murder or was planning to in the near future. Prosecutors alleged that Carpenter was devastated by the possible loss of Crane as a friend because he knew he would no longer be able to have sex with as many young women as he had been previously once he was out of Crane's orbit.

After Crane's body was discovered, the police were called, but the crime scene was tragically compromised by shoddy evidence-handling, improper crime-scene practices, and the failure to follow up on leads and clues.

In a 1994 article in the *Arizona Republic,* reporter Pamela Manson detailed the mistakes made by the Scottsdale Police Department:

The actress who found the body was permitted to answer the phone at the crime scene, possibly before technicians could dust for prints. Her large handbag was never searched.

Officers trooped in and out of the Scottsdale apartment where Crane's body was discovered on June 29, 1978. Evidence was dumped into one garbage bag, allowing for the possibility of tainting individual items.

Moving men working at the complex the morning of the slaying were never questioned.

The next day, Crane's business manager and son were allowed to remove items from the apartment before all of the items had been checked for fingerprints.

Investigators already were focusing on Carpenter as a suspect, but they never searched his hotel room.[3]

In 1994, after Carpenter's acquittal, Scottsdale, Arizona, police department spokesman Sgt. John Cocca, admitted that the department had not done a very good job of handling Crane's crime scene. "To say we didn't make mistakes would be naive," Cocca said. "However, the department has grown and matured. We're more professional because the public demands it. The officers demand it, too."[4]

Carpenter was charged with the crime after a photo surfaced showing a piece of *something* on his car door shortly after the murder. It was a fatty substance that the prosecution claimed was a piece of Crane's brain. The piece was lost, however, and the only physical evidence the prosecution had was a spot of blood that had been taken from Carpenter's car shortly after the murder. The blood type of this spot matched Crane's. But this was in the days before DNA testing, and the blood type (B) actually matched one in every seven people. The jury acquitted.

Carpenter died of a heart attack in September 1998 at the age of 70. His wife told a reporter, "He did some really stupid things in his life, but I don't think killing Bob Crane was one of them."[5]

When Bob Crane's son Scott Crane was asked if he thought Carpenter had killed his father, he said, "I don't know whether Carpenter did it. Only he knows."[6] And John Carpenter took that knowledge with him to the grave.

Postscript: On Tuesday, July 16, 2002, Bob Crane's son, Bob Scott "Scotty" Crane, was ejected from an advance screening of the Sony biopic about his father, *Auto Focus*, starring Greg Kinnear as Bob Crane. Scotty's half-brother, Robert David Crane, remained in the screening and also has a small role in the film. Scotty Crane had long objected to the movie's script, in which is suggested that Bob Crane may not have been Scotty's biological father. His lawyer later issued a statement that they had DNA evidence that Bob Crane was, indeed, Scotty Crane's father.[7]

Bob Crane Filmography[8]	
The Donna Reed Show (1958) TV Series	*The Delphi Bureau* (1972) TV
Return to Peyton Place (1961)	*Make Mine Red, White and Blue* (1972) TV
Man-Trap (1961)	
Hogan's Heroes (1965) TV Series	*Herbie Day at Disneyland* (1974) TV
The Wicked Dreams of Paula Schultz (1968)	*Superdad* (1974)
	The Bob Crane Show (1975) TV Series
Arsenic and Old Lace (1969) TV	*Gus* (1976)

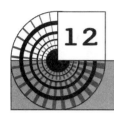

Jefferson Davis

ASSASSINATED ___

SURVIVED ✓

I am sure I feel no hostility to you, Senators from the North. I am sure there is not one of you, whatever sharp discussion there may have been between us, to whom I cannot now say, in the presence of my God, I wish you well; and such, I am sure, is the feeling of the people whom I represent towards those whom you represent. I therefore feel that I but express their desire when I say I hope, and they hope, for peaceful relations with you, though we must part.

—Jefferson Davis[1]

VICTIM: Jefferson Davis

BORN: June 3, 1808

DIED: December 6, 1889

AGE WHEN ATTACKED: 56

OCCUPATION: U.S. senator, president of the Confederate States of America,[2]; Union soldiers' prisoner for two years after 1865

Davis

capture; indicted for treason in 1866 after the Civil War (but never prosecuted), writer of a history of the Confederacy

UNSUCCESSFUL ASSASSINS: Ulric Dahlgren (1843–1864), 21, Union colonel (youngest ever to rise to rank of colonel), battle amputee, son of Admiral John Dahlgren (who was known as the "Father of American Naval Ordnance" and was a personal favorite of President Lincoln); Hugh Judson Kilpatrick (1836–1881), Confederate General, leader of the Kilpatrick-Dahlgren raid

DATE & TIME OF ATTACK: March 1864

LOCATION OF ATTACK: Richmond, Virginia

WEAPONS: Firearms

ASSASSINATION OUTCOME: Dahlgren was killed in a raid to free Union soldiers before he could implement his assassination plan.

JUDICIAL OUTCOME: When Confederate President Jefferson Davis learned of the Dahlgren assassination plot, he authorized Confederate terrorist attacks on the North, specifically arson, bank robberies, and sabotage. It is also believed that the Dahlgren plan convinced the Confederate high command to sanction the kidnapping of Abraham Lincoln (Chapter 42), which they later abandoned, leading to Booth's solo plot to kill the president.

The plan was for a cavalry raid on Richmond, Virginia, to free 10,000 Union soldiers being held as prisoners of war at Belle Isle. Hugh Judson Kilpatrick would come in from the north; Ulric Dahlgren would come in from the south. After the raid on Belle Isle, they would then hit the Libby Prison, where Union officers were being held, and free them as well. They would then set fire to Richmond and depart triumphantly for the north as the Confederate capitol of Virginia burned to the ground.

This raid had been personally approved by President Lincoln, and there was no doubt in the Union high command that the young Dahlgren could pull it off. Things did not work out as planned, however.

In early March 1864, Dahlgren and his invading troops were ambushed by a Confederate battalion outside of Richmond and Dahlgren was killed. The *Richmond Examiner* of March 5, 1864 reported that Dahlgren commanded between 300 and 400 men and that the Confederates took "90 prisoners and 35 Negroes and 150 horses." The hatred for Dahlgren was evident: "The wretch who commanded them was the son of Commodore Dahlgren, of ordnance notoriety. It would have been well if the body of the land pirate had been gibbeted in chains on the spot where he fell."[3]

Confederate soldiers searched Dahlgren's body and found documents that revealed the true nature of the raid: the assassination of Jefferson Davis and his cabinet. This note by Dahlgren was addressed to his men:

> *You have been selected from brigades and regiments as a picked command to attempt a desperate undertaking—an undertaking which, if successful, will write your names on the hearts of your countrymen in letters that can never be erased, and which will cause the prayers of our fellow-soldiers now confined in loathsome prisons to follow you and yours wherever you may go...We hope to release the prisoners from Belle Island first, and having seen them fairly started, we will cross the James River into Richmond, destroying the bridges after us and exhorting the released prisoners to destroy and burn the hateful city; and do not allow the rebel leader Davis and his traitorous crew to escape...The men must keep together and well in hand, and once in the city it must be destroyed and Jeff. Davis and cabinet killed.*[4]

The reaction in the South was, in hindsight, naive and risible. *How dare the enemy scheme to kill our leader! This is a gentleman's war; such unpleasantness is not warranted.* Yes, it seems that the Confederates were actually *insulted* that Dahlgren and Kilpatrick had planned to attack Jefferson Davis, he the secessionist, a supporter of slavery, and an enemy of the Union. Dahlgren and company had simply taken to heart the wisdom of the adage that opined that if you want to kill a dog, you don't cut off its tail, you cut off its head—and the Southerners were horrified.

After the failure of the raid, the South retaliated with terrorist acts and also sanctioned the kidnapping of Abraham Lincoln.

As for Dahlgren, it was rumored that his body was desecrated by Confederate soldiers after the assassination plot was uncovered. This caused great consternation to his father, Admiral Dahlgren, and, in response, Union Major-General Benjamin Butler wrote the senior Dahlgren a letter:

> *[T]he statements in the Richmond papers of any indignities to the remains of your son are false; that they were decently and properly buried under the direction of an officer of equal rank in the Confederate service. Secondly, I have the most positive assurances from him that you shall receive the remains of your son by next flag-of-truce boat.*[5]

Jefferson Davis lived quietly after the war (steadfastly refusing to take the oath of allegiance to the reunited United States, however), and died in 1889 at the age of 80.

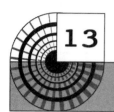

Charles De Gaulle

| ASSASSINATED | —— |
| SURVIVED | ✓ |

The French will only be united under the threat of danger. Nobody can simply bring together a country that has 256 kinds of cheese.

—Charles De Gaulle[1]

VICTIM: Charles André Joseph Marie De Gaulle

BORN: November 22, 1890

DIED: November 9, 1970

AGE WHEN ATTACKED: 69–79

OCCUPATION: General, president of France (1959–1969), leader of the French Free Resistance Movement during World War II, staunch anti-Communist, supporter of the French withdrawal from colonial Algeria, strengthener of France's international position, including its acquisition of nuclear weapons, writer

UNSUCCESSFUL ASSASSINS: There were 31 documented assassination attempts against Charles De Gaulle during his life, most of them by the OAS (the Organisation De L'Armée Secrète), specifically by French

De Gaulle

— 50 —

Air Force Lieutenant Colonel Jean-Marie Bastien-Thiry (1927–1963) and George Watin, the Algerian head of the Mission Three branch of the OAS who was responsible for the August 1962 attempt against De Gaulle. There is also evidence that the U.S. CIA briefly plotted to assassinate De Gaulle after he expelled American troops from France.

DATE & TIME OF ATTACK: Most attempts were made during De Gaulle's presidential administration (1959–1969), with the last documented attempt made on July 1, 1966.

LOCATION OF ATTACK: Various sites in France

WEAPONS: Butane bombs, machine guns, plastic explosives

ASSASSINATION OUTCOME: None of the assassination attempts against De Gaulle were successful. De Gaulle died at home at the age of 79 of a heart attack.

JUDICIAL OUTCOME: Jean-Marie Bastien-Thiry was sentenced to death for his attempts on De Gaulle's life and was executed by firing squad on March 11, 1963. George Watin was arrested in Switzerland in 1964 and expelled, and he then moved to South America. He was condemned to death by French authorities while he was expatriated, but later pardoned. He died in Paraguay.

Charles De Gaulle was tough, and he never panicked. There is no better example of his mettle than his behavior during an August 1963 assassination attempt in Notre Dame Cathedral. Assassins actually opened fire on De Gaulle inside the church during services. Did De Gaulle flee the cathedral or duck down in a pew? Negative. The General stood tall facing the altar and continued to sing the *Te Deum*, a sacred hymn of praise to God.

Here is a rundown of some of the more notable assassination attempts against De Gaulle.

▶ September 5, 1961: A 54-pound butane bomb and 20 pounds of plastic explosives were buried in sand near a bridge over the Seine River. The plan was to explode the bomb at the precise moment that De Gaulle's car passed by as a number of OAS terrorists then opened fire with machine guns on the (hopefully blown-up) car to gild the assassination lily, so to speak. The OAS assassin who was assigned to push the "detonate" button as the car passed by essentially chickened out, and De Gaulle's car passed by without incident.

▶ September 8, 1961: Three days after the September 5th attempt, the OAS decided to try again. The explosives were still buried so they retook their positions and again waited for De Gaulle's car to pass by. This time the button man did his job, and the butane bomb exploded, but the plastic explosives failed to detonate because of their age. They were from the World War II era and had lost their combustibility. The butane bomb resulted in De Gaulle's car being surrounded by flames, but his equally unshakable driver simply drove through the inferno and no one was harmed.

▶ June 23, 1962: On this day, De Gaulle was to be ambushed in his car on the road on his way to a wedding in Rebrechien. Unaware of this plot, he took a helicopter to the ceremony instead.

▶ June 25, 1962: On this day, another auto ambush was planned, but the French police saw the OAS cars and, to prevent being arrested, the hapless terrorists were forced to flee the scene.

▶ August 8, 1962: The OAS planned to shoot De Gaulle in his car as he traveled on his way to the airport to meet former U.S. president Dwight D. Eisenhower. Fortunately for De Gaulle, and unfortunately for the OAS, a civilian car got in the way of their attack. Remarkably, the OAS assassins wouldn't endanger a civilian, so they backed off for the day.

▶ August 22, 1962: While De Gaulle and his wife were on their way to Villacoulbay Airport, their presidential limousine was ambushed by 15 members of the OAS on an avenue in the Paris suburb of Petit Clamart. The assassins all had automatic weapons, and more than 100 rounds were fired. Twelve bullets entered the car and two struck the tires but, remarkably, no one was hurt. De Gaulle did, however, cut his finger brushing a piece of broken glass off his coat. This is the attack when De Gaulle reportedly made the famous remark "They shot like pigs," but what he actually said was "Quels maladroits!" which loosely translates to "What idiots!"[2]

▶ February 1963: A plot was uncovered to assassinate De Gaulle during ceremonies at the Ecole Militaire in Paris. A sniper with a rifle was to pick off the president from a rooftop. For unknown reasons, the plan was never carried out.

▶ August 26, 1963: This attempt, described previously, began as the president's motorcade pulled up to Notre Dame Cathedral and then continued inside. Two or three civilians were killed, but De Gaulle didn't flinch and even sang the *Te Deum*.

On November 9, 1970, De Gaulle, 79 and retired, sat down in front of the television to play a game of solitaire before the evening news started. He suddenly shouted, "I have a pain, a pain here, in my back!"[3] He then fell forward onto the table, unconscious. Those were his last words. A doctor and priest were summoned. The doctor could do nothing, but the priest managed to administer Last Rites to De Gaulle before he died.

After his death, a sealed letter to French President Pompidou was opened.

De Gaulle had spelled out his wishes for his funeral:

My grave shall be that in which my daughter Anne lies and where, one day, my wife will also rest. Inscription: Charles de Gaulle (1890–). Nothing else....I do not wish for a State funeral. No presidents, no ministers, no parliamentary delegations, no representatives of public bodies...No oration shall be pronounced, either at the church or elsewhere. No funeral oration in parliament...I declare that I refuse in advance any distinction, promotion, dignity, citation, decoration, whether French or foreign. If any whatsoever were conferred upon me, it would be in violation of my last wishes.[4]

De Gaulle did not specify the music for his funeral Mass, but he probably would not have protested if they sang the *Te Deum*.

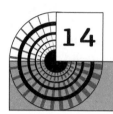

14

Thomas Dewey

ASSASSINATED	—
SURVIVED	✓

The son-of-a-bitch has got to be killed! If you won't go with me on this, I'll do it myself!

—Dutch Schultz[1]

VICTIM: Thomas Edmund Dewey

BORN: March 24, 1902

DIED: March 16, 1971

AGE WHEN ATTACKED: 33

OCCUPATION: New York City district attorney (1937–1941), unsuccessful Republican Presidential candidate (1944 and 1948), governor of New York (1943–1955), lawyer, special prosecutor for racketeering in 1935

CONSPIRING ASSASSIN: Dutch Schultz (1902–1935), 33, gangster, friend/associate of mob boss Lucky Luciano

DATE & TIME OF ATTACK: October 25, 1935 (planned date)

LOCATION OF ATTACK: A pharmacy phone booth in New York City was the planned location. (The hapless pharmacist on duty at the time was to be killed after Dewey was shot so as to eliminate the only witness.)

WEAPON: A pistol with a silencer

ASSASSINATION OUTCOME: The assassination was never carried out because mob boss Louis Lepke, who was very displeased with Schultz's stated

— 54 —

plan to kill Dewey, ordered Schultz killed, and in the fall of 1935, mob hitman Charlie "The Bug" Workman whacked Dutch Schultz and three of his henchman in the Palace Chop House, a New Jersey restaurant.

JUDICIAL OUTCOME: Because Dutch Schultz was eliminated by his own team, there was no judicial outcome to his planned assassination of Thomas Dewey. Lucky Luciano, however, was imprisoned in June 1936 on 62 various counts and given a 30- to 50-year sentence—thanks to the efforts of Thomas Dewey.

Dutch hated Dewey. The gung-ho district attorney was going full throttle investigating Dutch Schultz and his boys, and Dutch wanted him gone. Dewey had already indicted Dutch in 1933, but back then Dutch was cocky enough to show up at the opening of a Times Square nightclub three days after his arraignment. Things were different now. There was too much money at stake to risk Dewey suddenly coming down on the operation and shutting it down while locking them up. Schultz knew his phones were tapped, and one of his standard farewells before he hung up was, "I hope your ears fall off!"[2]

Dewey was making enormous headway cracking Schultz's loan-sharking and restaurant money-laundering business, and there was talk in the wind of a grand jury being impaneled in the not-too-distant future. As Richard H. Smith stated in *Thomas Dewey and His Times*, "One way or another...Dewey [was] determined to drag Schultz into a courtroom where his money and influence would be impotent."[3]

A man can't earn in prison, and that is where Dewey wanted to put Dutch, Lucky, and all the other arch-criminals that made up the New York/New Jersey underworld in the Roaring Twenties and the Big-Money Thirties.

Dutch decided to eliminate Dewey, and he offered the job to Albert Anastasio, who not only declined but told Lucky Luciano about Schultz's plans. Schultz's fate (and by extension, Dewey's) was then placed in the hands of Lucky Luciano and a commission of powerful wiseguys.

It was learned that Schultz had been watching Dewey and knew the DA's schedule. Every morning he visited the same drugstore, where he used the same phone booth to call his wife. Every morning. On the morning of October 25, 1935, one of Schultz's men would follow Dewey into the drugstore, pretending to be a customer, and wait for him to enter the phone booth, which, at that point, would become a death trap.

The gunman would then shoot Dewey in the booth, using a gun with a silencer, and then, as soon as he was dead, turn around and blow away the pharmacist. As long as there was no one else in the pharmacy at the time, the plan would work perfectly, and the gunman could simply walk out of the store, leaving behind one dead district attorney and one dead pharmacist.

The plot meeting lasted six long hours, and in the end, Schultz's plan was determined to be unsafe and stupid and would result in long-term harm to the influence and faux respectability that many of the wiseguys had achieved over the previous 10 years.

Charlie "The Bug" Workman was given the assignment of rubbing out Dutch Schultz and eliminating one of Lucky Luciano's headaches.

The Bug and two associates opened fire on Dutch in a Chinese restaurant. That same night, one of Dutch's lieutenants was blown away in a barbershop. Over the next five days, 10 more of the Dutchman's boys would get popped.

As for Schultz himself, he lingered in semiconsciousness in the hospital for almost a full day, finally dying at 8:30 p.m. on the night of October 24, 1935. These were his last words:

Please help me up. Henny. Max. Come over here. French-Canadian bean soup. I want to pay. Let them leave me alone.[4]

As for his nemesis, Thomas E. Dewey, he was not gunned down in a drugstore phone booth, and he went on to become governor of New York and also to run for president twice. In addition to his crime-fighting work, history will always remember Dewey as the politician who beat Harry Truman in the 1948 presidential election—if only on the front page of the *Chicago Daily Tribune.*

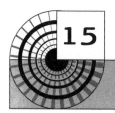

15

Medgar Evers

ASSASSINATED   ✓

SURVIVED   ___

For two and one half years I endangered my life as many other Negro Americans, on the far away battlefields, to safeguard America and democracy, only to return to our native country and state and be denied the basic things for which we fought...I have been told that "resistance to tyranny is obedience to God," and for that reason, if for no other, we shall not cease to press forward relentlessly, until every vestige of segregation and discrimination in America becomes annihilated.

—Medgar Evers[1]

If I die, it will be in a good cause. I've been fighting for America just as much as the soldiers in Vietnam.

—Medgar Evers[2]

VICTIM: Medgar Evers

BORN: July 2, 1925

DIED: June 12, 1963, at 3:14 a.m. at University Hospital

AGE WHEN ATTACKED: 37

OCCUPATION: Local field secretary for the Mississippi chapter of the National Association for the Advancement of Colored People (NAACP)

ASSASSIN: Byron De La Beckwith (1921–2001), 42, White Supremacist

DATE & TIME OF ATTACK: Wednesday, June 12, 1963, shortly after midnight

— 57 —

LOCATION OF ATTACK: Outside Evers's house in Jackson, Mississippi

WEAPON: A .30.06-caliber Enfield rifle with a telescopic sight

ASSASSINATION OUTCOME: Evers returned home around midnight after attending a rally for the NAACP's Jackson, Mississippi, civil rights campaign. He parked his 1962 light-blue Oldsmobile in his driveway behind his wife's station wagon, got out and began walking into a side entrance that opened onto a carport. He carried a pile of t-shirts that were printed with "Jim Crow Must Go!"[3] on them. Beckwith fired from a sniper's lair about two hundred feet away and struck Evers below his right shoulder blade. The bullet passed through Evers, went through a living room window, hit the kitchen wall, ricocheted off the refrigerator, struck a coffeepot, and came to rest beneath a watermelon on a kitchen counter. Evers staggered to the door, where he was met by his frantic wife and three children. A neighbor who had been awakened by the gunshot rushed over. Someone called the police. When the police arrived, Evers was placed in a station wagon owned by Evers's neighbor, Houston Wells, and he was driven to University Hospital. Evers's last words were "Sit me up," and "Turn me loose."[4] He died three hours later at the hospital from loss of blood and internal injuries.

JUDICIAL OUTCOME: Eleven days after Evers's murder, the police arrested Beckwith and charged him with murder. A .30-06 rifle with his fingerprints on it had been found at the murder scene. Beckwith claimed that it was his rifle, but that it had been stolen. Two all-white, all-male juries couldn't convict him, and he remained free for 31 years, until the Mississippi Supreme Court ruled in 1993 that Beckwith could be tried a third time for Evers's murder. Beckwith's third trial began in February 1994 and included testimony from witnesses recalling Beckwith bragging at a Ku Klux Klan meeting, and also saying, "Killing that nigger gave me no more inner discomfort than our wives endure when they give birth to our children."[5] Beckwith, who wore a Confederate flag pin in his lapel, was found guilty in just less than seven hours of deliberation. The 72-year-old racist was sentenced to life in prison. He died in January 2001 in a Mississippi penitentiary.

Medgar Evers came from a poor family. The children rarely saw new clothes or shoes, and their father, James Evers, had never learned to read or write. But they always had food on the table, and Medgar's father taught him and his brother Charles not to tolerate disrespect, no matter what the color of the guilty party.

As a young child, Medgar Evers did not hate white people. He naively accepted the cruelties of 1920s Jim Crow Mississippi, reflexively deferring to his father's cautious wariness around white people. James Evers was constantly reminded of how quickly a white man could toss a lynching rope over the limb of a tree and, thus, he advised Medgar and his brother Charles to be patient and accept what Evers's biographer, Adam Nossiter, describes as the "fixed realities."[6] These realities—having to walk to school while white children rode on buses; having to order a hamburger in an alley behind the burger stand away from the white customers; passing by the bloody clothes of a lynched neighbor in a field every day on his way home from school—quickly became unacceptable to Medgar, and this social milieu could have easily justified lifelong rancor. (We all know of World War II-era Americans who admit to *still* hating all Japanese people, even now, because of Pearl Harbor.)

Medgar and his brother did fight back, mostly by pulling malicious pranks and throwing rocks at the white kids' bus, but it wasn't long before "anger and resentment at whites [turned] into hatred."[7] He joined the Army to, he said half-jokingly, learn how to kill white people. But the military, even though it was still segregated in the 1940s, showed Evers a world where skin color didn't matter. Europeans (he was stationed in France at one point) didn't care that he was black. He even dated a white French girl for a time.

When he returned to Mississippi after serving in the Army, he was horrified at just how bad the situation was for blacks, now that he could view it with some detachment and distance.

Medgar became an insurance salesman for a company owned by blacks and he joined the NAACP. He soon left insurance to become a field agent for the NAACP, and he was working to advance the organization's goals at the time of his assassination. His efforts were to get crossing guards for black schoolchildren, allow blacks to eat at lunch counters, allow blacks to try on clothes and hats in department stores, and, of course, to win blacks the right to vote.

Medgar Evers's assassination was the first of a turbulent decade, which included the killing of Martin Luther King Jr., Robert Kennedy, John F. Kennedy, and many others less well-known who were also working for racial equality.

Medgar Evers's legacy is that his dreams have come true...for the most part.

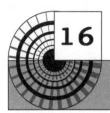

16

Louis Farrakhan

ASSASSINATED	—
SURVIVED	✓

The great recording companies that portray our people in such a filthy and low-rating way, yet they would not allow such a man as Michael Jackson to say one word that they thought would besmirch their reputation, but they put us before the world as clowns and as purveyors of filth. No, I will fight that.

—Louis Farrakhan[1]

VICTIM: Louis Farrakhan, born Louis Eugene Walcott

BORN: May 11, 1933

DIED: n/a

AGE WHEN PLOTTED AGAINST: Unknown

OCCUPATION: Nation of Islam leader, minister

IMPLICATED ASSASSIN: Qubilah Shabazz, daughter of Malcolm X, 34, implicated and clandestinely recorded by FBI informant Michael Fitzpatrick, indicted after a seven-month investigation by a Federal Grand Jury on January 12, 1995, on eight counts of use of an interstate commerce facility (the telephone) in the course of a murder-for-hire scheme against Louis Farrakhan

DATE & TIME OF ATTACK: Undetermined

LOCATION OF ATTACK: Undetermined

WEAPON: Undetermined

ASSASSINATION OUTCOME: Any alleged planned attempt on the life of Louis Farrakhan was never carried out.

JUDICIAL OUTCOME: The case was dropped by the Feds before it went to trial with an agreement from Shabazz that she would seek treatment for her anger problem and that she would not get into any trouble for a period of two years.

Civil rights leader Malcolm X's daughter, Qubilah Shabazz, was 4 years old when her father was assassinated and, decades later, she was recorded as saying she thought Louis Farrakhan was responsible for the murder and that he should be killed.

Her words were recorded by an FBI informant named Michael Fitzpatrick, 34, who, for reasons of his own, seemed to coerce Shabazz into saying on tape what the government needed to indict her. There was a very strong case for entrapment against the Feds, and the case against Shabazz was dropped before it went to trial.

For years, Louis Farrakhan was implicated as being involved in the Black Muslim murder of Malcolm X. The CBS news program *60 Minutes* went so far as to point the finger at Farrakhan, which greatly angered the Nation of Islam leader, but which was also endemic of the pervasive view that Farrakhan had been a member of the radical faction of Black Muslims responsible for the murder. In an interview with *The Final Call* newspaper on May 15, 2000, when asked "How is your family handling Mike Wallace's implication of you in the murder of Malcolm X?" Farrakhan responded, "My family is very angry."[2]

An article in the *New York Post* in which Qubilah Shabazz's mother and Malcolm X's widow, Betty Shabazz, stated that it was "common knowledge" that Farrakhan had plotted the assassination, led to a multi-million-dollar lawsuit against the *Post*. Considering Mrs. Shabazz's outspoken comments, many were not surprised when it was revealed that her daughter was alleged to have plotted to have Farrakhan killed.

After Qubilah Shabazz's case was settled, Farrakhan went on to organize the 1995 Million Man March and the 2001 Million Family March and continue to work for the causes on his agenda. He has also made a great many provocative statements that many in the black community feel serves to fuel divisiveness rather than unity and tolerance. Some of his most volatile statements have targeted whites, and gays and Jews in particular:

White people are potential humans—they haven't evolved yet.[3]

The Jews have been so bad at politics they lost half their population in the Holocaust. They thought they could trust in Hitler, and they helped him get the Third Reich on the road.[4]

It seems like being gay or whatever sin you wish to be a part of is okay...but I have the duty to lift that gay person up to the standard to ask if they want to live the life that God wants them to or live the lifestyle that they want to live.[5]

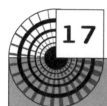

17

Archduke Franz Ferdinand

ASSASSINATED   ✓

SURVIVED   —

Worries and precautions cripple life. Fear is always one of the most damaging things. We are all constantly in danger of death. One must simply trust in God."

—Franz Ferdinand[1]

Ferdinand

VICTIMS: Archduke Franz Ferdinand; his wife, Countess Sophie Chotek; Erik Merizzi, a staff officer accompanying Franz Ferdinand in the motorcade; almost 20 spectators injured by the grenade explosion

BORN: December 18, 1863

DIED: June 28, 1914

AGE WHEN ATTACKED: 50

OCCUPATION: Nephew of Austrian emperor Franz Joseph, next in line to the throne of the Austro-Hungarian empire

ASSASSINS: Gavrilo Princip (1894–1918), 19, member of the Serbian nationalist group, the Black Hand; Nedeljko Gabrinovic, another member. According to Borijove Jevtic, one of the conspirators who wrote his account[2] of the assassination 10 years after the event, there were a total of 22 members of the Black Hand involved in the conspiracy. They included Muhamed Mehmedbasic, Vaso Cubrilovic, Cvetko Popovic, and Trifko Grabéz. Princip fired the gun; Gabrinovic hurled the bomb.

DATE & TIME OF ATTACK: Sunday, June 28, 1914, around 10 a.m. (the grenade); and around 11:15 a.m. (the gunshots)

LOCATION OF ATTACK: In a motorcade on Appel Quay in Sarajevo, Yugoslavia (both attempts)

WEAPONS: A Browning automatic pistol and a grenade filled with nails and pieces of lead and iron.[3] These are the weapons that were actually used in the two attacks. The almost two-dozen conspirators were reportedly, however, *all* armed with pistols and grenades.[4]

ASSASSINATION OUTCOME: The grenade Gabrinovic hurled during the first attempt on Ferdinand did not injure the archduke or his wife, but it did injure Adjutant Erik Merizzi and a dozen or so spectators. At the ceremony following the grenade attack, Ferdinand said, "Mr. Mayor, we come to Sarajevo to make a friendly visit and we are greeted by a bomb. This is outrageous."[5] Shortly thereafter, as the archduke's motorcade retraced its route, Princip fired twice. The first bullet struck Ferdinand in the chest near his neck. The second bullet struck Ferdinand's pregnant wife Sophie in the abdomen. She collapsed to the floor beneath Ferdinand's knees and died almost immediately.

JUDICIAL OUTCOME: This assassination was the spark that started World War I. After hurling the grenade at the archduke's open car, Gabrinovic ran to a river and swallowed cyanide. All the conspirators had been provided with cyanide, and suicide was to be chosen over capture. Unexpectedly, the cyanide was ancient and all it did was make him violently ill and vomit. He was arrested. Later, after firing his two shots, Princip did likewise and swallowed his poison. His cyanide was no fresher, and he, too, became very sick and vomited. He was captured by military officers and beaten severely. They threw him to the ground and beat him on the head with the flat side of their swords; they kicked him; they sliced the skin from his neck with the razor-sharp blades of their swords; and they came up with a few other nasty tortures, resulting in Princip losing an arm and almost dying. He was ultimately sentenced to 20 years in prison (he was not eligible for the death penalty because he wasn't 21); and he died in 1918 from tuberculosis while behind bars. According to Jevtic, Princip was placed in leg irons that were never removed the entire four years he was in prison. At his trial, Gavrilo Princip said: "I do not feel like a criminal because I put away the one who was doing evil."[6] Of the other conspirators, 16 were found guilty. Some were imprisoned, and some were executed.

One single death can be profound in its influence; one single death can result in tens of millions more dead; one single death can start a world war. We know all this to be true, because the assassination of Archduke Franz Ferdinand started World War I, in which more than 20 million people worldwide were killed.

Austria-Hungary used Franz Ferdinand's assassination as an excuse to declare war on Serbia. Russia immediately gave its support to Serbia. Germany then declared its support for Austria and declared war on Russia and France. Great Britain then declared war on Germany. Austria then declared war on Russia, and World War I was on.

Ultimately, Great Britain, France, Russia, Belgium, Italy, Japan, the United States, and other allies defeated Germany, Austria-Hungary, Turkey, and Bulgaria.

Today, in Serbia, the Gavilo Princip Museum honors the assassin who made a stand for Serbian independence and killed the heir to the oppressor Austrian throne.

The Black Hand Society's Loyalty Oath

"By the sun which warms me, by the earth that feeds me, by God, by the blood of my ancestors, by my honor and life, I swear fidelity to the cause of Serbian nationalism, and to sacrifice my life for it."[7]

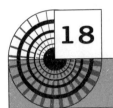

18

Larry Flynt

Assassinated	___
Survived	✓

I don't expect Time *magazine to nominate me Man of the Year. I do, however, hope that Americans will grant me some small measure of credit—however begrudgingly bestowed—for what I have done to protect their freedom of expression.*

—Larry Flynt[1]

We spared no one. We would intentionally try to offend people [by] lampooning blacks, whites, Jews, Christians, rich, and poor. I wanted to provide a forum for the kind of dark humor that characterized the mills, factories, workplaces of ordinary people.

—Larry Flynt[2]

VICTIM: Larry Flynt

BORN: November 1, 1942

DIED: n/a

AGE WHEN ATTACKED: 35

OCCUPATION: Publisher of many magazines, of which *Hustler* is one of his most famous

ADMITTED ASSASSIN: Joseph Paul Franklin (b. 1951), born James Clayton Vaughn, 27, white supremacist, anti-Semitic, shooter of civil-rights activist Vernon Jordan (Chapter 35)

DATE & TIME OF ATTACK: Monday, March 6, 1978, around noon

LOCATION OF ATTACK: On the street outside the Gwinnett County Courthouse in Lawrenceville, Georgia

WEAPON: A .44-caliber rifle

ASSASSINATION OUTCOME: Flynt survived, but ended up paralyzed from the waist down and with a permanent speech impediment. Doctors initially gave him a 50/50 chance of walking again, but Flynt has been wheelchair-bound since the shooting

JUDICIAL OUTCOME: While serving multiple life sentences in prison, Franklin confessed to shooting Flynt and was indicted, but never tried, for the crime. Franklin is currently incarcerated on Missouri's death row.

Larry Flynt and his attorney, Gene Reeves, had just finished eating lunch at the B and J Cafeteria in Lawrenceville, Georgia, and were walking back to the courthouse for the afternoon session in Flynt's latest obscenity trial when shots rang out. From a sniper's perch, bullets flew. Reeves was hit in the arm, and then Flynt was struck in the stomach. Flynt was rushed to the hospital, where doctors removed his spleen and part of his perforated intestines. Flynt's spinal cord was intact, but the bullet had passed through a bundle of nerves at the base of his spine and, his doctors' cautious optimism notwithstanding, Flynt would never walk again. Reeves recovered fully. Flynt experienced excruciating pain for several years and became addicted to prescription painkillers.

Larry Flynt holds the dubious notoriety of reportedly being the only person who has ever made Courtney Love blush. Love, widow of Nirvana leader Kurt Cobain and leader of all-girl band Hole, has been known to perform sans panties and with one leg propped up on a monitor, affording fans in the first row quite a, uh, view. Clearly, this is not a woman who blushes easily.

And yet Larry, often referred to as a self-taught gynecologist (given that *Hustler* is known for its "gynecological-themed" photo spreads), made Courtney go red in the face.

Love played Flynt's wife, Althea Leasure, in the 1996 Milos Forman biopic of Flynt, *The People vs. Larry Flynt.* (Woody Harrelson played Flynt.)

One day on the set, Flynt nonchalantly said to Love, "Althea had a hairy muff. What's yours like, Courtney?"

It didn't seem to matter to Courtney that Flynt could have answered that question for himself if he had simply planted himself in a front row at one of her concerts. Asked on a movie set, the question was *in* context for purposes of the film, but *out* of context for Courtney Love herself, whose megawatt sexuality is most commonly turned on during Hole performances.

Thus, the blush.

Flynt's no-holds-barred question to Love is indicative of the man's style—and also of the editorial impulse of his magazine, *Hustler*. This "nothing is sacred" attitude motivated Flynt to include previously taboo pics in his mag, including photos of elderly women, pregnant women, disabled women, and amputees, as well as photo features on naked celebrities (most notoriously, Jacqueline Kennedy Onassis) and seemingly every perversion known to man. Flynt touched on S&M, threesomes, bestiality, and, most disturbing to his shooter, interracial sex.

Flynt ran a photo spread in *Hustler* of a white woman and a black woman having sex. James Clayton Vaughn, a.k.a. Joseph Franklin, former member of the Ku Klux Klan and the American Nazi Party, was not happy about these pictures. To Vaughn, Flynt was guilty of promoting miscegenation and he needed to be punished and killed.

Flynt was not singled out by Franklin, however. It was later learned that Franklin had committed between 15 and 20 similar hate crimes, all of which were fueled by his hatred for blacks and Jews, as well as by his passionate belief that God was instructing him to mete out punishment in his name. He believed his divine mission was to clean the world by ridding it of blacks.

Franklin had killed two black men in Utah in 1980 for the "crime" of jogging with two white women; he had bombed a synagogue in Chattanooga, Tennessee, in 1977; he had killed an interracial couple in Wisconsin in 1986 (described by Wisconsin prosecutors as "the closest thing to killing for sport"[3]); and was suspected of 10 other hate-driven murders in five states (Georgia, Indiana, Ohio, Oklahoma, and Pennsylvania).

He also was convicted of shooting a 42-year-old father standing outside a synagogue after his son's bar mitzvah, as his young daughters stood by and watched. Franklin also confessed to the shooting of Vernon Jordan, the head of the National Urban League (page 118).

Because Franklin was serving sentences for many of his crimes (including four life sentences), the Georgia District Attorney's office declined to try him for Flynt's shooting.

Franklin later apologized for shooting Larry Flynt, saying, "I have nothing in my heart but love for Larry now. I really regret what happened. Larry has some faults, but I don't hate him anymore. It's the only shooting I've committed that I've ever cried about."[4]

Franklin's remorse has an ironic twist to it, considering his commitment to racial hatred, bigotry, and anti-Semitism. He is sorry for his actions because he now believes that he may have been a Jew in a former life.

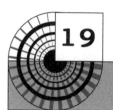

19

Gerald Ford

ASSASSINATED ___

SURVIVED ✓

I don't think any person as President ought to cower in the face of a limited number of people who want to take the law into their own hands. If we can't have that opportunity of talking with one another, shaking hands with one another, something has gone wrong in our society.

—President Gerald Ford, after the attempts on his life[1]

VICTIM: Gerald Ford

BORN: July 14, 1913

DIED: n/a

AGE WHEN ATTACKED: 62

OCCUPATION: 38th president of the United States

Assassination Attempt No. 1

UNSUCCESSFUL ASSASSIN: Lynette "Squeaky" Alice Fromme (b. 1948), 26, ecology fanatic, follower of Charles Manson[2], *The Ed Sullivan Show* guest (as a member of a youth dance troupe called *The Lariats*)

DATE & TIME OF ATTACK: Friday, September 5, 1975, shortly before 10 a.m.

LOCATION OF ATTACK: On the sidewalk in Sacramento, California, between the Senator Hotel and the California Capitol building. Ford was shaking hands with the public as he walked the 150 yards to the Capitol to deliver a speech on crime in America.

WEAPON: A .45-caliber Colt semi-automatic pistol, concealed in a holster strapped to her leg beneath a long red robe (The gun belonged to Harold Eugene Boro, 65, a civilian engineering draftsman at McLellan Air Force Base. Boro was later described as Fromme's "sugar daddy," a slang term defined as "a wealthy, usually older man who gives expensive gifts to a young person in return for sexual favors or companionship."[3] The gun had four bullets in the clip but none in the chamber when Fromme pulled the trigger the first time. She was swarmed and taken into custody before she could pull the trigger a second time.)

ASSASSINATION OUTCOME: A Secret Service agent, Larry M. Beundorf, grabbed the gun from Fromme as she lifted her arm and took aim at the president. She managed to pull the trigger once, but the agent stuck his finger in front of the firing pin and prevented a second pull. President Ford was unhurt but was shaken up at the scene. Witnesses reported that Ford's face drained of color, but he recovered very quickly and went on to deliver his planned speech shortly thereafter.

JUDICIAL OUTCOME: Fromme was found guilty of attempting to assassinate the president and was sentenced to life in prison. She managed to escape from prison in West Virginia in 1987, but she was apprehended 40 hours later. She is currently serving her sentence in a maximum-security prison in Texas. She is still a Manson follower.

Charles Manson disciple Lynette "Squeaky" Fromme wanted to shoot President Gerald Ford to call attention to Manson's "unjust" imprisonment for the Tate-LaBianca murders. She believed that if she was charged with the attempted assassination of Ford, Manson would be called to testify at her trial (she was very vocal to the FBI and Secret Service about her devotion to Manson) and, once he was on the stand, he would be able to speak out and regale the world with his philosophies and beliefs.

This was not enough to win a not guilty by reason of insanity verdict, so her lawyer also tried to convince the jury that, because Ford reminded her of her father, she therefore did not really intend to kill Ford because the firing chamber was empty. Neither defense worked.

Assassination Attempt No. 2

UNSUCCESSFUL ASSOCIATION: Sara Jane Moore (b. 1930), 45, married five times (twice to the same man), mother of four children, former bookkeeper for the *San Francisco Examiner,* former FBI informant, shopper (as a teenager) at a grocery store in West Virginia where Charles Manson's mother was a cashier

DATE & TIME OF ATTACK: Monday, September 22, 1975, around 3:30 p.m.

LOCATION OF ATTACK: On the corner of Post and Powell streets in San Francisco, California, as Ford was walking to his limousine

WEAPON: A .38-caliber Smith & Wesson revolver

ASSASSINATION OUTCOME: Moore was able to fire one shot at the president before being apprehended. A retired Marine, Oliver Sipple,[4] 33, saw the chrome-plated barrel of the weapon, yelled "Gun!," and struck at Moore's arm as she fired. Sipple's blow caused Moore to miss the president, and her bullet hit the front wall of a hotel, ricocheted to the right, and struck a cab driver, slightly wounding him. The bullet missed the president by a distance of two to three feet. President Ford was uninjured; the cab driver recovered.

JUDICIAL OUTCOME: Moore was immediately arrested and at her arraignment said, "I did indeed willfully and knowingly attempt to murder Gerald R. Ford, the President of the United States, by use of a handgun and would now like to enter a guilty plea."[5] The judge tried to persuade Moore to retract her guilty plea, because she was, in effect, guaranteeing herself a life sentence in prison. She refused and, a week after her arraignment, the judge accepted her plea and she was sentenced to life in prison. She is currently serving her sentence at the Dublin Federal Prison Camp in northern California.

Sara Jane Moore tried to kill President Ford to reestablish her connections with a number of radical left-wing groups that had shunned her after she briefly became an FBI informant. She had led a troubled personal life prior to the assassination attempt, and neighbors spoke of her fits of rage, multiple marriages, and financial difficulties. Apparently she believed that things would improve for her if she ended up back in the good graces of organizations with ties to the Symbionese Liberation Army (the group that kidnapped heiress Patty Hearst) and other fringe political factions.

Moore seemed serious about wanting to kill the president, even remarking to the Secret Service, "If I had had my .44, I would have caught him."[6] Moore's .44-caliber pistol had been confiscated by the police the day before the shooting and the Secret Service had interrogated her, but they let her go.

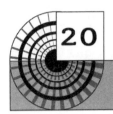

20

Henry Clay Frick

ASSASSINATED	
SURVIVED	✓

Whatever I engage in, I must push inordinately.

—Andrew Carnegie[1]

VICTIM: Henry Clay Frick

BORN: December 19, 1849

DIED: December 2, 1919

AGE WHEN ATTACKED: 42

OCCUPATION: Pittsburgh steel magnate, art collector, chairman of the Carnegie Steel Company (1889–1900)

UNSUCCESSFUL ASSASSINS: Alexander Berkman (1870–1936), 22, anarchist; Emma Goldman (1869–1940)[2], writer and anarchist, bought Berkman the gun he used to shoot Frick.

DATE & TIME OF ATTACK: Saturday, July 23, 1892, 1:55 p.m.

Frick

LOCATION OF ATTACK: Frick's office in the Carnegie Steel Company in Homestead, Pennsylvania, a suburb of Pittsburgh

WEAPONS: A pistol and a dirk knife (dagger)

ASSASSINATION OUTCOME: Berkman shot Frick in the neck two times and then stabbed him at least seven times with a short dagger. Frick's wounds were not fatal, and he returned to his office within a week. The other man in Frick's office at the time of the attack, Frick's chief aide John Leishman, was unhurt, except for minor cuts and bruises sustained while grappling on the floor with Berkman. The struggle, the arrest, and the removal of Frick and Berkman from the office took quite some time and, ultimately, close to 2,000 people watched from the sidewalk as the afternoon drama unfolded.

JUDICIAL OUTCOME: Frick was almost shot and lynched at Frick's office, but Frick himself shouted at the police not to hurt or kill him. "Don't shoot! Don't kill him! The law will punish him!" Frick shouted.[3]

The scene was surreal. Passersby stopped and stared as three men, one of them dripping blood, fought and struggled behind the second-floor window of an office building. The window was enormous and could easily be seen into from the opposite side of the street.

Anarchist Alexander Berkman had told Frick's receptionist that he was an agent for a New York employment firm and that he needed to meet with Henry Frick, chairman of the enormous and powerful Carnegie Steel Company.

As soon as he entered the office, Berkman pulled out a pistol and fired at Frick, who was seated behind his desk, his right leg thrown over the arm. Berkman had been aiming for Frick's brain, but the bullet struck him in the neck because he turned slightly in the chair when Berkman entered the room. The shot stunned Frick, and Leishman leaped up out of his chair and moved towards Berkman, who then immediately fired again, once more striking Frick in the neck.

As Berkman prepared to fire his third shot, Leishman grabbed his arm and pointed it towards the ceiling, which was where the bullet came to rest. By now Frick was on his feet, and the three-man struggle began. Leishman kicked out Berkman's knees and the three tumbled to the floor. Berkman pulled a dagger out of his pocket and began stabbing wildly, hitting Frick at least seven times.

At that point, a sheriff who had been visiting the building burst into Frick's office with his gun drawn. As he took aim at Berkman, Frick ordered him not to shoot.

Six people—some of whom were the very steelworkers whose oppression Berkman was attempting to avenge—then jumped Berkman and piled on top of him. He wasn't going anywhere after that and within minutes the police arrived and carted him off to jail.

Berkman served 14 years for the attempted murder of Henry Clay Frick.

After getting out of prison, anarchist Berkman published his autobiography, *Prison Memoirs of an Anarchist*. In the following excerpt, he describes the moment that he understood what his mission was and why he then resolved to eliminate Henry Clay Frick:

> *My purpose is quite clear to me. A tremendous struggle is taking place at Homestead: the People are manifesting the right spirit in resisting tyranny and invasion. My heart exults. This is, at last, what I have always hoped for from the American workingman: once aroused, he will brook no interference; he will fight all obstacles, and conquer even more than his original demands. It is the spirit of the heroic past reincarnated in the steel-workers of Homestead, Pennsylvania. What supreme joy to aid in this work! That is my natural mission. I feel the strength of a great undertaking. No shadow of doubt crosses my mind. The People—the toilers of the world, the producers—comprise, to me, the universe. They alone count. The rest are parasites, who have no right to exist. But to the People belongs the earth—by right, if not in fact. To make it so in fact, all means are justifiable; nay, advisable, even to the point of taking life.*[4]

If there is a hell on earth (and we rule out the inside of a volcano), it would have to be a steel mill in the late 19th century. Workers put in 12-hour shifts for 14 cents an hour, and they put their lives in jeopardy every time they walked through the doors of the mill. There were enormous cauldrons of molten metal; giant saws cutting steel ingots, spitting flames and slag; and areas around furnaces that were so dangerous the workers called them the deathtraps.

In July 1892, the steel workers went on strike at the Carnegie plant in Homestead, Pennsylvania, to protest not only inhumane and deadly working conditions, but also the eviction of workers and their families from company-owned houses and the reduction of already-too-low wages.

The catalyst for Berkman's assassination attempt—the absolute last straw for both Berkman and his lover, fellow anarchist Emma Goldman— was the slaughter of the striking steelworkers by Pinkerton detectives on the banks of the Monongahela River on July 6, 1892. Carnegie's position was simple: There was nothing to negotiate. The workers must accept these conditions completely or lose their jobs. The union must be crushed, and he gave the job of keeping things under control to Henry Clay Frick.

The striking workers were attacked on the banks of the Monongahela on Frick's orders. He called in a group of Pinkerton thugs euphemistically called "detectives" that were, in reality, more like a private militia. These mercenaries opened fire on the crowd without warning, killing 16 workers and wounding scores more. A little boy was killed in the crossfire, as were three Pinkerton detectives.

In the end, Berkman's assassination attempt did nothing, and he did not even gain the support of the workers. They shunned him for giving the company something to use as a weapon against them. The National Guard occupied the factories, the company hired scab replacement workers, and the Homestead Strike was of no import for Carnegie and company.

Regardless of Berkman's and Emma Goldman's altruistic motives, their efforts were futile, and Berkman committed suicide in 1936 at the age of 66.

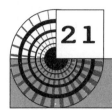

21

Indira Gandhi

ASSASSINATED   ✓

SURVIVED   ___

We were ready with the mike and camera. A secretary had gone to fetch her, and then it happened. I heard three single shots. We looked alarmed but the people in the office said it must be firecrackers. Then there was a burst of automatic fire as if the attackers were making sure of it. I didn't think she had a chance in hell. We saw soldiers running. They kept us there for five hours. It became like a prison.

—Peter Ustinov[1]

VICTIM: Indira Priyadarshini Gandhi[2]

BORN: November 19, 1917

DIED: October 31, 1984

AGE WHEN ATTACKED: 66

OCCUPATION: Prime minister of India (1966–1977, 1980–1984)

ASSASSINS: Beant Singh (1950–1984), 34; Satwant Singh,[3] 25

DATE & TIME OF ATTACK: Wednesday, October 31, 1984, just past 9:10 a.m.

LOCATION OF ATTACK: On a walkway in Mrs. Gandhi's compound between her residence at 1 Safdarjang Road and her office building at 1 Akbar Road in New Delhi, India

WEAPONS: A revolver (Beant Singh, type unknown), a Sten sub-machine gun (Satwant Singh)

— 76 —

ASSASSINATION OUTCOME: Indira Gandhi was rushed to the hospital with dilated pupils and no pulse. She was clinically dead but the doctors (perhaps realizing that their efforts were futile but recognizing the need to appear to have done everything they could to save her) operated and removed between 16 and 20 bullets, while giving her numerous blood transfusions. As part of the charade, the hospital even put out a call for blood donations, which resulted in riots as people fought to be one of the first to donate blood for the prime minister. Mrs. Gandhi was pronounced dead at 4:30 p.m.

JUDICIAL OUTCOME: Beant Singh was shot to death during an escape attempt. Satwant Singh was also shot, but he recovered, was tried, and was executed. Indira Gandhi's son, Rajiv Gandhi, was immediately sworn in as prime minister. He was assassinated in 1991.

Indira Gandhi was on her way to a television interview with the British actor Peter Ustinov for his show *Peter Ustinov's People* when she was gunned down by two of her bodyguards, Sikh separatists who had been accepted onto the security force by the Prime Minister herself. She felt it would be a unifying gesture for the country to allow two of her avowed enemies to guard her.

Mrs. Gandhi, a staunch advocate of a unified India, refused to recognize the Sikh demand for autonomy in the Punjab region of northern India, an area that had been controlled by Sikhs from 1799 to 1849 and that had been split up between India and Pakistan in 1949. (Sounds reminiscent of the Indian demand for autonomy from the British, doesn't it?)

In June 1984, Mrs. Gandhi ordered a raid of one of the holiest of Sikh sites, the Golden Temple in Amritsar, an offensive (an appropriate word considering the Sikh response) known as Operation Blue Star. The Sikh resistance was unexpectedly fierce, and between 600 and 1,200 people died. Mrs. Gandhi was universally loathed by Sikhs following this raid. Her assassination was a direct retaliation for the Golden Temple raid. A Sikh revolutionary leader, Dr. Jagjit Singh Chohan, immediately warned of increased Sikh terrorist attacks against the Indian government following the murder of Mrs. Gandhi.[4]

Immediately after the murder was publicly confirmed, Hindus began terrorizing Sikhs on the streets of India. Sikhs were randomly beaten and, in some cases, their long beards were set on fire. In Punjab, however, Sikhs celebrated, shouting "Indira Gandhi deserved to die!"[5] and giving money to the families of the assassins.

At around 9:30 in the morning, Mrs. Gandhi exited her residence and began walking the short distance to her office to meet Peter Ustinov for a scheduled TV interview. She was wearing a saffron sari. She had chosen this color specifically because she had been told it looked quite nice on television. Whether or not she realized that saffron was traditionally considered in India to be the color of martyrdom will never be known. That morning she had also eschewed her bulletproof vest, because she did not want to appear on TV wearing a bulky vest beneath her garments. Mrs. Gandhi almost always wore a protective vest following the Golden Temple raid, which Sikhs perceived as a desecration of their holiest place. She, her son, and her grandchildren received death threats on a daily basis.

As she walked, she came upon Sub-Inspector Beant Singh, a Sikh who had been one of her bodyguards for nine years. As she greeted him, he pulled out a revolver and shot her in the abdomen. Mrs. Gandhi screamed in pain and fell to the ground. Constable Satwant Singh then pulled out a Sten sub-machine gun and emptied it into the frail woman lying on the ground.

Commandos of the Indo-Tibetan Border Police, the security people who guarded the perimeter of Mrs. Gandhi's compound, stormed the scene and took the two assassins into custody. They were taken to a nearby security hut, at which time they both tried to escape. Beant Singh was shot and killed on the spot. Satwant Singh was seriously wounded by gunfire, but he survived to stand trial. He was found guilty and executed by hanging in January 1989.

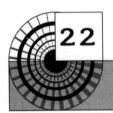

22

Mohandas Gandhi

ASSASSINATED   ✓

SURVIVED   ___

If I am to die by the bullet of a mad man, I must do so smiling. There must be no anger within me. God must be in my heart and on my lips.

—Mohandas Gandhi[1]

VICTIM: Mohandas Karamchand Gandhi, a.k.a. "Mahatma" (Great Soul) Gandhi

BORN: October 2, 1869

DIED: January 30, 1948

AGE WHEN ATTACKED: 78

OCCUPATION: Spiritual leader of India

ASSASSIN: Nathuram Vinayak Godse (1910–1949), Hindu nationalist, 36

Gandhi

DATE & TIME OF ATTACK: Friday, January 30, 1948, 5:15 p.m.

LOCATION OF ATTACK: The Birla House Gardens in Delhi, India

WEAPON: A Beretta 7-chamber automatic pistol

ASSASSINATION OUTCOME: Gandhi was hit by two bullets and collapsed. He was taken back to his house, where he died 25 minutes later.

JUDICIAL OUTCOME: Godse did not flee after shooting Gandhi and he was quickly taken away by Indian police to prevent the crowd from lynching him. Godse and his conspirator, Narayan Apte, were both convicted of the murder of Gandhi and sentenced to death. They were hanged on November 15, 1948. Nathuram Godse's brother Gopal was convicted of conspiracy and sentenced to life in prison. He was paroled after serving 18 years of his sentence and now lives in Pune, India.

A man who preached nonviolence his entire life is violently gunned down on his way to a prayer service.

Every evening, Mohandas Gandhi would leave his home and walk a short distance to a pergola in the Birla Gardens nearby where he would lead a prayer service, often attended by as many as a thousand people who supported the Mahatma's guiding principle of peace through nonviolent protest and "non-cooperation" with civil authorities. On the day he was assassinated, Gandhi walked slowly to the Gardens, where on this day approximately 500 people waited. Gandhi was supported on each side by one of his adoring grandnieces. Gandhi was frail and weak because he had just completed a five-day fast for peace.

Nathuram Godse, a Hindu extremist who believed that Gandhi's policies were dangerous for India and that he was encouraging Muslims to kill Hindus, waited in the crowd. As Gandhi slowly approached the spot where Godse was standing, the assassin withdrew a revolver from his pocket and concealed it in his hands. Godse saw that one of Gandhi's grandnieces was very close to the Mahatma, and he was concerned that he would accidentally hit the young girl if he fired at Gandhi. He then stepped forward, pushed the girl away from her uncle with his left hand, and fired at Gandhi at point-blank range.

Three bullets hit the Mahatma, two in the right side of his abdomen and one in his chest. Gandhi immediately collapsed to the ground, and many sources report that he uttered the words, "Hey Ram!"—which is Hindi for "Oh, God!"—and that these were his last words. In February 2000, in a rare interview with *Time* magazine, Nathuram Godse's surviving brother and co-conspirator Gopal Godse denied that this was true:

GOPAL GODSE: *After his death the government used him. The government knew that he was an enemy of Hindus, but they wanted to show that he was a staunch Hindu. So the first act they did was to put "Hey Ram" into Gandhi's dead mouth.*

TIME: *You mean that he did not say "Hey Ram" as he died?*

GG: *No, he did not say it. You see, it was an automatic pistol. It had a magazine for nine bullets but there were actually seven at that time. And once you pull the trigger, within a second, all the seven bullets had passed. When these bullets pass through crucial points like the heart, consciousness is finished. You have no strength....You see, there was a film and some Kingsley fellow had acted as Gandhi. Someone asked me whether Gandhi said, "Hey Ram." I said Kingsley did say it. But Gandhi did not. Because that was not a drama.*[2]

Gopal Godse's views represent the anti-Gandhi faction that was against Gandhi's support of a Muslim Pakistan. Nathuram Godse's last words as he walked to the gallows were, "Akhand Bharat" which translated to "Undivided India." (Also, only three bullets were fired at Ghandiji.[3]) Regarding the execution of Godse and his conspirator, Apte, it has been rumored that the hangman deliberately tied the knot for Godse's rope incorrectly so that the fall would not immediately kill him. Apte died instantly from a broken neck. Godse, his head covered in a black hood, on the other hand, twisted and writhed at the end of the rope for a full 15 minutes, slowly strangling to death.

Mohandas Gandhi was born in British-ruled India in 1869 and, in 1888, at the age of 19 (after his father died), he was sent to England to study law. He passed the bar in 1891 and returned to India, where he attempted to establish a law practice, with little success. Frustrated, he accepted a position assisting on a lawsuit in South Africa, and he planned to spend a year there. While in South Africa, in addition to his legal work, Gandhi got involved in trying to end the oppression against Indians in the country (they were a small minority), and he ended up commanding a volunteer Indian medical corps that served on the side of the British in the Boer War, a war between British and Dutch settlers that was fought from 1899 to 1902. (The British won.)

Gandhi ultimately remained in South Africa until 1914. His wife and children had joined him in 1896. During these years, Gandhi became very interested in the principle of nonviolent non-cooperation and began to live an ascetic life, abstaining from sex and most pleasures, and devoting himself to prayer and ending Indian oppression.

Gandhi returned to India in 1915, where he quickly became known as the Mahatma. He began practicing nonviolent civil disobedience, was imprisoned several times, and developed an enormous following. Gandhi played an important role in achieving Indian independence, but he had to reluctantly agree to the establishment of a separate Muslim state, Pakistan, which caused great turmoil and animosity between the Hindus and the Muslims.

Nathuram Godse believed the Muslim/Hindu problem would be solved if Gandhi were killed. As we know from the recent escalation of tensions between India and Pakistan over the contested area of Kashmir, Godse could not have been more wrong. His actions, however, robbed the world of one of its true peacemakers.

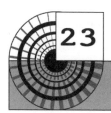

23

James Garfield

ASSASSINATED   ✓

SURVIVED   ___

To General Sherman: I have just shot the President. I shot him several times as I wished him to go as easily as possible. His death was a political necessity. I am a lawyer, theologian, and politician. I am a stalwart of the Stalwarts. I was with Gen. Grant, and the rest of our men in New York during the canvass. I am going to the Jail. Please order out your troops and take possession of the Jail at once. Very respectfully,

—Charles Guiteau[1]

VICTIM: James Garfield

BORN: November 19, 1831

DIED: September 19, 1881

AGE WHEN ATTACKED: 49

OCCUPATION: 20th president of the United States (1881)

ASSASSIN: Charles J. Guiteau (1841–1882), 40, deranged lawyer, petty thief, religious lecturer, and political malcontent. "He was also a liar, a swindler, an embezzler, a lecher, a wife abuser, and an obnoxious egomaniac."[2] At the

Garfield

— 83 —

time of the shooting, Guiteau was reportedly attempting to obtain a consulship to Paris or Vienna in Garfield's administration. A newspaper review of one of his "speeches" said that Guiteau had "fraud and imbecility plainly stamped upon his countenance."[3]

DATE & TIME OF ATTACK: Saturday, July 2, 1881, 9:20 a.m.; died 79 days later on September 19, 1881

LOCATION OF ATTACK: The Baltimore and Potomac Depot in Washington, D.C.

WEAPON: A .44-caliber British Bulldog revolver

ASSASSINATION OUTCOME: Guiteau fired two bullets at Garfield and hit him with both. The first bullet caused a superficial arm injury. The second entered the right side of his chest, fractured his 11th rib, traveled left, hit his spinal column (without touching the spinal cord), and lodged 2 1/2 inches to the left of his spine behind his pancreas. The location of this bullet was never found while Garfield was alive, even after Alexander Graham Bell used his newly invented "induction balance" (metal detector) on the president. Garfield's physician, Dr. D.W. Bliss, did not believe in the radical new theory of the potential danger of bacteria and germs on open wounds. Antiseptic conditions for surgery were almost unknown in 1881, and for weeks 15 different doctors explored the president's wounds with their bare, unwashed hands, trying to find the second bullet. They also fed the president "nutritional enemas." These concoctions consisted of an egg, bouillon, milk, whiskey, and opium. Because the anus does not have any digestion or absorption capabilities, it is likely Garfield also began to suffer from dehydration and malnutrition after several days of this kind of treatment. By the time Garfield died, his original 3 1/2-inch wound track was 20 inches long and grossly infected. Garfield developed sepsis (blood poisoning) from the unsanitary probing of his wound, and it is believed that he died from either a ruptured aneurysm or a massive coronary infarction (heart attack), either of which were likely worsened by his severe case of blood poisoning. Garfield's medical treatment following the shooting has been described as one of the most botched medical events in American history. Garfield suffered greatly toward the end, and his last words—a desperate plea to his doctor for relief from his pain—were "Swaim, can't you stop this? Oh, Swaim!"[4] as he grasped his chest above his heart.

JUDICIAL OUTCOME: Guiteau was indicted for murder on October 14, 1881, and put on trial. At the trial, Guiteau himself proved to be the most compelling evidence for an insanity verdict. He shouted at witnesses, quizzed prospective jurors on biblical passages, and repeatedly told the court that he could speak for God. Ironically, this display of insanity did nothing for his defense or his attorney's hope for a not guilty by reason of insanity verdict. Guiteau was found guilty on January 23, 1882, after the jury deliberated for little more than an hour. The assassin of the beloved President James A. Garfield was hanged on June 30, 1882. His body was left swinging for almost 30 minutes.

Charles Guiteau was insane, that is a given. But as is often the case with those so deemed, sometimes the truly crazy manifest shrewd, sly behavior. Guiteau went out of his way to specifically buy an expensive British Bulldog revolver for his shooting of James Garfield. Why? Because he wanted it to look impressive when it finally ended up in a museum.

Before he stalked and shot President Garfield, Guiteau wrote the following letter, found in his papers after his arrest:

Washington June 16, 1881.
To the American People:
I conceived the idea of removing the President four weeks ago. Not a soul knew of my purpose. I conceived the idea myself and kept it to myself. I read the newspapers carefully for and against the Administration, and gradually the conviction settled on me that the President's removal was a political necessity, because he proved a traitor to the men that made him, and thereby imperiled the life of the Republic. ...This is not murder. It is a political necessity...

Garfield's presidency is one of the shortest in American history: only nine months, tragically cut short by a lunatic whose last words before he swung from the scaffold were, "I saved my party and my land! Glory hallelujah!"

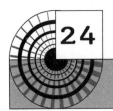

24

Germaine Greer

| ASSASSINATED | — |
| SURVIVED | ✓ |

Ever since I published The Female Eunuch *there has always been an off-chance that someone was going to pick me off. Somewhere. Some nutter. Seeing some of the hostility we get in letters. I feel a bit like Caesar. The brave man dies but once. The coward dies many times. In this case it is a brave woman. I refuse to be afraid.*

—Germaine Greer[1]

VICTIM: Germaine Greer

BORN: January 29, 1939

DIED: n/a

AGE WHEN ATTACKED: 61

OCCUPATION: Australian-born writer, teacher, author of the best-selling seminal feminist apologia, *The Female Eunuch*

ASSAILANT: Karen Burke (b. 1981), 19, obsessed student

DATE & TIME OF ATTACK: Monday, April 24, 2000, late afternoon

LOCATION OF ATTACK: In Greer's home near Saffron Walden, in Great Chesterford, Essex, England

WEAPON: A fireplace poker

ASSASSINATION OUTCOME: Greer was tied up and physically struggled with Burke over a two-hour period, but she was uninjured.

JUDICIAL OUTCOME: Burke was charged with unlawful imprisonment and assault occasioning actual bodily harm. In July 2000, she pled guilty to harassment, and the unlawful imprisonment and assault charges were dropped. She was given two years probation, agreed to seek psychiatric treatment, and was ordered not to contact Greer or go within five miles of Greer's home.

Would obsessed student Karen Burke have killed Germaine Greer if her hostage-taking of the feminist writer and professor had not been interrupted?

Greer's friends investigated when she was almost three hours late for a planned dinner, and they came upon a volatile situation in which Burke had smashed things in Greer's home with a fireplace poker, tied her up, and had held Greer captive in the house for close to two hours.

Karen Burke, a Bath University student studying Italian, German, and European Studies, was known to Germaine Greer, although they had never actually met prior to the April 2000 incident, which began on Friday, April 21st and ended on Monday, April 24th.

Burke, who was from Wollaton, Nottingham, England, became utterly obsessed with the author after studying her works in school and, shortly thereafter, in early 2000, Burke began writing letters to Greer that have been described by Greer and the police as distressing and disturbing. Greer wrote back to Burke and asked her to stop writing to her, but this failed to sever the emotional tie Burke felt with Greer.

On April 21, 2000, Burke showed up at Greer's home in Essex. Greer (in hindsight, unwisely) apparently felt sympathetic towards the delusional, fixated young woman and allowed her to spend the night in her garden shelter on the grounds of her farm. The following morning, Greer drove Burke to a train station and asked her to please leave and not come back.

Two days later, as Greer was walking down her driveway on her way to a dinner engagement, Burke burst out of the bushes bordering the drive, frightening Greer. Greer screamed and turned to run back to her house to call the police, but Burke jumped onto the 61-year-old writer's back, and began shouting, "Mummy, Mummy, don't do that! Mummy, Mummy, don't do that!"

Somehow, Burke managed to move Greer back into the house and, for the next two hours, a bizarre and violent psychodrama took place, during which both women were injured and many items in Greer's home were destroyed by Burke, maniacally wielding a fireplace poker.

When Greer's academic friends visited to inquire as to why she was late for their dinner, they immediately called the police and Burke was arrested.

During Burke's arraignment, the prosecutor for the case, Dinah Walters, told the court, "[Miss Greer] gathered from the conversation [on the 21st] that Karen Burke was infatuated with her and wished to adopt her as some form of spiritual mother figure."[2] According to Walters, when Greer's friends arrived, "They found Miss Burke holding on to Professor Greer by the legs and screaming."[3]

Walters then read to the court a statement by Burke in which she said, "I know this was extremely stupid and I should not have done it. I don't know what got into me. I just wanted to get all this stuff out of my head. It is an emotional thing. I wanted to hug her."[4]

Again, this begs the question: What would have happened to Greer if her friends had not shown up when they did? Would Burke have had a complete psychotic break and tried to kill Greer? Burke later claimed to be aware that her actions were daft and that she was agreeable to the mandate to stay away from Greer, but history shows that obsession is not so easily vanquished. Since her conviction, Burke has not harassed Professor Greer (or, if she has contacted her, it has not made the media). Germaine Greer did not allow the attack to rattle her, and she continues to teach comparative literature at Warwick University in England. She has not published a new book since 1999's *The Whole Woman*, but she continues to speak out and write about women's issues.

Germaine Greer Bibliography	
1970 *The Female Eunuch* 1979 *The Obstacle Race: The Fortunes of Women Painters and Their Work*	1984 *Sex and Destiny: The Politics of Human Fertility* 1991 *The Change: Women, Aging and the Menopause* 1999 *The Whole Woman*

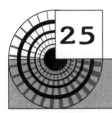

25

George Harrison

ASSASSINATED	
SURVIVED	✓

After what happened to John, I'm absolutely terrified.
—George Harrison in 1984[1]

VICTIM: George Harrison

BORN: February 25, 1943

DIED: November 29, 2001

AGE WHEN ATTACKED: 56

OCCUPATION: Musician, actor, writer, producer, former member of The Beatles

UNSUCCESSFUL ASSASSIN: Michael Abrams, 33, mentally ill heroin addict

DATE & TIME OF ATTACK: Thursday, December 30, 1999, approximately 3:30 a.m.

LOCATION OF ATTACK: Inside Harrison's home on his estate Friar Park in Henley-on-Thames, England

WEAPON: A 6-inch-long knife

ASSASSINATION OUTCOME: Harrison was stabbed in the chest, suffered a punctured lung, and was bruised, but his wounds were not life-threatening and he survived. His wife Olivia was treated for cuts and bruises sustained during her struggle with Abrams.

JUDICIAL OUTCOME: In November 2000, Abrams was found not guilty by reason of insanity and committed to a psychiatric hospital "indefinitely."

George Harrison's English neighbors jokingly referred to his 34-room, 32-acre Gothic estate as "Fort Knox" because of the elaborate security precautions (supposedly) protecting the place.

Friar Park had bright floodlights, barbed wire atop high fences, video camera surveillance, electronically controlled gates, and routine dog patrols. Harrison was always worried about himself and his family being hurt or killed and, following John Lennon's assassination (Chapter 41) in 1980, he took his protection concerns very seriously. Harrison seemed to always understand how vulnerable artists were to their fans and how easy it would be for someone in an audience to attack a performer on stage (or anywhere else, actually). The Beatles final live performance as a group—the lunchtime rooftop concert in London on January 30, 1969—happened only because Harrison adamantly refused to play in front of an audience, no matter how many times the other Beatles asked him to.

Security is as security does, however, and in the early morning hours of December 30, 1999, George Harrison's secure manse was anything but.

To this day, fans of the former Beatle still ask many tough questions about the assassination attempt on George—specifically, how could a mentally ill drug addict get onto the grounds of Harrison's estate, break a kitchen window, enter the house, climb the stairs to George and Olivia's bedroom, and attack them with a knife? If there was video surveillance of the grounds, why wasn't someone monitoring the cameras? If there were "elaborate" alarm systems, why didn't sirens go off and lights explode on when the downstairs window was broken? If the security system was so air-tight, why didn't George have a panic button that would have summoned help immediately, instead of him having to telephone the police and lock himself and his wife in his bedroom until they arrived?

George and Olivia were awakened by the sound of breaking glass, not by an alarm going off. While Olivia called for help, George got up and, clad only in pajama bottoms, went downstairs where he was confronted by Michael Abram, who then attacked the former Beatle with a knife. George was stabbed in the chest during a violent struggle, and his life was saved when his wife came downstairs and struck Abrams in the head with a heavy brass lamp, knocking him unconscious. "Olivia gave him a good clocking and probably saved George's life," said an unidentified police source following the attack.[2]

George and Olivia were taken to nearby Royal Berkshire Hospital, where they were both treated. Dr. William Fountain, the surgeon who treated George's stab wound and collapsed lung, described the stabbing as "a narrow escape that was little short of miraculous."[3] Abram's knife barely missed cutting George's superior vena cava, a critically important artery that carries blood from the entire upper body to the heart. George was later moved to Harefield Hospital, which was better equipped to treat chest injuries. George was alert and in good spirits while in the hospital and he even joked with the staff, telling them that he did not think that Abrams was a burglar, but "he certainly wasn't auditioning for the Traveling Wilburys."[4]

Abram's mother later told the authorities that her son was severely mentally ill—a paranoid schizophrenic—and that he had become obsessed with The Beatles (after a short flirtation with the Beatles-inspired band Oasis) and that he believed them to be proponents of black magic and that George himself was the "phantom menace" described in the writings of Nostradamus. Following his arrest, his mother expressed relief that her son would get the help he so desperately needed, and she blamed the British medical establishment for not recognizing the severity of his illness and for allowing him to wander the streets.

George was released a few days after the attack and spent several weeks recovering from his injuries.

Although he fully recovered from the knife attack, George experienced a recurrence of the cancer that had begun with throat cancer several years prior and that moved to his brain in early 2000. Harrison died of brain cancer in November 2001, and his ashes were scattered in the Ganges River in India.

And then there were two.

George Harrison Solo Discography	
1968 *Wonderwall*	1977 *The Best of George Harrison*
1969 *Electronic Sound*	1979 *George Harrison*
1970 *All Things Must Pass*	1981 *Somewhere In England*
1972 *The Concert For Bangladesh*	1982 *Gone Troppo*
1973 *Living In The Material World*	1987 *Cloud Nine*
1974 *Dark Horse*	1989 *Best of Dark Horse 1976–1989*
1975 *Extra Texture*	1992 *Live In Japan*
1976 *Thirty Three And A Third*	2002 *Brainwashed*

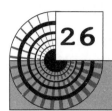

26

Phil Hartman

ASSASSINATED $\checkmark$

SURVIVED ___

Phil, while he was a wonderful listener, didn't offer a lot. He was pretty tight-lipped about his own problems, if he were having some. I can't honestly say that he shared a lot with me about his home life. But Brynn was always very sweet to me, and she would come to the shows, and bring the children into rehearsal. To me, it just seemed like a lovely, happy family.

—*Saturday Night Live* alumni Jan Hooks[1]

VICTIM: Phil Hartman

BORN: September 24, 1948

DIED: May 28, 1998

AGE WHEN ATTACKED: 49

OCCUPATION: Canadian-born comedian, writer, actor, best known for his virtuoso performances on *Saturday Night Live*, his starring role in the sitcom *Newsradio*, and several movie roles

ASSASSIN: Brynn Hartman (1958–1998), 40, Hartman's wife

DATE & TIME OF ATTACK: Thursday, May 28, 1998, probably around 3 a.m.

LOCATION OF ATTACK: On the king-sized bed in the bedroom of Hartman's mansion (which he had nicknamed "The Ponderosa") in Encino, California

WEAPON: A Smith & Wesson revolver

ASSASSINATION OUTCOME: Phil Hartman was killed in his sleep by being shot three times by his wife, Brynn, in the early hours of May 28, 1998. There were no signs that Hartman awakened during the shooting. Brynn Hartman committed suicide around 6:30 that morning.

JUDICIAL OUTCOME: None. The Hartmans' estate went to their children, who are being raised by Brynn Hartman's sister and her husband in Eau Claire, Wisconsin.

The assassination of Phil Hartman by his wife, Brynn, who later committed suicide, occurred while the couple's two children, Sean, 9, and Birgen, 6, were asleep in their beds. Brynn Hartman shot her husband three times in the head and neck as he slept and then fled the house, leaving behind their still-sleeping children and the corpse of their father.

After killing Phil, Brynn went immediately to the home of her friend Ron Douglas, and she confessed to him that she had had just murdered her husband. At first, Douglas did not believe her, but he became very concerned and suspicious when he found a Smith & Wesson revolver in her purse. She reportedly fell asleep at Douglas's house for a couple of hours and then accompanied Douglas back to her and Phil's home at around six o'clock that morning.

Upon their arrival, Douglas found Hartman's kids awake, terrified, and huddled together inside the front door of the house. (It is highly likely that at least Sean, the older child, saw his father's body. He may have then prevented his sister from seeing it—or they both could have visited their parent's bedroom upon awakening and together seen what happened. Either or both of the children may choose to talk about the deaths of their parents when they are adults, but for now, this is all speculation.)

In the bedroom, Douglas found Hartman's dead body, and he called 911 at 6:20 a.m. "She said she had killed her husband and I didn't believe her," Douglas told the 911 dispatcher. The dispatcher then asked Douglas where Hartman had been shot and he replied, "I think around the head and the neck. I just got here."[2]

When the police arrived at around 6:30, Brynn Hartman quickly locked herself in the bedroom with her husband's body. The police ushered Sean out to a police car and, as they were carrying out Birgen, they heard a single gunshot from inside the house.

The police broke open the bedroom door and found Hartman's body on the bed and Brynn Hartman's body beside the bed on the floor. Brynn had shot herself in the head, the bullet almost blowing her head off her body.

Autopsies were performed and the toxicology report revealed that alcohol, cocaine, and the antidepressant drug Zoloft were found in Brynn Hartman's blood. An over-the-counter cold medication was found in Phil Hartman's blood.

Why did Brynn Hartman kill her husband in his sleep and then commit suicide, leaving behind two young children? This is the question Hartman's family and friends asked, and yet probably have not been able to answer. No one truly knows what goes on between a married couple and, surface appearances aside (they were a glamorous, loving couple often in the public eye), there were obviously some deep-seated problems (at least in Brynn's mind) that consumed her and pushed her to the point of killing her husband and herself.

The evening of the murder, Brynn had dinner with a female friend at Buca di Beppoa, an Italian restaurant she and her husband frequented. She drank two Cosmopolitans, and her dinner companion later told police that Brynn had seemed "friendly and calm."[3]

During dinner, at approximately 9:45 p.m., Phil called Brynn's cell phone. She answered the call, hung up, said, "Phil's home, I'm going,"[4] and left the restaurant.

Several hours later, she murdered her husband. What happened between Phil and Brynn between approximately 10 o'clock that evening and three in the morning? Did they fight? Did Phil tell her he wanted a divorce or that he was having an affair? Did Brynn have some kind of psychotic breakdown that convinced her that death was the only solution to her problems? We don't know the answers to these questions, and we will likely never know.

This horrible tragedy robbed two children of their parents and deprived the world of one of its funniest citizens.

Phil and Brynn Hartman's bodies were not embalmed, and both were cremated. According to their death certificates, Phil's ashes went to his mother, Doris, and Brynn's ashes went to her mother, Constance.

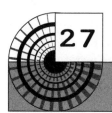

27

Wild Bill Hickok

ASSASSINATED   ✓

SURVIVED   __

I have seen many dead men on the field of battle and in civil life, but Wild Bill was the prettiest corpse I have ever seen. His long moustache was attractive, even in death, and his long tapering fingers looked like marble...

—Ellis T. "Doc" Pierce[1]

VICTIM: James Butler "Wild Bill" Hickok

BORN: May 27, 1837

DIED: August 2, 1876

AGE WHEN ATTACKED: 39

OCCUPATION: The "Prince of Pistoliers," frontier figure, entertainer with Buffalo Bill Cody's Wild West Show, Civil War-era spy, stagecoach driver, occasional scout for 10th U.S. Cavalry, United States Marshall

ASSASSIN: John "Jack" McCall (real name Bill Sutherland) (1850? –1877), 26?, drifter and scoundrel, possibly a buffalo hunter

DATE & TIME OF ATTACK: Wednesday, August 2, 1876, sometime shortly before 3 p.m.

LOCATION OF ATTACK: Nuttal & Mann's No. 10 Saloon, Deadwood, South Dakota Territory

WEAPON: A .36-caliber 1851 Colt Navy cap and ball plack powder single action pistol (Later, most accounts of the assassination would state that the pistol used was a Colt .45 Peacemaker single action pistol, but in 1876 there were only 25,000 of these expensive weapons in use, and it is unlikely that McCall possessed one. Accounts of the shooting, including the size and shape of Hickok's wound and the failure of the gun to discharge when McCall tried to fire at others in the saloon, support the cap and powder pistol theory.)

ASSASSINATION OUTCOME: McCall's bullet, fired point blank, entered the base of Hickok's brain at the back of his head and exited through his right cheek. Hickok died instantly. After exiting Hickok, the bullet struck the wrist of one of his fellow poker players, a Mississippi riverboat captain named William R. Massie.

JUDICIAL OUTCOME: After he shot Hickok, McCall fled the saloon, but he was chased and quickly captured by a group of men who had witnessed him kill Wild Bill. A Miner's Court was convened the following day, and McCall was acquitted after explaining that he shot Hickok in retribution for Hickok's alleged murder of his brother. Set free, McCall then fled the area and traveled around the South Dakota Territory bragging about getting away with murdering Wild Bill. His hubris was short-lived, however, because he was re-arrested a couple of weeks later, thanks to the efforts of Hickok's friend George May. He was retried at the end of August 1876, found guilty of murder, and hanged the following March.

I have a friend who always used to say to me, "It only takes once." Basically a variation of the Marines' motto "ever vigilant," his constant reminder that one single oversight can lead to tragedy always struck me as a worthy principle to live by. The one time you leave your car unlocked is the one time your tape deck will get stolen. The one time you forget to set your home alarm system is the one time your house will get broken into. And the one time you sit with your back to the door is the one time someone will put a bullet in your brain.

Wild Bill Hickok always poured his drinks with his left hand so his gun hand was free at all times. When he played poker, he always sat with his back to a wall. After an article about his exploits appeared in *Harper's New Monthly Magazine*, Wild Bill became a celebrity around Kansas, and, subsequently, Bill "acquired" lots of enemies. Such safety practices were employed because he didn't want anyone sneaking up behind him.

His precautions kept Wild Bill alive until he was 39 years old. On August 2, 1876, he entered the No. 10 Saloon in Deadwood in the South Dakota Territory and saw that a poker game was already in progress. Bill loved to gamble, and he especially loved five-card draw poker. There was one open spot at the table, but it faced the back of the room, leaving whomever sat in it blind to anyone walking in the door of the tavern. Bill asked another player to switch seats, but the man told him his seat had been lucky for him so he'd rather stay put.

Bill probably argued with himself a bit, but he did so love a good card game that, finally, he abandoned—just this one time—his long-held security practices—and took the stool with his back to the front door.

Shortly before 3:00 in the afternoon, Jack McCall entered the tavern and saw Wild Bill sitting at a table in the center of the room.

McCall was cross-eyed and drunk (not "cross-eyed drunk"; literally cross-eyed *and* drunk).

He walked up behind Hickok and, when he was within three feet of the frontier legend, pulled out a pistol, said, "Damn you, take that!" and fired one bullet into the back of Wild Bill's head.

Wild Bill fell off the chair, still holding his hand of cards, supposedly consisting of a pair of black aces, a pair of black eights, and the red Jack of Hearts (or Diamonds, or Queen of Diamonds, depending on the source). This hand—aces and eights—soon became known as the Deadman's Hand, although many historians now claim that the story of the cards was a fabrication of later chroniclers of the Wild Bill legend and that there is no contemporary evidence of what hand Hickok was holding when he was shot. The only confirmed account of the cards came from Ellis Pierce, a local barber and witness to the shooting. In a letter to Frank J. Wilstach, Pierce wrote, "Bill's hand read 'aces and eights'—two pair, and since that day aces and eights have been known as 'the Deadman's hand' in the Western country."[2]

The legend of Wild Bill Hickok only grew following his death, and today reenactments of his shooting and McCall's trial take place four times a day in Deadwood, South Dakota.

> Wild Bill
> J.B. Hickok
> Killed by the Assassin
> Jack M'Call
> In Deadwood, Black Hills
> Aug. 2d 1876
> Pard, we will meet
> Again in the Happy
> Hunting Ground
> To part no more,
> Goodbye

Wild Bill's Epitaph

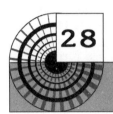

28

Adolf Hitler

ASSASSINATED ___

SURVIVED ✓

Those who joined in the plots to remove Hitler were true heroes. They listened to their conscience, and the majority of them paid for their decision with their lives. In many cases, friends and family members who were not directly involved in the plots were punished as well. Being a part of the hidden resistance was not a decision that anyone took lightly. They knew the risks, but they also believed that their actions were necessary.

—Michael C. Thomsett[1]

VICTIM: Adolf Hitler

BORN: April 12, 1889

DIED: April 30, 1945

OCCUPATION: Austrian-born founder of the Nazi Party, Fuehrer, Reich chancellor of Germany, fascist dictator of Germany (1933–1945), Roman Catholic, writer (published more than six volumes of writings), member of the German Army 16th Reserve Infantry Regiment of Bavaria, spy, recipient of two Iron Crosses for Bravery (presented to him by a Jew), architect of the mass annihilation of Jews and homosexuals now known as the Holocaust, most evil person who ever lived[2]

Hitler

— **98** —

How would history have been written if one of the many assassination attempts against Adolf Hitler had succeeded? How much pain would have been prevented? How many lives would have been saved? How would the world be different?

Hitler's own economic minister, Albert Speer, plotted to assassinate Hitler with the deadly nerve gas tabun.

In 1921, gunmen opened fire on Hitler during a speech he was giving called, ironically, "Who Are the Murderers?" Reportedly, Hitler himself returned fire.

In 1929, an SS soldier planted a bomb underneath a speaking platform where Hitler was to give a speech but then locked himself in bathroom and could not trigger the bomb before Hitler left the building.

In 1932, gunmen opened fire on Hitler as he rode on a train from Munich to Weimar.

That same year, his car was ambushed and fired upon near the town of Straslund.

A month later, a group of unknown malcontents threw stones at Hitler's car and hit the Fuehrer in the head.

There are too many more similar accounts to include in this limited space, but suffice to say that the resistance to Hitler was obviously "local," as well as global.

Here are three of the most notable attempts to kill Adolf Hitler.

The Beer Hall Bombing

UNSUCCESSFUL ASSASSIN: Johann Georg Elser (1903–1945), 36, carpenter, electrician, member of the Woodworker's Union

DATE & TIME OF ATTACK: Wednesday, November 8, 1939, 9:20 p.m.

LOCATION OF ATTACK: In the Lowenbrau Beer Hall (formerly called the Burgerbraukeller, and the site of Hitler's unsuccessful 1923 *putsch* to overthrow the German government) on Rosenheimer Strasse, in Munich, Germany

WEAPON: A 110-pound time bomb hidden in the main support column of the Beer Hall

ASSASSINATION OUTCOME: Hitler, 50, left the Beer Hall earlier than anticipated and was not on the premises when the bomb went off. Eight people were killed, 63 were injured, and "Hitler's table was buried under more than six feet of timbers, brick and rubble, and fallen ceiling beams."[3]

JUDICIAL OUTCOME: Elser was caught at the Swiss/German border and sent to a concentration camp. He was treated quite well, though, because the German high command believed that he might have been part of a conspiracy, and they hoped to learn its secrets from him. Elser even built them a duplicate of the bomb he used. It was eventually determined that Elser acted alone and it was reported that he died in an Allied bombing raid. It is more likely that Heinrich Himmler, Hitler's second-in-command, ordered his execution after he had exhausted his usefulness.

Operation Flash

UNSUCCESSFUL ASSASSIN: Fabian von Schlabrendorff (1907–1980), 36, lawyer, Wehrmacht reserve officer, part of the resistance movement

DATE & TIME OF ATTACK: Saturday, March 13, 1943

LOCATION OF ATTACK: On Hitler's personal plane, on approach to an airfield in Smolensk, Germany

WEAPON: A time bomb disguised to look like two brandy bottles

ASSASSINATION OUTCOME: The bomb failed to detonate when triggered due to a faulty British-made detonator. The plane landed safely and Hitler, 54, never learned about the failed attempt on his life. (Earlier, Schlabrendorff had attempted to plant a bomb in Hitler's personal car but was foiled by tight security. He did not have that problem planting a bomb on the plane.)

JUDICIAL OUTCOME: Schlabrendorff was never charged with this assassination attempt, although he was arrested by the Gestapo on August 17, 1944, as a member of the resistance. He was brutally tortured and put on trial on February 3, 1945, but an air raid blew up the courtroom and killed the judge. At his second trial on March 16, 1945, he was acquitted on grounds of unlawful torture. Nonetheless, the Gestapo interred him in a concentration camp, but he was freed by the Allies during the last days of the war.

The Valkyrie Plan

UNSUCCESSFUL ASSASSIN: Colonel Count Klaus Schenk von Stauffenberg (1907–1944), 37, Roman Catholic, a natural leader, main architect of the Valkyrie plan

DATE & TIME OF ATTACK: Thursday, July 20, 1944, 12:42 p.m.

LOCATION OF ATTACK: In the Map Room in Hitler's headquarters in Rastenburg, East Prussia

WEAPON: A 2-pound bomb hidden under a uniform shirt in Stauffenberg's suitcase

ASSASSINATION OUTCOME: The bomb exploded successfully but Hitler, 55, who was knocked unconscious, received only superficial wounds and burns, ruptured eardrums, and shredded pants. Others in the room were thrown to the floor with their hair and uniforms on fire. Several officers died, and many more were wounded. Hitler was treated by his doctor and spoke to the German people on the radio a few hours after the bombing.

JUDICIAL OUTCOME: Stauffenberg was arrested, court-martialed, and executed by firing squad the evening of July 20, 1944, less than twelve hours after the assassination attempt. His last words were, "Long live sacred Germany." Close to 7,000 people were later arrested and punished for conspiring with Stauffenberg against Hitler, and 2,000 death sentences were issued. Eight complicit officers were strung up with piano wire and suspended from meat hooks at the Ploetzdensee Prison. Hitler had their hanging filmed, and it showed them suspended from the hooks, stripped to the waist, writhing violently as they slowly died. As they swung, their pants dropped off, leaving them naked. The film was rushed to Hitler for a private viewing and, reportedly, the footage was so grisly that Joseph Goebbels had to cover his eyes to prevent himself from fainting. The investigation into the Valkyrie Plot remained ongoing until the collapse of the Reich nine months later.

Adolf Hitler committed suicide in his bunker on April 30, 1945, as the Nazi regime crumbled around him and the Allies were on the verge of winning World War II. He shot his dog and his mistress, Eva Braun, first.

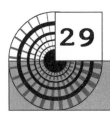 **29**

Herbert Hoover

ASSASSINATED ⎯

SURVIVED ✓

I see Mr. Hoover first, I kill him first. Make no difference, presidents just the same bunch—all same.

—Giuseppe Zangara[1]

VICTIM: Herbert Hoover

BORN: August 10, 1874

DIED: October 20, 1964

AGE WHEN ATTACKED: n/a

OCCUPATION: 31st president of the United States (1929–1933), Republican

CONSPIRING ASSASSIN: Giuseppe Zangara (1900–1933), Italian-born bricklayer with stomach problems that he blamed on Hoover, assassin of Chicago Mayor Anton Cermak during an assassination attempt on President Franklin Delano Roosevelt (page 208)

Hoover

DATE & TIME OF ATTACK: Undetermined

LOCATION OF ATTACK: Somewhere in Washington. D.C.

WEAPON: Likely a pistol that Zangara bought for $20

ASSASSINATION OUTCOME: Zangara never acted on his plan to assassinate President Hoover.

JUDICIAL OUTCOME: Zangara was executed in the electric chair on March 20, 1933 at the Florida State Penitentiary in Railford, Florida, for the death of Chicago Mayor Anton Cermak, but never faced charges for his planned assassination of Hoover.

Giuseppe Zangara was a disturbed, misanthropic Italian immigrant who once admitted, "I don't like no peoples."[2]

History remembers Zangara for his attempted assassination of President Franklin Roosevelt and his successful assassination of Chicago Mayor Anton Cermak, but Zangara later admitted also plotting to assassinate President Herbert Hoover with a cheap pistol he bought for $20.

Due to a terrible diet and poor eating habits as a child, the adult Zangara developed a number of stomach ulcers that caused him constant, agonizing abdominal pain. He once said he felt like he had a drunk man's stomach, so we can conclude that he was also nauseated a great deal of the time, as well as suffered the burning, stabbing pain so common to ulcers. An autopsy later revealed that Zangara also had a diseased gallbladder, which contributed to his stomach troubles. (No wonder he hated everybody.)

For some reason, Zangara blamed President Hoover for his stomach pains, and he also disliked him because Hoover was the leader of the most capitalistic nation in world history. Zangara hated capitalism and believed it was the source of all his problems, as well as being the reason the world knew so much suffering. In his twisted thinking, then, the kings and presidents and leaders who supported such policies were to blame, they needed to be eliminated, and he was the man for the job.

Even though Zangara personally hated Hoover, he was not committed to assassinating him in particular. When FDR beat Hoover in the 1932 election, Zangara dropped his plans to kill Hoover and instead moved on to developing a plot to assassinate Roosevelt. As far as we know, President Hoover was never in any actual danger from Giuseppe Zangara. (For more information on Zangara and his attempted assassination of President Roosevelt, see pages 208-210.)

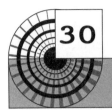

30 Hubert Humphrey

ASSASSINATED ___

SURVIVED ✓

The Vice President will be and is what the President wants him to be.

—Hubert Humphrey[1]

VICTIM: Hubert Humphrey

BORN: May 27, 1911

Died: January 13, 1978

AGE WHEN PLOTTED AGAINST: 55

OCCUPATION: Vice president of the United States (1965–1969) under President Lyndon Johnson (1963–1969)

AVOWED ASSASSIN: Peter Kocan (b. 1947), 19, schizophrenic, sporadic factory worker, failed assassin of Australian Labour Party leader Arthur Calwell

DATE & TIME OF PLOTTED ATTACK: August 1966

LOCATION OF ATTACK: Australia

WEAPON: Probably a sawed-off shotgun

ASSASSINATION OUTCOME: Kocan could not get close to Humphrey due to his extremely tight security. The Secret Service is especially vigilant on foreign soil and, in this case, it prevented an assassination attempt on the vice president.

JUDICIAL OUTCOME: Kocan was never charged with anything pertaining to his stated intent to assassinate Hubert Humphrey. He was, however, sentenced to life imprisonment in Australia in 1966 for his attempt on the life of Arthur Calwell. He has been institutionalized in an asylum for the criminally insane in Morisset, Australia, since December 30, 1966. In 1968, he wrote to Calwell and apologized for shooting at him with a sawed-off shogun. Calwell forgave him. It is not believed he expressed any regret for plotting to kill Vice President Humphrey.

This is technically not a specific assassination attempt on the life of Vice President Hubert Humphrey, because Peter Kocan did not act on his stated intent; however, if Humphrey's Secret Service detail had been even a little lax that day in Australia in August 1966, then it is extremely likely that Kocan would have taken a shot at Humphrey and possibly killed him.

Kocan's desire to kill Humphrey is included here as an illustration of the randomness with which an assassination attempt can occur. Humphrey's trip was designed to assure the Australian government (a strong American ally) that the war in Vietnam was being run by Peking and Hanoi. Arthur Calwell had recently come out in opposition to drafting Australian soldiers for the war in Vietnam and Humphrey went to the land down under to soothe Aussie nerves.

Humphrey made it back to America safely.

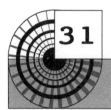

Andrew Jackson

ASSASSINATED ___

SURVIVED ✓

You are uneasy; you never sailed with me before, I see.
—President Andrew Jackson[1]

VICTIM: Andrew Jackson

BORN: May 15, 1767

DIED: June 8, 1845

AGE WHEN ATTACKED: 67

OCCUPATION: 7th president of the United States (1829–1837)

UNSUCCESSFUL ASSASSIN: Richard Lawrence (1800/1801? –1861), 34/35?, mentally disturbed, unemployed house painter

DATE & TIME OF ATTACK: Friday, January 30, 1835, late morning

Jackson

LOCATION OF ATTACK: The rotunda of the Capitol Building in Washington, D.C.

WEAPONS: Two single-shot derringer dueling pistols

ASSASSINATION OUTCOME: President Jackson was uninjured, thanks to both of Lawrence's guns misfiring. It is estimated that the odds of two single-shot pistols misfiring at the same time are hundreds of thousands to one. Experts now believe that the gunpowder failed to

— 106 —

ignite due to moisture. The day is recorded as being very humid and foggy, and the type of pistol Lawrence used was known to malfunction in damp weather. (It should be noted (and probably admired) that President Jackson was so infuriated by the audacity of someone trying to shoot him that he went after Lawrence with his walking cane, presumably to wale him into stupefaction.)

JUDICIAL OUTCOME: Lawrence was immediately arrested and went to trial on April 11, 1835 for attempting to assassinate the President of the United States. During the proceedings, Lawrence was unruly, disruptive, disrespectful, and incoherent. It took the jury five minutes to find him not guilty by reason of insanity, and he was sentenced to confinement in a mental institution for the remainder of his days. Lawrence died in a mental institution in 1861.

Richard Lawrence was the first person to attempt to assassinate a United States president. His reason? He believed that he was King Richard III of England, that the United States Congress owed him an enormous sum of money, and that President Andrew Jackson was gumming up the works and preventing him from receiving what was rightfully due him.

Yes, Richard Lawrence was as crazy as a loon, yet this did not prevent him from carefully planning his attack, stalking the president, and getting close enough to kill him—if both of his guns had not misfired.

The president went to the Capitol to attend funeral services for recently deceased South Carolina congressman Warren R. Davis. Lawrence had watched Jackson enter the Capitol building but could not get close enough to fire. He waited until the ceremony was over and the mourners began to file out before making his move. As Jackson walked slowly across the rotunda, his cane in one hand and his other hand resting on the arm of Secretary of the Treasury Levi Woodbury, Lawrence waited patiently behind a pillar, his guns cocked.

When Jackson got close enough, he burst out from behind the column, aimed the gun in his right hand at Jackson's heart, and fired.

Nothing.

He then dropped the pistol and moved the gun in his left hand to his right, and fired again.

Nothing again.

By then, it was all over for Richard Lawrence, and he ended up being taken into custody with a few welts from President Jackson's cane.

Interesting facts about the assassination attempt against President Jackson

▶ The prosecutor in the case against Richard Lawrence was Francis Scott Key. Yes, *that* Francis Scott Key, the composer of "The "Star-Spangled Banner."

▶ One of the politicians who subdued Lawrence after his guns misfired was Davy Crockett. Yes, *that* Davy Crockett, the frontiersman who was also known as Congressman David Crockett from the great state of Tennessee.

▶ Lawrence's attempt on Jackson's life was not only the first time someone tried to kill a U.S. president, but it was also the first time a conspiracy theory about a presidential assassination attempt was born. As soon as Lawrence was in custody, President Jackson began telling anyone who would listen that he believed Lawrence was hired by some of his Whig opponents—specifically Senator Poindexter of Mississippi—to kill him. There was even talk that members of Jackson's own cabinet had plotted against him. In the end, it was accepted that Richard Lawrence was nothing more than a man we would describe today as a paranoid schizophrenic, attacking the most visible representative of his imagined oppression.

▶ The hospital where Lawrence was confined for his entire life was originally called the Government Hospital for the Insane. It is now known as St. Elizabeth's Hospital and is the institution where another presidential assassin, John Hinckley, is now in custody.

▶ Would-be assassin Richard Lawrence was a house painter and a landscape painter, and there was serious inquiry into the possibility that his insanity came from being poisoned by the lead pigment in the paints he used on a daily basis.

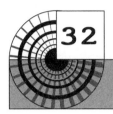

32

Reverend Jesse Jackson

ASSASSINATED	___
SURVIVED	✓

Our flag is red, white, and blue, but our nation is a rainbow— red, yellow, brown, black, and white—and we're all precious in God's sight. America is not like a blanket—one piece of unbroken cloth, the same color, the same texture, the same size. America is more like a quilt—many patches, many pieces, many colors, many sizes, all woven and held together by a common thread...Even in our fractured state, all of us count and all of us fit somewhere.

—Jesse Jackson[1]

VICTIM: Reverend Jesse Jackson

BORN: October 8, 1941

DIED: n/a

AGE WHEN PLOTTED AGAINST: 47

OCCUPATION: Candidate for Democratic presidential nomination, founder of the Rainbow Coalition, religious leader, civil-rights activist, founder of Operation PUSH (People United to Save Humanity), recipient of the Martin Luther King, Jr. Nonviolent Peace Prize, recipient of Presidential Medal of Freedom

CONSPIRING ASSASSINS: Londell Williams, 30, member of the Neo-Nazi organization, the Covenant, the Sword and the Arm of the Lord (CSA); Tammy Williams, 27, his wife

DATE & TIME OF ATTACK: Probably sometime in 1988

LOCATION OF ATTACK: Somewhere on Jackson's campaign trail. (The Williamses lived in Washington, Missouri.)

WEAPON: An AR-15 automatic rifle with telescopic sight

ASSASSINATION OUTCOME: Unsuccessful. Londell and Tammy Williams were surveilled, arrested, tried, convicted, and imprisoned before they could take a shot at Reverend Jackson. He was unhurt.

JUDICIAL OUTCOME: The Williamses were arrested and charged with threatening a presidential candidate, threatening a government informant, and possession of an illegal weapon. In August 1988, Londell Williams pled guilty to threatening a presidential candidate and possession of an unregistered weapon. The threatening an informant charge was dropped in a plea agreement. He was sentenced to two years in prison and fined $100. A few months later, his wife Tammy was sentenced to 20 months in prison for her complicity and participation in the plot to assassinate Jesse Jackson.

The Reverend Jesse Jackson[2] made it possible for Americans to conceive of a black president.

He ran for the Democratic nomination for president in 1984 and 1988 and, by his second attempt, it was clear that *he* was serious and that his possible candidacy was also being taken seriously by Americans.

Londell Williams and his wife, Tammy, had three children and lived in Washington, Missouri, 50 miles or so from St. Louis. In 1988, Londell was on probation for a gun charge; his wife was on probation for a marijuana possession charge.

Londell was not happy about Jesse Jackson attempting to run for president of the United States. He just did not see this as a good thing for white America. He was a proud member of a Neo-Nazi organization called *The Covenant, the Sword and the Arm of the Lord*, and the members of this group agreed that Jesse Jackson did not belong in the presidential race. Londell reportedly spoke out about his membership in the CSA, and he also bragged that he planned to kill Jesse Jackson. An obviously more-tolerant citizen of Missouri tipped off the police about Williams's boasts and, because Jackson was a legitimate candidate for the nomination, the Secret Service was notified.

The Franklin County, Missouri, Sheriff's Department, working with wiretaps, informants, and the Secret Service, recorded Williams talking about being a member of the CSA, and this was enough to get a search warrant for his house.

Inside Williams's home, they found a powerful—and illegal—AR-15 assault rifle, specially equipped with a telescopic sight, and Williams was arrested. Tammy Williams was also arrested, and they both ended up going to prison for their intent to assassinate Jesse Jackson.

Jesse Jackson was told about the Williamses as he traveled the campaign trail. Revealingly, he described the two racists as "dream busters," which is an extremely apt perception of their overall mission. They did not simply want to kill Jesse Jackson; Londell and Tammy Williams wanted to kill the dream of African-Americans running for higher office in America—and of a tolerant America welcoming their participation in the democratic process.

How have things changed since 1988 when the Williamses wanted to eliminate Jesse Jackson from the Democratic ticket?

Colin Powell is now Secretary of State, and there was serious talk about him one day running for president.

Dr. Condoleeza Rice is now National Security Advisor, and there is an unofficial Web site called "Condoleeza Rice for President 2008."

Jesse Jackson's son is now a Congressman, and it is believed he will definitely seek higher office one day.

The efforts of the CSA and similar groups have been, for the most part, for naught.

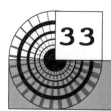

33

Jesse James

ASSASSINATED   ✓

SURVIVED   ___

THE FORD BROTHERS INDICTED, PLEAD GUILTY, SENTENCED TO BE HANGED, AND PARDONED ALL IN ONE DAY

St. Louis, April 17—A report gained circulation here that the Ford brothers, who killed Jesse James, were hanged at St. Joseph this morning. Inquiry proves this to be false, but elicited the fact that the Grand Jury found an indictment against them for murder in the first degree this noon. About an hour later the boys were brought into court and pleaded guilty, and were sentenced to be hanged May 19.

—*The New York Times*[1]

VICTIM: Jesse Woodson James

BORN: September 5, 1847

DIED: April 3, 1882

AGE WHEN ATTACKED: 34

OCCUPATION: Legendary Western outlaw, bank robber, train robber

ASSASSINS: Robert Newton Ford (1860–1892), a member (with his brother Charley) of James's gang of outlaws, 22; Charley Ford (1862–1884), 20, had his gun out but did not fire

DATE & TIME OF ATTACK: Monday, April 3, 1882, early morning

LOCATION OF ATTACK: The living room of the James' home at 1318 Lafayette Street in St. Joseph, Missouri (The house has since been moved two blocks south to the Belt Highway in St. Joseph and is now a popular tourist attraction.)

WEAPON: A .44-caliber Smith & Wesson No. 3 nickel-plated revolver with a 6 1/2-inch barrel

ASSASSINATION OUTCOME: In hopes of collecting a $10,000 reward, Bob Ford, a member of Jesse James's gang, fired one .44-caliber bullet at James as the famous outlaw stood on a chair to dust a picture.[2] The bullet entered the back of James's head and exited over his left eye. He fell backwards off the chair, hit the floor, and died within seconds.

JUDICIAL OUTCOME: The Ford brothers turned themselves in to police almost immediately, but, instead of collecting the $10,000 reward, they were both charged with murder. They were both convicted and sentenced to hang, but then Governor Thomas Crittenden immediately pardoned them. Charley committed suicide in 1884; Bob was killed in a bar fight in 1892.

During his "career," Jesse James, his brother, Frank, and their boys robbed 13 banks, 11 trains and stagecoaches, and even the gate receipts of the Kansas City Fair. The James gang stole hundreds of thousands of dollars in cash, gold, and securities, and at least a dozen people were killed during the commission of these crimes.[3]

And yet Jesse James was beloved by many of those of his time. He was often referred to as Jesse the Brave and Jesse the Kind, and the annals of history are filled with folk legends of good deeds done by Jesse James. He once gave his best coat to an old man freezing by the side of the road. He once gave all the proceeds of one of his robberies to an orphanage so that the little ones would have vittles through the winter.

One of the most famous Jesse James stories has been told of many other legendary outlaws, but it is believed to have started with a true episode from Jesse James's career.

After one of their hold-ups, the James gang stopped at a small cabin occupied by a widow. She lived alone and was desperately poor, but she welcomed the boys into her home and managed to feed them all with what little food she had. As she was bustling about, Jesse saw that she was crying and, being the considerate soul that he was, he asked her what was wrong. She told him that the bank had demanded payment of her $3,000 mortgage and that, because she did not have the money, the banker was coming out that afternoon to either collect the money or foreclose on her home and throw her out into the desolate, cold, cold wild.

Jesse reached into his pocket, pulled out a roll of bills, and peeled off $3,000, which he handed to the tearful woman. She accepted the money with enormous gratitude, and he warned her to be sure and obtain from the banker the mortgage note marked "Paid" before the banker left her house.

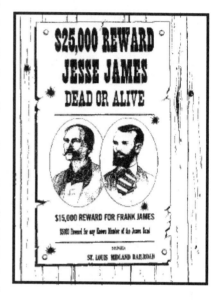

Jesse and his boys finished their meal and headed on their way.

Later that afternoon, the banker arrived, prepared to throw the woman out of her home and take possession of the house and property. He was stunned when she handed him the $3,000 and she did as Jesse told her to, making sure she had the paid mortgage note before the gleeful banker left.

As he rode back into town, about three miles from the widow's cabin, Jesse and his boys ambushed the banker, who was suddenly terrified to have the notorious Jesse James's revolver pointed at his head. Jesse recovered his $3,000, and also took the banker's pocket watch, before sending him on his way.

This story is just one illustration of the pervasive, romantic "Robin Hood" legend that evolved around Jesse James during his heyday.

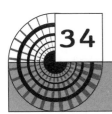

34 Andrew Johnson

ASSASSINATED	___
SURVIVED	✓

After mature consideration of the evidence adduced in the case of the accused George A. Atzerodt, the Commission find the said accused of the specification GUILTY. And the Commission do, therefore sentence him, the said George A. Atzerodt, to be hanged by the neck until he be dead, at such time and places as the President of the United States shall direct; two-thirds of the Commission concurring therein.

—Atzerodt's Finding and Sentence, June 29, 1865[1]

VICTIM: Andrew Johnson

BORN: December 29, 1808

DIED: July 31, 1875

AGE WHEN PLOTTED AGAINST: 56

OCCUPATION: Vice president to Abraham Lincoln, 17th president of the United States (1865–1869), Democrat

Johnson

ASSASSIN: George A. Atzerodt (1832–1865[2]), 33, carriage builder, Lincoln assassination conspirator.

DATE & TIME OF ATTACK: The planned time of attack was Thursday, April 13, 1865, at 10:15 p.m.

LOCATION OF ATTACK: The planned site of attack was Suite 68 of the Kirkwood House on Pennsylvania Avenue in Washington, D.C.

WEAPON: A large Bowie knife (planned weapon)

ASSASSINATION OUTCOME: On the night President Lincoln was shot (page 142), the conspirators had also planned to kill Lincoln's vice president, Andrew Johnson. Atzerodt was given the assignment of killing Johnson, but he lost his nerve and spent the afternoon getting drunk. He then abandoned his knife (he had traded his pistol for $10 drinking money) in an alley and, later on the evening of the assassination, fled on horseback to Maryland. Johnson was never in danger, and he learned of the threat to his life after Lincoln's assassination.

JUDICIAL OUTCOME: Atzerodt was arrested and charged with conspiracy in the murder of Abraham Lincoln, along with Mary Surratt, Lewis Paine (Paine also conspired against William Henry Seward, page 227), and David Herold. They were all found guilty and all four were hanged at the same time on July 7, 1865. Mary Surratt's hanging was the first time a woman had been executed in the United States.

George Atzerodt was a coward who was given the daunting assignment of assassinating the vice president of the United States.

The witnesses who testified at his trial *in his defense* were merciless in their portrayal of Atzerodt as a yellow-streaked, lily-livered chicken.

Defense witness Alexander Brawner said, "I never considered Atzerodt a courageous man, by a long streak... His reputation is that of a notorious coward."[3]

Defense witness Louis B. Harkins testified, "I have known Atzerodt for probably ten years...We never gave him credit down our way for much courage. I call to mind two difficulties in which I saw him—one happened in my shop, and the other in an oyster saloon—in both of which I thought he lacked courage."[4]

Defense witness Washington Briscoe told the court, "I have known the prisoner, Atzerodt, six or seven years at Port Tobacco. He has always been considered a man of little courage, and remarkable for his cowardice."[5]

But, ironically, the world-class, major-league, lily-gilding regarding Atzerodt's pluck (or lack thereof) came from none other than William E. Doster, Atzerodt's *own attorney*, who opened his defense of his client with, "May it please the Court, I intend to show that this man is a constitutional coward; that if he had been assigned the duty of assassinating the Vice-President, he never could have done it; and that, from his known cowardice, Booth probably did not assign him to any such duty."[6]

Atzerodt's plan was to wait until President Lincoln was in his booth at the Ford Theater, watching the play *Our American Cousin*, and then climb the stairs to the room in the Kirkwood House Hotel where Vice President Johnson was staying. He would knock on the VP's door, and then, as soon as Johnson opened it, he would plunge a large Bowie knife into his chest, aiming for the heart, and then flee. At the same time as Atzerodt was killing Johnson, John Wilkes Booth would be killing Lincoln and Lewis Paine would be killing Secretary of State William Seward. The plot hatched by Booth and company, if successful, would have cut the head off the current administration and afford the Confederates a chance to move into power.

Seward's assassination was botched; Johnson's wasn't even attempted. Booth was the only one of the conspirators to succeed in assassinating his target. And he may have also killed a future American president, General Ulysses S. Grant, if Grant had attended the performance with President Lincoln as originally planned.

Grant's life was likely saved because Mrs. Grant did not like Mrs. Lincoln.

Mary Todd Lincoln was a volatile, moody woman who was prone to emotional outbursts and irrational behavior. The president was extraordinarily patient and tolerant with her, but many others, who had a choice as to whether or not to spend time in her company, were not. Mrs. Grant had been witness to Mrs. Lincoln's "explosions," and she was the one who vetoed her and her husband's attendance the night Lincoln was shot. Major Henry Rathbone and his fiancée went in Grant's place, and Rathbone was stabbed by Booth after he shot the president. History would have been written quite differently if the two wives got along and Ulysses S. Grant had also been murdered that April night in Washington.

Following Booth's arrest, the other conspirators were quickly arrested, and all were tried before a military tribunal, justified by the fact that Lincoln was Commander in Chief of the United States Armed Forces, and he had died "in actual service in time of war."

On July 7, 1865, less than three months after Lincoln's death, Atzerodt was hooded and the noose was placed around his neck as he stood next to Surratt, Paine, and Herold. The executioner opened the platform beneath them and all four fell and died at the same time.

They were left hanging long enough for someone to take a picture for posterity. Atzerodt was on the far right.

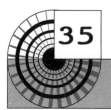

35

Vernon Jordan

ASSASSINATED	___
SURVIVED	✓

Our nation cannot call for respect for human rights when it lacks the moral courage to save its own cities, its own poor, its own minorities whose rights are trampled upon.

—Vernon Jordan[1]

VICTIM: Vernon Eulion Jordan, Jr.

BORN: August 15, 1935

DIED: n/a

AGE WHEN ATTACKED: 44

OCCUPATION: Civil rights activist, lawyer, former executive director of the United Negro College Fund (1970), former executive director of the Urban League (1971–1981), advisor to President-elect Jimmy Carter and his transition team, director of President-elect Bill Clinton's transition team

UNSUCCESSFUL ASSASSIN: Joseph Paul Franklin (b. 1951), 29, white supremacist, anti-Semite, shooter of *Hustler* publisher Larry Flynt (page 66)

DATE & TIME OF ATTACK: Friday, May 29, 1980, 2:05 a.m.

LOCATION OF ATTACK: In the parking lot of a Marriott Inn motel in Fort Wayne, Indiana

WEAPON: A .30-06 Remington 700 rifle

ASSASSINATION OUTCOME: Franklin fired two shots at Jordan from a sniper's lair in a grassy area near the hotel. One hit Jordan in the back, exploding inside of him; a fragment of the second bullet ricocheted off something and also struck Jordan, causing damage to the rear of his right thigh. Jordan cried out, "Help me! I've been shot!"[2] He was rushed to the hospital, where he was listed in critical condition, and surgeons operated on him for 4 1/2 hours to remove the bullet and close the wound. The exploding bullet created three exit wounds that needed to be surgically repaired. Jordan had grave internal injuries, and part of his intestine had to be removed. The doctor later said that the bullet barely missed Jordan's spinal column and that, if it had exploded a millionth of a second later, he would have had zero chance for survival. Jordan fully recovered and is now active in corporate law and fund-raising for civil-rights causes.

JUDICIAL OUTCOME: A .30-06-caliber shell casing was found in the grassy area near the Marriott where Jordan was shot, so the FBI searched for suspects and took into custody anyone who was found to be in possession of a .30-06-caliber rifle. (Apparently a .30-06 rifle is popular enough that many people were taken into custody.) Franklin was arrested and it was learned that he was also wanted for questioning for the murders of a black man and white woman in Oklahoma City, the killing of two black teenagers in Salt Lake City, and the killing of a black man and a white girl in Pennsylvania, as well as a threatening letter to President Carter. Franklin was ultimately indicted for the Salt Lake City murders, as well as the Jordan shooting. He was acquitted of the Jordan shooting, but by then he was already serving six life sentences for other murders. He has since confessed to shooting Larry Flynt and is currently on death row in Missouri.

It's impossible to know how many times Vernon Jordan and Charlayne Hunter heard the word *nigger* shouted at them that Monday morning in January 1961 as they walked through crowds of protesters to the Registrar's Office at the University of Georgia. But it didn't shake him or sway him from his mission. The Georgia Supreme Court had just ruled that the University's segregationist policies were illegal, and Vernon Jordan was going to see to it that Charlayne Hunter was granted her rightful place in the school's freshman class.

And he did.

Jordan was born in Atlanta, Georgia, in 1935, the son of a postal worker and a caterer. He earned a bachelor's degree in political science from DePauw University, and then a law degree from Howard University in 1960. He became executive director of the United Negro College Fund in 1970 and president of the National Urban League in 1972.

He worked diligently throughout his life for voter-registration programs and civil rights, and he became a powerful Washington insider. His nickname was "Mr. Smooth." He has often been seen golfing with Bill Clinton, and he reportedly helped the former president through the Monica Lewinsky scandal and his impeachment.

Following his assassination attempt, which required months of recuperation and physical therapy, Jordan left the civil-rights movement for the world of corporate law.

Joseph Paul Franklin did not like blacks and Jews, and he once wrote a threatening letter to President Carter in which he accused him of "selling out to the blacks." When Franklin was arrested in October 1980 for the shooting of Vernon Jordan, it was learned that he had once been a member of the American Nazi Party, as well as being a member of the white supremacist organization, the Ku Klux Klan. Even so, he told police in Florida, "I'm innocent," and "They're trying to pin it on me because of my racist views."[3]

Franklin was *not* innocent and he shot Jordan because he was black and because Jordan espoused policies that he opposed, such as integration and religious tolerance.

Jordan had just stepped out of a red Grand Prix parked about 50 feet from the entrance to his room. With him was Martha C. Coleman, 36, a member of the Urban League organizing committee that had scheduled Jordan's speech that evening at their annual dinner. Ms. Coleman, while still in the car, reported hearing a thud, as though something had hit the car's windshield, and then she saw Vernon Jordan fall. Ms. Coleman got out of the car, went to Jordan, saw that he had been shot, and then ran into the motel lobby. Shortly thereafter an ambulance and police cars arrived. By then, Joseph Franklin was long gone.

It wasn't long before political bigwigs began flying to Indiana to visit the well-known and well-liked Jordan in the hospital, including Senator Edward Kennedy and President Carter. It also wasn't long before the police questioned Martha Coleman at length, looking for a domestic angle to the shooting.

Ultimately, the only angle to the shooting was a racist filled with hatred who is now sitting on death row.

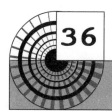

36

Edward Kennedy

| ASSASSINATED | — |
| SURVIVED | ✓ |

Based on some estimates, guns are statistically like rats. They outnumber our population. Not surprisingly, our output of ammunition for civilian firearms almost staggers the imagination. American industry outdoes all other nations in the production of bullets. Nearly 5 billion rounds of ammunition flow through the marketplace each year. That is enough, laid end to end, to stretch a bandoleer of ammunition three times around the equator. All of those bullets could not only wipe out the world's entire human population, but they could decimate practically most of the world's species of wildlife.

—Edward Kennedy[1]

VICTIM: Edward "Ted" Kennedy

BORN: February 22, 1932

DIED: n/a

AGE WHEN PLOTTED AGAINST: Unknown

OCCUPATION: U.S. senator from the state of Massachusetts

CONSPIRING ASSASSIN: John W. Hinckley (b. 1955), future attempted assassin of President Ronald Reagan

DATE & TIME OF ATTACK: Never carried out

LOCATION OF ATTACK: Unknown

WEAPON: Probably a handgun

ASSASSINATION OUTCOME: Hinckley abandoned the notion of assassinating Ted Kennedy and subsequently turned his attention to President Reagan.

JUDICIAL OUTCOME: None.

Presidential assassin John Hinckley (see page 201) also appears in *In the Crosshairs* as the potential killer of both Jimmy Carter (page 20) and Edward "Ted" Kennedy.

Hinckley came closest to making an attempt on Jimmy Carter, stalking him and being photographed in the crowd at a Carter campaign rally, but he never actually took a shot at him.

Hinckley's threats to Edward Kennedy, the brother of assassinated Kennedys, John and Robert, appear to be even more tenuous. After his arrest for shooting President Reagan, Hinckley revealed that he had concocted a few other ghastly scenarios with which to impress Jodie Foster.

One was to open fire on the campus of Yale in New Haven, Connecticut. Hinckley had regularly traveled to New Haven and had been on the Yale campus several times before he traveled to Washington to shoot Reagan. Obsessed with Foster, Hinckley even enrolled in a writing course at Yale and, once he could justifiably be on campus, began leaving notes for the actress in her campus mailbox. He even had two telephone conversations with her, but she cut off the contact after the second call.

If he had carried out the Yale plan, he likely would have shot randomly and killed whomever was in his crosshairs.

His second idea was to assassinate Edward Kennedy. This was likely abandoned because he probably realized he would become more famous for shooting a president than a senator. If he had carried out his plan to shoot Kennedy and succeeded, all three political Kennedy brothers would have died from assassination.

Hinckley's third idea was to shoot up the Senate Chamber. This would have been extremely difficult to carry out, although he might have been able to wound and possibly kill many high-profile politicians, but he would have had to smuggle a gun into the Capitol Building, which was not an easy task. Plus he would be indoors after the shooting. The Yale plot and the Reagan assassination attempt were both outdoors, suggesting that Hinckley may have been considering escape after he opened fire.

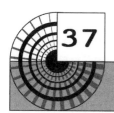

37

John F. Kennedy

| Assassinated | ✓ |
| Survived | — |

This is a sad time for all people. We have suffered a loss that cannot be weighed. For me it is a deep personal tragedy. I know the world shares the sorrow that Mrs. Kennedy and her family bear. I will do my best. That is all I can do. I ask for your help—and God's.

—Lyndon Johnson[1]

VICTIM: John Fitzgerald Kennedy

BORN: May 29, 1917

DIED: November 22, 1963

AGE WHEN ATTACKED: 46

OCCUPATION: 35th president of the United States (1961–1963)

ASSASSIN: Lee Harvey Oswald, 24, former U.S. Marine

DATE & TIME OF ATTACK: Friday, November 22, 1963, 12:30 p.m.

Kennedy

LOCATION OF ATTACK: Shot in a motorcade in front of the Book Depository in Dallas, Texas; later died at Parkland Memorial Hospital

WEAPON: A 6.5-mm Mannlicher-Carcano bolt-action carbine rifle

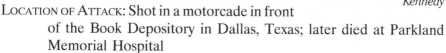

ASSASSINATION OUTCOME: Kennedy was shot in the neck and the head, and his wounds were so grave that there was no chance of recovery. He was pronounced dead at Parkland Memorial Hospital 30 minutes after he was shot. Lee Harvey Oswald fired three shots at the presidential motorcade from an open window on the sixth floor of the Texas School Book Depository. The first shot missed completely, and it is believed that oak trees and a traffic light pole blocked Oswald's view. The only evidence of the first bullet was a nick on a concrete curb near the Triple Underpass. A piece of flying concrete from the first shot cut witness James Tague on the cheek. The second shot entered the back of the president's neck and exited through his throat, chipping a vertebra in his neck. This shot caused the president's arms to fly up, elbows out, with his hands at his chin. This is a neurological reflex common in spinal-cord injuries called the Thorburn Reflex. This bullet, after exiting the president, then struck Governor Connally in the right shoulder, shattered his right rib, and exited below his right nipple. The bullet then fractured Connally's right wrist and came to a stop in Connally's left thigh. The third shot, the most devastating, struck Kennedy in the back of the head above the right ear and exited at the right front of his head, blowing off part of his skull and destroying the right front section of his brain. From the Warren Report:

> *Dr. Carrico was in the emergency area, examining another patient, when he was notified that President Kennedy was en route to the hospital. Approximately 2 minutes later, Dr. Carrico saw the President on his back, being wheeled into the emergency area. He noted that the President was blue-white or ashen in color; had slow, spasmodic, agonal respiration without any coordination; made no voluntary movements; had his eyes open with the pupils dilated without any reaction to light; evidenced no palpable pulse; and had a few chest sounds which were thought to be heart beats. On the basis of these findings, Dr. Carrico concluded that President Kennedy was still alive.*

His clothes and back brace were cut off, a breathing tube was inserted into his throat, and he was placed on a respirator. Three IVs were inserted for drugs and fluids, and he was hooked up to an electrocardiogram. Dr. Malcolm Perry then performed a tracheotomy, creating an artificial airway in the president's throat. This procedure obliterated the neck exit wound. A tube was also inserted into Kennedy's chest to drain blood and fluid. Kennedy was then administered 300 milligrams of steroids, specifically a cortisone drug called Solu-Cortef.

Because the president's pulse was still erratic, one of the doctors began closed-chest massage. Opening the president's chest for open heart massage was considered but later rejected.

The doctors concluded that Kennedy was beyond resuscitation and asked a priest to perform Last Rites before pronouncing him dead. The priest did as requested, and Kennedy was pronounced dead at 1 p.m. The doctors had worked on him for approximately 20 minutes before giving up.

The room emptied, and First Lady Jacqueline Kennedy then kissed the president's toe, stomach, and his lips. She then removed one of her rings and placed it on her husband's little finger.[2]

Several nurses and residents then re-entered the room. The tracheotomy, IVs, and EKG leads were removed. The nurses and residents then wrapped the president's body in white sheets, a plastic mattress cover, and several pillowcases. The body was then placed in a casket, transported to Air Force One, and flown to Washington.[3]

JUDICIAL OUTCOME: Oswald (Chapter 55), Kennedy's presumed assassin, did not survive to stand trial. He was assassinated two days after Kennedy's assassination by Dallas nightclub owner Jack Ruby while being transferred by the police. The Warren Commission released a 26-volume report that concluded that Lee Harvey Oswald had acted alone. Many conspiracy theories suggesting that others were involved in Kennedy's killing have been put forth over the years, but no one has ever been charged with the murder of John F. Kennedy and the wounding of Governor John Connally, and no one other than Lee Harvey Oswald has ever been officially regarded as the assassin of the president.

Hundreds of books have been written about the assassination, and dozens of theories have been offered to explain what happened. The Mafia, Fidel Castro, the Russian KGB, the CIA, and even Lyndon Johnson and the Secret Service have all been hinted at as being responsible for Kennedy's death.

Some theories ask legitimate questions:

- ► If the shots came from above and behind, then why is there video evidence of several people turning towards the grassy knoll in front and to the right of the presidential limousine after the shots were fired? (The echoing of Oswald's shots is believed to have been responsible for this response by witnesses.)

- ► Isn't it possible that the KGB ordered Kennedy's assassination as payback for Russian humiliation during the Cuban Missile Crisis?

- ► Couldn't Castro have ordered the assassination as retribution for the failed Bay of Pigs invasion?

- ► We know that Kennedy and his brother, Attorney General Robert Kennedy (page 128), were cracking down on organized crime. Couldn't the Mob have decided to get rid of JFK to scare Bobby into backing down?

- ► Reportedly, the CIA was concerned that Kennedy was going soft on Communism and that he was considering pulling the United States out of Vietnam. Getting rid of him would make Lyndon Johnson president, along with, it is assumed, policies concerning these matters of which the CIA approved.

- ► Isn't the Single Bullet Theory (that is, that a single bullet hit both Kennedy and Connally, a seeming impossibility) a valid rejection of the Lone Assassin theory? (No, as was disproved convincingly, and in great detail, in *Case Closed*.)

- ► Why was the Press Car, which is usually in front of the presidential limousine in order to facilitate photographic documentation of presidential visits, several cars back in the procession that day in Dallas (an explainable, logistical mix-up)? This resulted in the Zapruder film being the only visual record of the assassination.

There are logical common-sense answers to almost all of these questions, and the most recent attempt to calm the hysteria and debunk the wild theories permeating this American tragedy is Gerald Posner's aforementioned book *Case Closed*, in which he analyzes all the major conspiracy theories and comes to the conclusion that, the American people's suspicions aside, the Warren Report was correct and Lee Harvey Oswald was the lone gunman in the assassination of John F. Kennedy.

A great deal of the controversy and madness surrounding the assassination could have easily been prevented if a thorough autopsy on the president had been performed. The brief post-mortem examination, which should have taken two or three days, was rushed through in a few hours because Bobby and Jacqueline Kennedy insisted on staying at Bethesda Naval Hospital during the autopsy, and they reportedly made it known that they wanted it done quickly. Also, it is believed that Kennedy's brain, which would have provided answers to many questions about the head shot (and which was discovered missing from the National Archives in 1966), was believed to have been disposed of by Robert Kennedy for fear it would become "a lurid public exhibition."[4]

The assassination of John F. Kennedy was a seminal moment in American history, and its mysteries continue to fascinate.

Postscript: Abraham Zapruder received $25,000 from *Life* magazine for his color footage of the assassination of President Kennedy. Zapruder gave the entire $25,000 to the widow of Dallas Police Officer J.D. Tippit, who was slain by Lee Harvey Oswald shortly after he shot the president. In 1999, the U.S. government paid the Zapruder family $16 million for the film, which was declared a permanent possession of the American people in 1997.

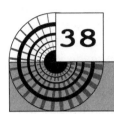

38

Robert F. Kennedy

ASSASSINATED   ✓

SURVIVED   ___

My brother need not be idealized, or enlarged in death beyond what he was in life, to be remembered simply as a good and decent man, who saw wrong and tried to right it, saw suffering and tried to heal it, saw war and tried to stop it.

Those of us who loved him and who take him to his rest today, pray that what he was to us and what he wished for others will some day come to pass for all the world.

As he said many times, in many parts of this nation, to those he touched and who sought to touch him: "Some men see things as they are and say why. I dream things that never were and say why not."

—Senator Edward Kennedy[1]

VICTIM: Robert Francis Kennedy

BORN: November 20, 1925

DIED: June 6, 1968

AGE WHEN ATTACKED: 42

OCCUPATION: U.S. Attorney General, U.S. Senator, Democratic candidate for president. Bobby Kennedy was his brother Jack's campaign manager and later served as President Kennedy's Attorney General from 1961 to 1964. During his tenure as Attorney General, Bobby promoted the Civil Rights Act of 1964 and also pursued a racket-busting policy that created enormous animosity between the Kennedys and organized-crime factions. After J.F.K.'s assassination, President Johnson chose Hubert Humphrey as his vice-presidential running mate instead of Bobby. R.F.K. then resigned and was elected Senator in New York.[2]

ASSASSIN: Sirhan Bishara Sirhan (b. 1944), 24, deranged Palestinian-born (Jerusalem) anti-Semitic, arrived in the United States with his family in 1956

DATE & TIME OF ATTACK: Wednesday, June 5, 1968, 12:15 a.m.; died almost 26 hours later on Thursday, June 6, 1968, at 1:44 a.m.

LOCATION OF THE ATTACK: In the kitchen of the Ambassador Hotel in Los Angeles, California

WEAPON: A .22-caliber Iver Johnson Cadet revolver

ASSASSINATION OUTCOME: Kennedy was hit by three bullets; a fourth went through his jacket but did not hit his body. One bullet entered his brain at the back of his head near his ear. This bullet severed the cerebral artery and was the bullet that did the gravest, and most immediate serious damage. Amazingly, after he was shot, Kennedy reportedly was able to ask if everyone was all right and also how bad his injuries were. The other two bullets that hit him caused minor injuries. After surgery, Kennedy did not regain consciousness or breathe on his own, and his wife and family made the decision to turn off the respirator. One doctor admitted that if Kennedy had survived, he would have been in a vegetative state for the rest of his life.

JUDICIAL OUTCOME: Sirhan was restrained (and beaten) at the scene by several people in the kitchen at the time, including football great Rosie Greer. He was ultimately tried, convicted of murder, and sentenced to death. Before his execution could be carried out, however, the state of California abolished the death penalty, and Sirhan's sentences was commuted to life with the possibility of parole. He was turned down for parole in 2000, and his next parole hearing is 2004. He currently resides in Corcoran State Prison in California and is actively working to have his next parole request approved.

There are several questions regarding the assassination of Robert F. Kennedy that have never been satisfactorily answered for many conspiracy theorists who have studied the crime.

One of them involves the entrance wound. If all the witnesses to the shooting state with certainty that Sirhan Sirhan fired at Kennedy *from the front*, then why did the Senator have an entrance wound on the *back* of his neck, complete with powder burns to the skin, suggesting that the gun barrel was within 1 1/2-inches of Kennedy's head? Was there a second shooter? All of the eight bullets from Sirhan's Iver Johnson revolver were accounted for by the Los Angeles Police Department, and one was determined to have entered Kennedy's brain at the neck. Yet no one saw Kennedy turn his back towards Sirhan, which would have allowed a bullet to enter his neck at the spot where it did. Complicating the matter is a report that there were two bullet holes found in a wooden divider in the pantry of the kitchen where Kennedy was shot. Photographs showing the holes were discovered later, but the wooden panel had by then been removed and destroyed. Were 10 shots fired instead of eight?

There is another seemingly puzzling question as well. Why did bullets fired from Sirhan Sirhan's gun in 1975 bear different markings than the bullets recovered from the scene of the assassination?

All of this leads to the key question: Were two guns fired at Robert Kennedy? And if so, was the assassination a plot to kill Kennedy, instead of simply the anti-Semitic hatred of an Arab who did not agree with R.F.K.'s pro-Israel stance?

In his 1995 book, *The Killing of Robert F. Kennedy*, author Dan Moldea answers these questions and closes the case on the assassination. There was no conspiracy, he tells us, and his research—along with prison interviews with Sirhan Sirhan himself—led Moldea to the conclusion that Sirhan acted alone.

What about the entry wound in the back of the head?

In 1968, an investigator on Sirhan's defense team asked Sirhan why he didn't shoot Kennedy between the eyes. He was definitely close enough to the senator and, because it was accepted that he was in front of Kennedy, it would have been the most effective shot to take. Apparently, shooting Kennedy in the face was precisely what Sirhan had intended to do. Sirhan immediately replied, "Because that son of a bitch turned his head at the last second."[3]

What about the different markings on the 1975 bullets?

Moldea interviewed several police officers who admitted that Sirhan's gun had been reloaded and fired privately after the shooting so that officers could have *souvenir bullets* fired from the gun that killed Robert Kennedy. These extra shots—the exact number of which is not known—created a residue in the barrel of Sirhan's pistol that resulted in the 1975 bullets bearing different markings than the eight fired by Sirhan.

Regarding the mysterious disappearing bullet holes, Moldea believes that the bullet holes in the wooden door panel that were seen in photographs of the crime scene were not actually bullet holes and that untrained eyes probably identified them incorrectly.

America was still reeling from the assassination of Martin Luther King, Jr. (page 132) when Robert Kennedy was killed only two short months later, and the memory of the 1963 assassination of John F. Kennedy was still fresh in the minds of many Americans, as well as people around the world. R.F.K. was the Democrat's best chance to retain the White House, and his death got Republican Richard Nixon elected with 301 electoral votes to Hubert Humphrey's 191.

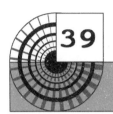

39

Martin Luther King, Jr.

ASSASSINATED   ✓

SURVIVED   —

Well, I don't know what will happen now. We've got some difficult days ahead. [But] I've been to the mountaintop. I won't mind. Like anybody, I'd like to live a long life. Longevity has its place but I'm not concerned about that now. I just want to do God's will, and He's allowed me to go up to the mountain. And I've looked over. And I've seen the Promised Land. I may not get there with you, but I want you to know tonight that we as a people will get to the Promised Land. So I'm happy tonight. I'm not worried about anything. I'm not fearing any man. Mine eyes have seen the glory of the coming of the Lord.

—Martin Luther King, Jr.[1]

VICTIM: Martin Luther King, Jr.

BORN: January 15, 1929

DIED: April 4, 1968

AGE WHEN ATTACKED: 39

King

OCCUPATION: Civil rights leader; vocal advocate of nonviolence and racial equality; Baptist minister; founder and President of the Southern Christian Leadership Conference; *Time*'s Man of the Year (1963); winner of the Nobel Peace Prize (1964);

organizer of the Montgomery, Alabama, bus boycott; author of one of the most famous speeches in U.S. history ("I have a dream"), delivered in front of the Lincoln Memorial on August 28, 1963

ASSASSIN: James Earl Ray (1928–1998), 39, ex-con, a.k.a. Eric Starvo Galt, Ramon George Sneyd, and Paul Edward Bridgeman

DATE & TIME OF ATTACK: Thursday, April 4, 1968, 6:01 p.m.

LOCATION OF ATTACK: On the balcony outside King's room in the Lorraine Motel in Memphis, Tennessee

WEAPON: A .30-06-caliber Remington 760 Gamemaster pump rifle with a Redfield 2 x 7 telescopic sight

ASSASSINATION OUTCOME: A single bullet struck King on the right side of his face near his jaw, fracturing his lower mandible, severing his jugular vein, vertebral artery, and subclavian artery, and shattering to pieces several vertebrae in his cervical spine (neck) and back. The force of the bullet ripped his necktie completely off his shirt and hurled King backwards against a wall. King could have been shot in this manner in a fully equipped operating room with a team of surgeons standing by and there would have been nothing they could have done to save his life. King was pronounced dead at St. Joseph Hospital in Memphis at 7:05 p.m., just more than an hour after he was shot. He never spoke after the bullet ripped through him.

JUDICIAL OUTCOME: James Earl Ray was arrested at Heathrow Airport in London on June 8, 1968 while trying to board a plane for Brussels, Belgium. His phony "Sneyd" passport had been linked to his real identity, and Scotland Yard made the arrest on the U.S. charge of murder. Reportedly, Ray put his head in his hands and wept when told he was under arrest and that he was wanted in the United States for the murder of Dr. Martin Luther King, Jr. U.S. officials immediately requested Ray's extradition, but Ray protested the extradition, which required the FBI to make a case against him in the British courts, which they did. Some of the evidence they offered included the fact that a man named James Earl Ray had bought a rifle identical to the one used to kill Dr. King; a man named James Earl Ray had booked a room in the rooming house opposite the Lorraine Hotel shortly before Dr. King was killed by a shot fired from that same rooming house; witnesses reported seeing Ray himself fleeing the scene of the shooting shortly after Dr. King was shot, leaving behind the weapon with his prints on it;

and, equally damning, Ray's fingerprints were found in a car identical to the one seen racing away from the scene of the assassination. Ray was extradited and, after meeting with his lawyers, learned that he couldn't plead not guilty without risking a death sentence. Because he did not want to be executed, Ray pled guilty and was sentenced to 99 years in prison. He immediately recanted his guilty plea and spent the rest of his life angling for a new trial and telling anyone who would listen that he did not kill Martin Luther King, Jr. and that there was a conspiracy involving the FBI and the U.S. government to murder the civil-rights leader. King's family ultimately believed Ray, who died in prison in 1998 of liver failure before his allegations could be proven. To this day he still has supporters who do not believe he killed Martin Luther King, Jr.

Who killed Martin Luther King, Jr.?

Many would answer "James Earl Ray" to that question, and yet that very question is the title of a book by none other than James Earl Ray himself, who most assuredly does not answer "I did" in its pages.

It is well known that FBI director J. Edgar Hoover hated Martin Luther King, Jr. Hoover put King under surveillance, he had his phones tapped, he leaked information about King's sexual adventures, and he was livid when King was awarded the Nobel Peace Prize in 1964.

So did the FBI assassinate King on Hoover's orders?

There are many who believe the answer to that question is yes. And yet the evidence that James Earl Ray pulled the trigger is compelling and convincing. A 1970s House Select Committee investigation into King's murder concluded that Ray fired the fatal shot but that there was a "likelihood" that he was part of a conspiracy. The Committee, however, did not point the finger at Hoover's FBI. Instead, they cited "right-wing racist" organizations in St. Louis, Missouri, as the probable culprits.

King was in Memphis on April 4, 1968 to try to ease tensions on both sides of a rancorous 1,300-strong sanitation workers' strike. Undercover law-enforcement instigators had caused conflicts between the police and the strikers that had resulted in the death of one man and the arrests of 238 strikers. The presence of Dr. King could easily have complicated the situation. If there was a conspiracy to kill King, was his involvement in the labor problem a contributing factor? We don't really know.

James Earl Ray went to his grave proclaiming that there was a conspiracy. As in the JFK assassination (Chapter 37), though, no matter how many theories are mounted, it is almost certain that there will never be a clear-cut resolution of the question of who killed Martin Luther King, Jr.

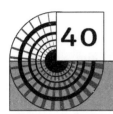

Vladimir Lenin

ASSASSINATED ___

SURVIVED ✓

*ALL SOVIET WORKERS, PEASANTS AND
RED ARMYMAN'S DEPUTIES,
ALL ARMIES, ALL, ALL, ALL*

*A few hours ago a villainous attempt was made on the life of
Comrade Lenin. The working class will respond to attempts on
the lives of its leaders by still further consolidating its forces
and by a merciless mass terror against all the enemies of the
revolution.*

—Decree following the assassination attempt on Vladimir
Lenin[1]

VICTIM: Vladimir Ilyich Lenin

BORN: April 10, 1870

DIED: January 21, 1924

AGE WHEN ATTACKED: 48

OCCUPATION: Marxist revolutionary founder of the
Bolshevik party, responsible for much of the
success of the Russian Revolution of 1917,
succeeded by Joseph Stalin

Lenin

UNSUCCESSFUL ASSASSIN: Fanya Kaplan (1883–
1918), 35, member of the anti-Lenin group, the Right Social Revolutionaries, a Socialist revolutionary party

— 135 —

DATE & TIME OF ATTACK: Friday, August 30, 1918, 7:30 p.m.

LOCATION OF ATTACK: Outside the Michelson factory in Moscow

WEAPON: A Browning pistol

ASSASSINATION OUTCOME: After Lenin exited the factory following a rousing and successful speech, Kaplan fired three shots at him. One went harmlessly through his coat, and two struck him. One bullet broke his left shoulder and injured his left arm. The other bullet punctured the top of his left lung, penetrated his neck from left to right, and lodged near the left side of his collarbone. Although both bullets missed vital arteries, if any of the elements of the shooting equation—specifically the positions and movements of both Lenin and the shooter—had varied even slightly, the second bullet might have deviated one millimeter in either direction, and Lenin would have died instantly. Instead, he was placed in his car and driven back to the Kremlin. He did not want to go to the hospital for fear of a plot. When he arrived at the Kremlin, blood was pouring from him and he was in great pain, yet he refused to allow his driver to carry him upstairs to his apartment. Summoning enormous determination and will, Lenin walked upstairs under his own power. All he asked was that someone help him remove his coat before he made the climb. Once he was upstairs, calls went out for doctors, and soon a small field hospital was set up in a room adjacent to Lenin's bedroom. Although the doctors knew the bullets should be removed, they did not even considering operating on him outside of a hospital. They decided to leave the bullets inside him, and they began to watch him carefully for signs of infection. Incredibly, with massive blood loss, a punctured lung, and a broken shoulder, Lenin recovered on his own, without surgery, and with the barest minimum of medication.

JUDICIAL OUTCOME: Fanya Kaplan was immediately arrested and brought to a basement cell in the Kremlin. She was interrogated constantly, but she adamantly refused to tell where she had gotten the gun with which she had shot. (Was she tortured? Perhaps we should ask if it is cold in Moscow in January?) Her refusal to talk was ultimately attributed more to mental incompetence than revolutionary fervor. Fanya Kaplan had been imprisoned for trying to kill a Czarist leader, and years of hard labor had resulted in her experiencing constant headaches, plus long periods of blindness. Soviet officials questioning her were frustrated by her demented responses. "Why did you shoot Comrade Lenin?" they asked her. Her reply? "Why do you have to know?"[2] Eventually, they tired of attempting to glean from her anything that even remotely made sense, so they took her into a room with a cement floor and a drain in the middle of the floor, and shot her in the back of the head. She never had a trial. Case closed.

After Lenin was shot, Soviet officials broadcast a decree (see page 135) that resulted in a mass slaughter of revolutionaries—including even those only *suspected* of being revolutionaries. The Petrograd division of the Soviet secret police (Cheka) executed more than 800 people in a single month. The Nizhny Novogord Cheka killed 46 people in one day. Soviet sailors in Kronstadt executed 500 prisoners in one day. Yakov Sverdlov, who acted as head of the Soviet government while Lenin was incapacitated, began a terror rampage that served more to exterminate those opposed to Lenin than to weed out whatever possible plot against the Soviet leader that might have existed.

The assassination attempt against Vladimir Lenin is believed to have drastically shortened his life—even though he recovered from serious gunshot wounds without surgery. Four years after the attempt, he began having seizures, possibly caused by lead poisoning from the bullets still inside his body, and became seriously incapacitated. In March 1923 he suffered a severe stroke that took his speech. A final stroke in January 1924 ended his life during a visit to the village of Gorki, near Moscow. Lenin's body still lies in state in a crystal casket in Red Square, although the honor guard that once stood watch at the entrance to his mausoleum have long gone.

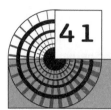

41

John Lennon[1]

ASSASSINATED   ✓

SURVIVED   ___

America is where it's at. I should have been born in New York...that's where I belong. Why wasn't I born there?

—John Lennon, 1971

VICTIM: John Ono Lennon

BORN: October 9, 1940

DIED: December 8, 1980

AGE WHEN ATTACKED: 40

OCCUPATION:
Musician; singer/songwriter; writer; artist; former member of The Beatles; environmental, political, feminist, and anti-war activist

ASSASSIN: Mark David Chapman (b. 1955), 25, deranged and obsessed Beatles/John Lennon fan, former maintenance man, former security guard

DATE & TIME OF ATTACK: Monday December 8, 1980, 10:49 p.m.

LOCATION OF ATTACK: Outside The Dakota Arms, 1 West 72nd Street in New York City

WEAPON: A .44-caliber Charter Arms Bulldog revolver

ASSASSINATION OUTCOME: One bullet hit John in the back, puncturing his right lung and aorta and exiting his body through his chest wall. One bullet hit John in the left shoulder, shattering the bone and then also exiting his body. The third bullet struck John in the left side of his neck. These three hits spun John around, and the fourth and final bullet struck John in the right upper arm, shattering the long bone and passing through his flesh to exit into his black leather jacket. Lennon was rushed to nearby Roosevelt Hospital in the back of a police car. He was gravely wounded and, after valiant efforts by the emergency team on duty, pronounced dead at 11:13 p.m.

JUDICIAL OUTCOME: Chapman—who George Harrison (Chapter 25) described as "the devil's best friend" in his tribute song to John, "All Those Years Ago"—was arrested at the scene and later pled guilty. He was sentenced to 20 years to life in prison, with the possibility of parole. He is currently incarcerated in Administrative Protective Custody (APC) at Attica State Prison in New York. Chapman was turned down for parole at his most recent parole hearing in October 2002.

The stunning Dakota Arms sits on the corner of West 72nd Street on Central Park West in New York, a massive, seemingly impenetrable stone fortress, home to the famous and the unknown, all of whom have in common a love for New York and, of course, loads of money.

John Lennon and Yoko Ono loved The Dakota. John and Yoko owned five apartments comprising thirty-four rooms in the building, and one of John's great joys was watching the sun set over Central Park from his windows. John was one of the most popular residents in the building and was beloved by the building's staff. He was a notoriously big tipper and often doormen would fight over who got to deliver a package to John.

John and Yoko also loved the city of New York. John felt safe in New York. He once told a reporter that one of the greatest joys of his new "post-Beatles" life was being able to walk out his front door, walk down the street, and walk into a restaurant without being chased or stopped for an autograph.

Monday, December 8, 1980, the day John was assassinated, was unusually warm in Manhattan. After a very productive recording session at the Hit Factory, John and Yoko returned home. Their limousine pulled up in front of the Dakota at precisely 10:49 p.m.

Yoko exited the rented limo first, followed by John, who was carrying a tape recorder and tapes from the day's session. The tapes were of Yoko's song "Walking on Thin Ice."

As John followed Yoko down the Dakota's carriageway, Mark David Chapman called out to John from the sidewalk, "Mr. Lennon?" Chapman did not shout, but his words were loud enough to be immediately heard by John and prompt him to instinctively turn towards the sound of them.

John half-turned towards the voice and saw what he had to have perceived as an odd sight: An overweight young man wearing glasses and a olive-green military jacket was down on one knee in a combat shooting stance, aiming a gun at him. We'll never know if John recognized Chapman and recalled signing his *Double Fantasy* album earlier in the day. Before John could react, Chapman fired five times from his Charter Arms .38 revolver, hitting John with four of the bullets.

The front-desk clerk on duty at the time, Jay Hastings, heard the shots and immediately ran out to see what had happened. Before he left his desk, though, he hit the alarm button that was connected directly to the 20th Precinct Station House (located 10 blocks away), which would summon the police almost immediately.

Hastings burst through the front door of the Dakota's lobby and ran into a scene from a nightmare. The legendary former Beatle John Lennon was lying face-up in a spreading pool of blood on the sidewalk. Yoko Ono was bent over John, screaming his name and looking around frantically for someone to help him. John's face was stark white and his eyelids fluttered rapidly. Hastings was certain he could see the whites of John's eyes. Hastings could also see that John was still breathing, and his immediate thought was to put on a tourniquet. Hastings ripped off his tie but then had a sudden realization of just how bad John was injured. Hastings recalled that John's eyes were open but unfocused and that he made a gurgling sound, after which he vomited blood and fleshy material.

John was bleeding heavily from his chest, shoulder, and neck. A squad car pulled up in front of the Dakota, its lights spinning, and two police officers jumped out. Officers Steve Spiro and Pete Cullen had been around the corner when the emergency call came in to the station and they were immediately dispatched to 1 West 72nd Street. As soon as Spiro got out of the front seat of the squad car, he saw Mark David Chapman sitting crosslegged on the sidewalk, his olive-green jacket folded neatly in front of him, calmly reading from a paperback edition of J. D. Salinger's *The Catcher in the Rye*. Spiro instantly recognized the dark red cover of the book. At the same time, Officer Cullen looked up the carriageway and saw two people bent over the body of a man who was obviously seriously wounded and bleeding.

Cullen bent back into the car, grabbed the radio microphone and barked out, "Shots fired 1 West 72nd Street. Radio car on scene. One victim down. Ambulance needed. Urgent."

Hastings pointed at Chapman and shouted, "He's the one who did the shooting!"

Spiro immediately pulled out his gun, pointed it at Chapman and shouted, "Don't move! Put your hands on the wall!"

Spiro handcuffed Chapman, who pleaded with the officer, "Please don't hurt me! Please!"

By this time, officers Herb Frauenberger and Tony Palma had arrived and moved to where Yoko stood in shock over her bleeding husband.

The two officers then made a command decision that is still being debated to this day. They picked up the mortally wounded Lennon, carried him the few feet to their squad car, and laid him down in the backseat. Some argue Lennon might have had a better chance of surviving if he had been left at the site until the EMTs arrived. Hastings later said that he heard John's bones creaking and that his body was limp and floppy.

Chapman was arrested, and John was brought to the emergency room of Roosevelt Hospital. John had almost no pulse and, although seven doctors worked on him furiously, it was impossible to resuscitate him. His aorta had been severed and he bled out. By the time he got to the hospital, John had lost 80 percent of his total blood volume. The official cause of death was shock caused by massive hemorrhaging.

Dr. Stephen Lynn walked into the room where Yoko was waiting and said to her, "We have very bad news. Unfortunately, in spite of massive efforts, your husband is dead. There was no suffering at the end."

Yoko looked up at the doctor and said, "Are you saying he is sleeping?"

Yoko was brought back to the Dakota where she reportedly called John's Aunt Mimi, his son Julian, and Paul McCartney.

John's body was cremated and his ashes were given to Yoko.

Mark David Chapman is currently in prison and, from interviews he has given, seems to consider himself a celebrity.

In October 2001, an all-star tribute to John Lennon took place at Radio City Music Hall. Sean Lennon performed and dedicated his father's song "Julia" to his mother.

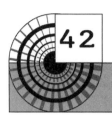

42

Abraham Lincoln

ASSASSINATED   ✓

SURVIVED   ___

This country was formed for the white, not for the black man. And looking upon African slavery from the standpoint held by the noble framers of our Constitution, I, for one, have ever considered it one of the greatest blessings (both for themselves and us) that God ever bestowed upon a favored nation.

—John Wilkes Booth, in a letter to his sister Asia[1]

Well, I guess I know enough to turn you inside out, old gal—you sockdologizing old man-trap.

—The last words Lincoln heard of the play *Our American Cousin* before he was shot[2]

His wound is mortal; it is impossible for him to recover.

—Dr. Charles A. Teale[3]

VICTIM: Abraham Lincoln

BORN: February 12, 1809

DIED: April 15, 1865

AGE WHEN ATTACKED: 56

Lincoln

— 142 —

OCCUPATION: 16th president of the United States (1861–1865), former member of the House of Representatives, lawyer, "Honest Abe," the "Great Emancipator," author of the Gettysburg Address

ASSASSIN: John Wilkes Booth (1838–1865), 26, actor, passionate defender of the Confederacy

DATE & TIME OF ATTACK: Friday, April 14, 1865, approximately 10:15 p.m.

LOCATION OF ATTACK: The presidential box in the balcony of the Ford Theater in Washington, D.C.

WEAPON: A .44-caliber Derringer

ASSASSINATION OUTCOME: From about 2 feet away, Booth pointed the muzzle of his derringer at Lincoln's head "to the left of the middle line, and below the line with the ear."[4] He then fired. One .44-caliber Britannia metal ball entered the president's skull, "ranged forward and upward toward the right eye, lodging within a half inch of that orbit."[5] Lincoln fell unconscious immediately and slumped forward, his chin dropping onto his chest. Booth then dropped his empty gun, pulled out a hunting knife with a 7 1/4-inch razor-sharp blade, and lunged at Lincoln's guest, Major Henry Rathbone, slashing open his left arm (through a thick jacket) from "the elbow nearly to the shoulder, inside—cutting an artery, nerves, and veins—he bled so profusely as to make him very weak."[6] Booth then shouted "Sic semper tyrannis!" (Thus be it ever for tyrants!"), climbed over the edge of the balcony box, and leaped 12 feet to the stage, landing crooked and breaking the smaller fibula bone just above his left ankle. As he fled through a back door, he shouted, "Revenge for the South!" Lincoln, who had no pulse and shallow respiration, was resuscitated by Dr. Charles A. Leale, who used a combination of mouth-to-mouth artificial resuscitation and closed chest cardiac massage. Lincoln was then carried across the street to the Petersen House, where he was taken to a first-floor back bedroom and, due to his height, was placed diagonally on a bed. (Incidentally, as legend would have it, Booth stayed at this boarding house on at least one occasion.) Even with several doctors in attendance monitoring him and allowing his head wound to drain, the president succumbed from his injuries at 7:22 a.m. on Saturday, April 16, 1865. After his death, Dr. Leale placed two of his own silver coins on Lincoln's eyelids and drew a white sheet over his face. Secretary of War Edwin

Stanton then spoke the immortal words, "Now he belongs to the ages." Lincoln's body was later moved to the White House and an autopsy was performed.

JUDICIAL OUTCOME: Lincoln's assassination was only one component of an assassination plot by John Wilkes Booth to destroy Lincoln's administration and allow the defeated Confederates to take control of the U.S. government. The other conspirators were David E. Herold (misidentified on the Wanted poster as "Daniel Harrold"), who conspired to assassinate Secretary of State William Seward; Lewis Paine, who stabbed Seward that night (page 227); George A. Atzerodt, assigned to assassinate Vice President Andrew Johnson (page 115); and Mrs. Mary Surratt, who was convicted of conspiracy and executed but whose actual involvement in carrying out the plot was never conclusively proven. Booth fled the theater on horseback and rode to a farm in Bowling Green, Virginia, where he hid out in a tobacco barn. Federal authorities tracked him down there and, after they set fire to the barn, he was shot in the back of his neck, either by Sergeant Boston Corbett, a Union soldier, or in a failed suicide attempt by Booth himself.

Booth was dragged from the barn and died on April 26, 1865. His last words, as he looked down at his hands, were "Useless, useless."[7] Herold, Paine, Atzerodt, and Surratt were hanged in unison on July 7, 1865.

The fatal shot

John Wilkes Booth was a Confederate racist who blamed Abraham Lincoln for abolishing the institution of slavery, one of the "greatest blessings" known to man. He was also against the Union government and *for* Southern secession, and he truly believed that the elimination of President Lincoln, Vice President Johnson, and other members of Lincoln's Cabinet would bring about a restoration of the Confederacy. General Robert E. Lee had recently surrendered to

Ulysses Grant after losing the Battle of Gettysburg, and this convinced Booth to abandon his original plan of kidnapping Lincoln (a live Lincoln no longer had any bargaining power) and, instead, kill him.

Booth was a well-known actor and was thus able to get into the theater before the evening performance and prepare the presidential box for the assassination. Booth cut a mortise into the door frame of the box so that he would be able to insert a board across the door, thereby preventing anyone from entering the box after he snuck in. He planned to escape by jumping down to the stage, which he did, but his spur caught in a portrait of George Washington and caused him to break his leg.

How did Booth manage to get inside the presidential box? Wasn't there a guard? Didn't the president have some kind of protection? Yes, he did. Lincoln's guard for the evening was John Parker. Parker arrived at the theater well before the presidential party's arrival at approximately 8:25 p.m. Parker investigated the balcony box (which had been doubled in size by having a partition removed) and realized that if he stood guard at the door to prevent unauthorized access, he would not be able to see the play. Parker saw the president, Mrs. Lincoln, and their guests to their seats and then remained at the door a short time, but only until the play started. He then left his post and moved to a spot from which he could see the evening's performance. He left the presidential box unguarded, and John Wilkes Booth made his way inside and bolted the door at approximately 10:13 p.m.

President Lincoln's murder was the first presidential assassination in America's history, and it plunged the nation into a period of widespread mourning and grief. It also put Andrew Johnson in office, making him responsible for the extremely difficult task of Reconstruction and fulfilling Lincoln's objective of making a "house divided" a house united.

Most presidential polls by historians rank Lincoln as one of the greatest U.S. presidents, along with George Washington, Thomas Jefferson, and Franklin Delano Roosevelt.

Astonishing Connection: In the early years of Lincoln's administration, Edwin Booth, John Wilkes Booth's brother and a fellow actor, once saved the life of Lincoln's son, Robert Todd Lincoln, when the boy fell between a train and a railway platform in Jersey City. Edwin Booth received a letter of gratitude from General Ulysses S. Grant and also was held in high regard by President Lincoln himself, who actually saw the actor perform several times following this incident. *Yes, Abraham Lincoln was a fan of the brother of the man who killed him.*

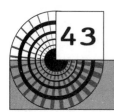

43

Huey P. Long

ASSASSINATED ✓

SURVIVED ___

And it is here, under this oak where Evangeline waited for her lover, Gabriel, who never came. This oak is an immortal spot, made so by Longfellow's poem, but Evangeline is not the only one who has waited here in disappointment. Where are the schools that you have waited for your children to have, that have never come? Where are the roads and highways that you send your money to build, that are no nearer now than before? Where are the institutions for the sick and the disabled? Evangeline wept bitter tears in her disappointment, but it lasted through only one lifetime. Your tears in this country, around this oak, have lasted for generations. Give me the chance to dry the tears of those who still weep here!

—Huey Long[1]

VICTIM: Huey Pierce Long, a.k.a. "the "Kingfish"[2]

BORN: August 30, 1893

DIED: September 10, 1935

AGE WHEN ATTACKED: 42

OCCUPATION: Governor of Louisiana (1928–1930), U.S. Senator (1932–1935), potential Democratic presidential candidate against Republican Herbert Hoover

ASSASSIN: Dr. Carl Weiss (1905–1935), 29; Roman Catholic; conservative; eyes, ears, nose, and throat specialist; considered a brilliant physician (His motive for assassinating Long remains unknown, although he was the son-in-law of one of Long's political foes, Judge Benjamin Pavy, a district judge whose office was threatened by a bill supported by Long.)

DATE & TIME OF ATTACK: Sunday, September 8, 1935, 9:22 p.m.; died Tuesday September 10, 1935, at 4:10 a.m.

LOCATION OF ATTACK: In a first-floor corridor of the Louisiana State Capitol in Baton Rouge

WEAPON: A .32-caliber Browning semi-automatic pistol

ASSASSINATION OUTCOME: Huey Long died 30 hours and 48 minutes after being shot in the abdomen. The direct cause of his death was probably from undetected, unrepaired damage to his right kidney from the gunshot. The doctor who performed the surgery, Dr. Arthur Vidrine, reportedly operated from the front, and he may have missed a nick to an artery that led to Long's kidney. This could have caused Long to bleed to death.[3] The assassin, Carl Weiss, died instantly at the scene after being shot 61 times by Long's bodyguards—30 times in the front, 29 in his back, and twice in his head.

JUDICIAL OUTCOME: None. The assassin was dead and Mrs. Long refused to allow an autopsy on her husband's body. Any errors during surgery, or possible evidence of more than one bullet causing the damage, all went to the grave with the Kingfish.

The Tulane University Medical School Yearbook prophecy for Carl Weiss read, "With knowledge aplenty and friends galore, he is bound to go out and make the world take notice." A few years later, Weiss would be shot and killed during an assassination attempt against Senator (and possible presidential candidate) Huey P. Long of Louisiana. The world did, indeed, take notice of Weiss.

Although Weiss is considered the "official" assassin of Huey Long, there has long been speculation (yes, the reflex conspiracy theory) that Weiss never actually fired at Long and only punched him in the mouth, either with his hand or his pistol. The alternative story is that Weiss waited for Long as the senator and his team of bodyguards walked down a first-floor corridor in the Capitol building in Baton Rouge. As soon as Long was close enough, Weiss leapt out from behind a marble pillar and struck the Senator in the mouth, either with his fist or his .32-caliber pistol.

As soon as Long was struck, his bodyguards drew their weapons and opened fire on Weiss. The first two (or 10) bullets probably killed Weiss, but the guards continued to fire, ultimately pumping 61 bullets into the doctor. Many of these bullets, so the theory goes, entered and exited Weiss's body, struck several of the marble surfaces in the corridor (walls, pillars, the floor, and so on) ricocheted, and struck Huey Long in the abdomen.

This conspiracy theory then merges with verifiable, uncontested fact, and the story goes on to tell how Long was helped down a flight of stairs to the basement where he and his men exited through a rear door. He was then put in a car and rushed to the hospital, yet even this part of the story has a few different versions. In one, Long was taken to the hospital by one of his bodyguards, in the bodyguard's car. In another, a cab was hailed. In another, Long's aide James O'Connor saw a parked Ford with a driver and ordered him to take Long to the hospital.

Whatever his mode of travel, upon his arrival, Long was examined and also questioned about the wound on his lip. "That's where he hit me," he reportedly said, according to witness Jewel O'Neal, a student nurse.[4] A rumor also has made the rounds that one of Long's bodyguards drunkenly sobbed to a friend a few days after Long's death that he had killed his only friend. Many believe this to be a reference to the Senator.

Long underwent surgery to repair damage to his colon caused by one bullet that entered his upper right side and exited through his back. The bullet had also apparently nicked a renal artery, but this may have been missed. Because Mrs. Long forbade an autopsy, we will never know the true cause of Huey Long's death.

An argument can be made, however, for the claim that Weiss never meant to kill Huey Long, a belief his family has embraced since 1935. We can check off the reasons why it was highly unlikely that Weiss went to the Capitol that evening to kill the Senator. He was married, and he and his wife had a 3-month-old son; he had a thriving medical practice; he was not politically vocal or involved; and his behavior the night of his death was not the behavior of a man who believed he might die within hours. It was learned that an hour before he died, Weiss had called an anesthesiologist who was scheduled to assist him in surgery the following morning to tell him the hospital had been changed. *This* Carl Weiss does not come across as a depressed, fatalistic political assassin.

Huey Long was called a demagogue and a dictator, yet his flamboyant, irreverent manner endeared him to the electorate, giving him a popular support that allowed him (and encouraged him) to push through programs and changes that, in the long run and with almost three-quarters of a century of hindsight, helped more than hindered. He got roads and bridges built, he taxed the oil companies, and he expanded the school system into rural areas. His "Share the Wealth" program made national headlines and, at the time of his death, he was gearing up for a probable bid for the Democratic presidential nomination.

Robert Penn Warren won a Pulitzer Prize for his 1946 novel *All the King's Men*, in which the character of Willie Stark was based on Huey Long.

In 1999, Dr. Donald Pavy published a book called *Accident and Deception: The Huey Long Shooting*, in which he insists that Weiss wasn't armed the night he went to the Capitol and that all he wanted to do was talk to Long. Pavy is the nephew of Judge Benjamin Pavy. Dr. Pavy's cousin Yvonne was Carl Weiss's wife.

The controversy continues to this day and the question "Who shot Huey Long?" remains unanswered for many. Bullet holes are still visible in the wall of the Capitol building in Baton Rouge.

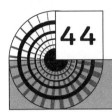

44

Malcolm X

ASSASSINATED   ✓

SURVIVED   ___

Being born here in America doesn't make you an American. Why, if birth made you American, you wouldn't need any legislation, you wouldn't need any amendments to the Constitution, you wouldn't be faced with civil-rights filibustering in Washington, D.C., right now. They don't have to pass civil-rights legislation to make a Polack an American.

No, I'm not an American. I'm one of the 22 million black people who are the victims of Americanism. One of the 22 million black people who are the victims of democracy, nothing but disguised hypocrisy. So, I'm not standing here speaking to you as an American, or a patriot, or a flag-saluter, or a flag-waver—no, not I. I'm speaking as a victim of this American system. And I see America through the eyes of the victim. I don't see any American dream; I see an American nightmare.

—Malcolm X[1]

VICTIM: Malcolm X, born Malcolm Little, later took the name El Hajj Malik El-Shabazz after a pilgrimage to Mecca in 1964

Born: May 19, 1925

Died: February 21, 1965

AGE WHEN ATTACKED: 39

OCCUPATION: Black nationalist; Muslim leader; founder of the Organization for Afro-American Unity; former drug dealer, pimp, and burglar; self-educated ex-con

ASSASSINS: Thomas Hagan, 22, real name Talmadge Hayer, later changed his name to Mujahid Abdul Halim; Normal Butler, 26, a.k.a. Norman 3X, later changed his name to Muhammad Abdul Aziz; Thomas Johnson, a.k.a. Thomas 15X, later changed his name to Khalil Islam all three members of the Nation of Islam

DATE & TIME OF ATTACK: Sunday, February 21, 1965, afternoon

LOCATION OF ATTACK: The Audubon Ballroom in Washington Heights, Harlem in New York City

WEAPONS: A 12-gauge double-barrel shotgun; a .45-caliber automatic pistol; a German Luger pistol

ASSASSINATION OUTCOME: Thomas Hagan shot Malcolm X in the chest with a double-barrel shotgun. Malcolm fell to the floor, and Butler and Johnson then ran up and fired several rounds into his body with handguns. The black leader was shot a total of 16 times and died two hours later during surgery.

JUDICIAL OUTCOME: Malcolm X's bodyguards shot Hagan in the thigh. He tried to flee, but the crowd restrained him and beat him bloody. When he was arrested, he had a bullet wound in his thigh, a broken ankle, and several bleeding wounds. The other two gunmen were also arrested. All three were found guilty and sentenced to life in prison. Butler was paroled in 1985. Hagan is on a work-release program. Johnson was released in 1987. Hagan maintained his innocence throughout his stay in prison, but no further arrests have been made.

Malcolm X's wife was pregnant with his twin daughters on the day her husband was killed. One of the most heart-wrenching moments from the Audubon Ballroom that cool Sunday in 1965 was the sight of his pregnant wife bending over his bleeding body, screaming, "They're killing my husband!"[2]

Malcolm X arrived at the Audubon Ballroom prepared to offer his usual diatribe against white America, hoping to rally the black community to passionate self-empowerment. Malcolm's rejection of his "slave name" set the tone for his rhetoric and also set a powerful example for the poor black class who were still reeling on a societal level from having ancestors not too many decades past that had been slaves.

Malcolm X and his associates radiated confidence and self-respect. They were always dressed impeccably, complete with bow ties, they also spoke calmly and intelligently, and they rarely raised their voices. They were courteous, dignified, proud, and insisted on being taken seriously. "A race of people is like an individual man," Malcolm X once said. "Until it uses its own talent, takes pride in its own history, expresses its own culture, affirms its own selfhood, it can never fulfill itself."[3]

The first words Malcolm X said upon entering the auditorium were his standard greeting: "As-salaam aleikum" ("Peace be with you"). He spoke of peace with his first utterances and, in stark contrast to his salutation, watched as a scuffle broke out in the first couple of rows of the audience. Two men were seemingly arguing over one accusing the other of picking his pocket. "Now brothers, be cool," Malcolm said to the two men in an attempt to defuse the situation. It was then that a smoke bomb went off in the back of the hall, adding to the confusion.

All of this was planned to distract, and it worked. Right after the smoke bomb went off, the assassins struck. Thomas Hagan stalked up the center aisle, pulling a double-barreled shotgun from his coat. The stock and the barrels had both been cut down so the gun could be concealed more easily. Hagan reached the front of the aisle, took aim, and pulled both triggers at once. The deafening explosion ripped a hole in the podium, behind which Malcolm was standing, penetrated the wood, and then tore into Malcolm's stomach and chest. Malcolm fell to the floor and then two of Hagan's accomplices, Butler and Johnson, ran up to the front, stood over the bleeding and critically wounded black leader, and emptied their handguns into him.

A photo of Malcolm X on a stretcher being carried to an ambulance appeared in the next day's newspapers. His face was uncovered, because he was being taken for emergency treatment, but he could have been declared dead at the scene, such was the fatal ferocity with which the assassin's bullets tore through him.

The Nation of Islam issued a statement affirming that it had nothing to do with Malcolm X's assassination. Nonetheless, a Nation of Islam mosque in New York was firebombed 36 hours later and it burned to the ground.

An estimated 22,000 people viewed Malcolm X's body. His eulogy was delivered by actor Ossie Davis. At his grave site, his followers took the shovels out of the hands of the cemetery workers and dug his grave themselves.

Today, Malcolm X is an icon for many African-Americans, especially after Spike Lee's laudatory 1992 eponymous biopic, starring Denzel Washington as the black leader.

45 Jean-Paul Marat

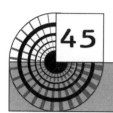

ASSASSINATED ✓

SURVIVED ___

Toute institution qui ne suppose pas le peuple bon, et le magistrat corruptible, est vicieuse.
Any institution which does not suppose the people good, and the magistrate corruptible, is evil.

—Maximilien Robespierre[1]

VICTIM: Dr. Jean-Paul Marat

BORN: May 24, 1743

DIED: July 13, 1793

AGE WHEN ATTACKED: 50

OCCUPATION: Physician, revolutionary journalist, author of *The Chains of Slavery* (1774), leader of the radical Jacobin party working to overthrow the French monarchy and establish a republic

Marat

ASSASSIN: Charlotte Corday (1758–1793), 24, member of the republican political party, the Girondists, a more moderate group that was against the violent excesses of Marat's camp

DATE & TIME OF ATTACK: Saturday, July 13, 1973, shortly after 7 p.m.

LOCATION OF ATTACK: In the bathtub of his apartment in Paris, France

— 153 —

WEAPON: A knife

ASSASSINATION OUTCOME: Marat died almost instantly from a knife wound to a major artery in his chest.

JUDICIAL OUTCOME: Corday was found guilty and executed, all within three days of her assault on Marat.

Naked and submerged in a tub filled with cold water and herbs is how the brilliant writer and revolutionary Jean-Paul Marat met his maker.

Charlotte Corday blamed Marat (along with his contemporary Robespierre) for unleashing the Reign of Terror, a systematic slaughter of all those who were opposed to the French revolution. "Enemies of the revolution" (particularly nobles and their supporters) were rounded up and guillotined, and much of the bloodshed was probably due to the inflamed writings of Marat and Robespierre.

Charlotte Corday had had enough of the massacring (nine were killed in the morning on the day she stabbed Marat), and she believed that eliminating Marat would remove one of the movement's de facto leaders.

Corday managed to finagle her way into Marat's apartment by refusing to leave when one of Marat's servants told her the master was sick and in the tub and could not see anyone. This conversation must have gotten somewhat loud because, suddenly, Marat shouted out from the bathroom inquiring what was going on. The servant went into the bathroom and told him that a young woman was here and that she insisted on seeing him to tell him of political goings-on in her town of Caen. Surprisingly, Marat agreed to see Corday, and the servant ushered her into the bathroom.

From all accounts, Corday was greeted by an altogether disgusting sight.

Marat was in a tub that had originally been painted a yellowish-brown color, but that was so filthy it looked black. Marat was naked in the tub, and a board lay across it, serving as a makeshift desk for the writer. Marat had a cloth wrapped around his head that he had soaked in vinegar, and the sour liquid dripped into his greasy black hair. Marat's facial features were swollen amidst sunken cheeks; his skin was gray and covered with scabs and sores; and his eyes bore the yellow tint of liver or kidney disease.

Next to the tub was a small window and on the sill were two small plates, one holding a serving of calf brains; the other sweetbreads (pancreas). Behind the tub, a map of France was pinned to the wall and beneath it was a piece of paper on which the word *Mort* (death) had been written.

Charlotte Corday—with her luminous beauty, radiant skin, and lustrous hair—must have been like a flower in a stinking pile of garbage in that small, foul bathroom. She maintained enough of her composure, though, to give him the information she had promised: the names of several Girondists in Caen, along with their movements.

Marat was delighted with her revelations and began to write down the names she had mentioned. As he wrote, Corday stood up, pulled a knife from a sheath in her pocket, and, with one quick movement, plunged it into Marat's chest, just above his heart, burying it all the way to the hilt.

Corday then withdrew the blade and dropped the knife onto the dirty bathroom floor.

Marat let out a scream when she stabbed him, and the people in his house came running. They found Marat with blood gushing out the hole in his chest, obviously dying, and they tried to get him out of the water. It was useless, though, as Corday had hit a major artery below his collarbone and nothing could be done to save him.

During this commotion, Charlotte Corday tried to flee the house to no avail. She was restrained by two men—a porter and another lodger in the building—who tied her hands behind her back with handkerchiefs and called the gendarmes.

Corday was arrested and quickly put to trial. Because she did not deny her actions, she was immediately found guilty and executed just days after the assassination.

After the executioner chopped off Charlotte Corday's head in the guillotine, he held the head up and slapped it in the face. (The *London Times* of July 30, 1793 reported that he "gave it a blow.") The crowd attending the public execution was unanimously approving.

Note: In 1964, a play by Paul Weiss, *Marat/Sade*, was published and performed for the first time. The play's full title was *The Persecution and Assassination of Jean-Paul Marat* as Performed by the Inmates of the Asylum of Charenton Under the Direction of the Marquis de Sade. The story concerned De Sade putting on a play in the asylum where he was confined, and it gave Weiss an opportunity to imagine a lengthy conversation between the two writers, in which the anarchist De Sade debated his philosophies with the pre-Marxist Marat. As of 2002, the play was still in active production in many venues around the world.

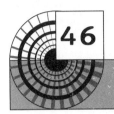

46

Imelda Marcos

ASSASSINATED ___

SURVIVED ✓

I am extravagant. In the material world, where everything is valued, when you commit yourself to God, beauty and love, it can be mistaken for extravagance.

—Imelda Marcos[1]

VICTIM: Imelda Marcos

BORN: July 2, 1929

DIED: n/a

AGE WHEN ATTACKED: 43

OCCUPATION: Philippines first lady, wife of Philippines President Ferdinand E. Marcos (1917–1989; deposed in 1986), former beauty queen, shoe fanatic, legislative representative of Leyte (elected in 1989), arrested and charged with corruption in October 2001

UNSUCCESSFUL ASSASSIN: Carlito Dimaali (1945–1972), 27, geodetic engineer from Cuenca, Philippines

DATE & TIME OF ATTACK: Thursday, December 7, 1972, 4:30 p.m.

LOCATION OF ATTACK: In a Pasay, Philippines, TV studio on live television as Mrs. Marcos was awarding prizes to the winners of a National Beautification and Cleanliness contest

WEAPON: A 12-inch-long dagger, hidden in a sheath in the assassin's left sleeve

ASSASSINATION OUTCOME: The assailant tried to stab Marcos in the chest, but she stooped, turned her body, and parried the blows with her arms and hands. She sustained serious cuts on her hands and arms, and tendons were severed in her arms. She was rushed by helicopter to the Makate Medical Center and needed 75 stitches for her injuries. Other than her hands and arms wounds, she was not injured anywhere else. She recovered fully. (Some of the more catty media accounts of the attack reported that Marcos was not seriously injured but that she did break some nails.) Two others were injured while grappling with the assassin: Philippines Congressman José Aspiras suffered a deep head wound, and Linda Amor Robles, the secretary of the beautification campaign, received a deep wound in the back. Both recovered.

JUDICIAL OUTCOME: There was no trial, and no charges were filed. Dimaali was killed at the scene, and no one else was implicated in the attack. Initially, there was suspicion that Dimaali could have had accomplices on the scene, because he had no problem accessing the live studio area, but this was later discounted. There was also talk that Dimaali had actually been targeting Imelda Marcos's husband, President Ferdinand Marcos, who had recently imposed martial law on the Philippines but, because he was not on the scene during the incident, this theory, too was ultimately dismissed. The Philippines Secretary of State Francisco S. Tatad issued a statement revealing that one hour before the television show, someone had called the palace to inquire whether or not Ferdinand Marcos would be at the broadcast. This fueled the Ferdinand-as-target theory for a time, but because the assassin was shot and killed at the scene his motives remain unknown.

The assassin was short, slim, and wore a dark suit. He milled around the television studio, waiting for the perfect opportunity to strike.

The enormously popular first lady of the Philippines, Imelda Marcos, she of the three thousand pairs of shoes and charismatic presence, was handing out awards to winners of a national contest to clean up unsightly, blighted neighborhoods.

The show was almost over and Mrs. Marcos was presenting an award to the delegation from Cobato City when the assassin lunged. He climbed onto the stage, withdrew his foot-long dagger, and ran at Mrs. Marcos.

Apparently trained in the martial arts, Mrs. Marcos moved in such a way as to shield her trunk from the knife, folding her arms to protect her internal organs. She fell to the floor and took the blows on her hands and arms, suffering deep wounds but protecting herself from a fatal injury.

Two others present—Aspiras and Robles—attempted to subdue the assailant, and he lashed out at them with his knife. They did manage to get him down onto the floor, though, briefly disabling him long enough for security guards from the wings to make their way onto the stage. One guard fired two shots into Dimaali's back, killing him instantly.

The entire incident was broadcast on live television.

Mrs. Marcos recovered fully, although her recuperation was marked by her trademark flair for fashion. When she attended President Richard Nixon's inauguration ball in January 1973, she wore a sling specially designed and covered with pearls.

Postscript: In a Manila court in November 2001, Imelda Marcos pled not guilty to four counts of corruption. She and her late husband were accused of stealing $352 million during their administration. Shortly after her arraignment, Mrs. Marcos filed a $400 million lawsuit against the Philippine government for slander. Both cases are still pending.

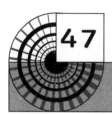

47 Christopher Marlowe

ASSASSINATED   ✓

SURVIVED   ___

[Ingram Frizer], in defence of his life, with the dagger afore-said of the value of 12d. gave the said Christopher then & there a mortal wound over his right eye of the depth of two inches & of the width of one inch; of which mortal wound the aforesaid Christopher Morley [sic] then & there instantly died.

—Court documents[1]

VICTIM: Christopher Marlowe

BORN: February 1564

DIED: May 30, 1593

AGE WHEN ATTACKED: 29

OCCUPATION: Poet, playwright, translator, contemporary of William Shakespeare

ASSASSINS: Ingram Frizer, personal businessman of Marlowe's patron, Thomas Walsingham, known for being a swindler and an all-around shady character; Robert Poley and Nicholas Skeres were also present and may have been accomplices/co-conspirators if the murder had been planned as a conspiracy, but they were only interviewed as witnesses.[2]

Marlowe Memorial, Collis, Canterbury

— 159 —

DATE & TIME OF ATTACK: Wednesday, May 30, 1593, evening, after dinnertime

LOCATION OF ATTACK: In the bedroom of a house owned by a widow named Eleanor Bull, in Deptford Strand, a small town about 3 miles from London (Marlowe and his colleagues were in Deptford because London was raging with the plague; it had not yet spread to Deptford Strand.)

WEAPON: A common dagger known as a poniard. It had a long, slender blade with a triangular or square cross-section.

ASSASSINATION OUTCOME: The poniard was plunged two inches deep into Marlowe's skull just above his right eye. Witnesses all reported that the renowned playwright died instantly, although there has long been strong medical skepticism[3] suggesting that a wound such as the one Marlowe sustained could not have possibly killed him so quickly.

JUDICIAL OUTCOME: Ingram Frizer claimed that he killed Christopher Marlowe in self-defense. The two witnesses to the altercation between Frizer and Marlowe, Robert Poley and Nicholas Skeres, both confirmed Frizer's story and signed affidavits in his defense. Frizer was granted a complete pardon 4 weeks and 1 day after Marlowe's murder.

Was the 16th-century playwright Christopher Marlowe, author of the acclaimed *Tamburlaine the Great*, assassinated as part of a conspiracy, or was he murdered in an out-of-control argument over who should pay a restaurant bill?

Marlowe's killer, as well as the two witnesses to the murder, tell the same story.

The four men arrived at Eleanor Bull's home in Deptford Strand at ten in the morning, apparently for an important, all-day business meeting. History does not tell us what the meeting was about, but there has been speculation that it was personal financial business among the men or some kind of government business. (Bull's house has sometimes been referred to as a kind of pub, but there is also evidence that it was something akin to a boardinghouse or hostel that the widow was allowing them to use, likely for a significant fee of course, for their meeting.[4])

The men had a private lunch in one of the house's bedrooms, with much wine being drunk, and then they walked in Eleanor Bull's garden discussing whatever they needed to discuss. They apparently spent much of the afternoon outside (and away from the widow's ears, it should be noted), and then they went back inside at dinnertime, around 6:00. They returned to the bedroom where they had eaten lunch and more wine was drunk with dinner.

After they ate, Marlowe lay down on the bed, and the other three men sat on a bench at the table across from the bed—with (according to the coroner's report) their back to Marlowe. Frizer, Marlowe's assassin, reportedly began playing backgammon with one of the other men.

Shortly thereafter, Frizer and Marlowe began to argue about le recknynge, in other words, they clashed over who would pay Mrs. Bull's bill.

Marlowe then leaped up off the bed, grabbed the dagger from a sheath Frizer was wearing on his belt, and stabbed Frizer in the head, giving him two wounds 2 inches in length and a 1/4-inch deep. A struggle ensued, Frizer grabbed back his own dagger and stabbed Marlowe in the skull, burying the dagger 2 inches into his brain at a spot just above his right eye.

Frizer did not flee, because in Elizabethan times that was considered an admission of guilt and, as history shows, after telling his story and having the other two men present corroborate it, he was given a pardon for killing Marlowe.

There may, in fact be some validity to the theory that Marlowe was plotted against. Some of the facts simply do not add up:

▶ How could there have been disagreement over who would pay the tab for an agreed-upon, day-long meeting? They carefully planned the meeting but left the payment of the bill up in the air?

▶ How could a minor argument among friends turn so deadly, so quickly? Granted, everyone was probably drunk, but it is likely that these men had all been drunk together before, and the situation had previously never ended up with somebody dead.

▶ Frizer's wounds were suspected of being self-inflicted. They were too insignificant to have been caused by an enraged, drunken man (Marlowe).

▶ The only witnesses were confederates of the killer, men who were known for shady dealings. It is not far-fetched to imagine them coordinating their story.

▶ Frizer and Marlowe had a blistering argument—while Marlowe was lying on the bed and Frizer had his back to him?

▶ Why didn't the other two men present try to "break it up?" If two friends get into a fight in the presence of other friends, it is a given that the non-combatants will try to stop the fight.

▶ Were Marlowe and company the *only* patrons in Mrs. Bull's restaurant/tavern/brothel that day? Also, why wasn't Mrs. Bull called to testify at Frizer's trial?

▶ Why did Marlowe's patron, Thomas Walsingham, and his wife remain friends with his killer?

Personally, this author believes Marlowe was definitely targeted, for some unknown reason, and that Frizer and company were the paid assassins.

Christopher Marlowe's contribution to English literature was huge, and he was surpassed only by his contemporary, Shakespeare. Many literary critics believe that if Marlowe had lived, he might have outdone the Bard himself—or at the very least created magnificent and memorable poetry. His death at the young age of 29 surely robbed the world of unimaginably great art.

Plays by Christopher Marlowe	
Dido Queen of Carthage, circa 1586 *Tamburlaine the Great, Parts 1 and 2,* 1587–1588	*The Jew of Malta,* circa 1590 *The Massacre at Paris,* circa 1590 *Edward II,* 1592 *Dr. Faustus,* 1594

48

William McKinley

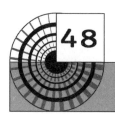

ASSASSINATED   ✓

SURVIVED   —

Unlike any other nation, here the people rule, and their will is the supreme law.

—William McKinley[1]

I have no enemies. Why should I fear?

—William McKinley[2]

VICTIM: William McKinley, Jr.

BORN: January 29, 1843

DIED: September 14, 1901

AGE WHEN ATTACKED: 57

OCCUPATION: 25th president of the United States (1897–1901)

ASSASSINS: Leon Czolgosz (pronounced "Colgosh") (1873–1901), 28, anarchist, disciple of Russian-born American anarchist Emma Goldman,[3] wire millworker

DATE & TIME OF ATTACK: Friday, September 6, 1901, 4:07 p.m.

McKinley

LOCATION OF ATTACK: In the Temple of Music at the Pan American Exposition in Buffalo, New York

WEAPON: A .32-caliber Iver Johnson Revolver

ASSASSINATION OUTCOME: The assassin fired twice and hit the president with two bullets. The first bullet hit him in the chest but bounced off a button above his breastbone and did no harm. The second bullet hit McKinley in the abdomen, about 5 inches below his left nipple, 1 1/2 inches to the left of the median line. This bullet entered and exited his stomach, gashed the top of his left kidney, and then entered and lodged in his pancreas. McKinley remained conscious but collapsed into the arms of a detective assigned to the presidential detail. He was rushed to a hospital on the grounds of the Exposition, and surgery was performed to repair the entry wound and the internal damage to his stomach. During the operation, doctors tried to find the bullet, but it was buried so deep in the pancreas that they could not find it, so it was left inside the president's body. (The hospital on the grounds of the Exposition had one of the first x-ray machines in the country, but the doctors still considered it an experimental device and felt McKinley's wounds were not serious enough to risk using it on him.) McKinley tolerated the operation well and, four days later, a second operation was performed to remove a small piece of clothing that had been inadvertently left in the president's abdomen. For five days, McKinley seemed to improve and there was hope he would survive. During this time, however, a deadly gangrenous infection was growing inside him from the lack of sterile conditions during his surgeries. On the eighth day after the shooting, September 14, 1901 at 2:16 a.m., McKinley died after saying goodbye to his wife. His last words were, "Goodbye. Goodbye to all. It is God's will. His will, not ours, be done."[4] The official cause of death was gangrene of the stomach and pancreas following the gunshot wound.

JUDICIAL OUTCOME: After firing his gun twice, Czolgosz was immediately set upon by Secret Service agents and police. A contingent of American soldiers from the U.S. 73rd Company was also in the Temple of Music at the time, and it seems that everyone who could get near him took a shot at the assassin. Czolgosz was beaten almost to the point of death, and then he was taken away to the police station, where he made a full confession, exhibiting no remorse and telling the authorities that he had willfully planned the shooting of McKinley. Remarkably, during the beating of Czolgosz, as the president lay bleeding, McKinley told his guards not to harm his assassin. Czolgosz admitted his guilt but refused a lawyer, because he rejected the right of any court to try him. A plea of not guilty (automatic in capital crime cases in New York) was entered for him, and he was found guilty on September 23, 1901, after 34 minutes of jury deliberation. He was electrocuted on October 29, 1901, at Auburn State Prison.[5] His last words were, "I killed the President because he was the enemy of the people—the good working people. I am not sorry for my crime."[6] Sulfuric acid was poured over Czolgosz's corpse before he was buried.

The president's eyes fluttered open and the doctors and nurses moved to his side. Weakly, he asked for his wife to be brought to him. His face bore the signs of great weakness and profound suffering, yet he rallied himself enough to maintain wakefulness until Mrs. McKinley could arrive.

A guard escorted the first lady from her room, and a chair was placed by the side of the president's bed. She sat and grasped his hand, and a small smile lit up the countenance of her dying husband. His lips moved and she bent to place her ear next to his mouth. Everyone in the room turned away from this poignant scene, except for one doctor and nurse who stood silent, watching the president at all times.

What McKinley said to his wife is not known, except for a single sentence overheard by the doctor. "Not our will, but God's will, be done."[7]

The President drifted in and out of consciousness, and Mrs. McKinley was returned to her room, wracked with unimaginable grief, knowing with certainty that the death of her beloved husband was moments away. As she wept in her room, never to see him again, the President began to fail rapidly. His doctor held his finger on the president's neck, monitoring his pulse until, at 2:16 a.m., he raised his head and, with tears pouring down his face, said, "It is over. The President is no more."[8]

McKinley's vice president, Theodore Roosevelt, was located vacationing in the Adirondacks, returned to Buffalo, and sworn in as president at the home of Ansley Wilcox, a friend and political supporter, on September 14, 1901. He was 42 years old and the youngest man ever to become president. (John F. Kennedy, at 43, was the youngest man ever *elected* to the presidency.)

William McKinley's killing was the first political assassination of the 20th century.

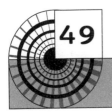

49

Harvey Milk[1]

ASSASSINATED   ✓

SURVIVED   ___

I cannot prevent anybody from getting angry, or mad or frustrated. I can only hope they'll turn that anger and frustration and madness into something positive, so that hundreds will step forward, so that gay doctors come out, the gay lawyers, gay judges, gay bankers, gay architects. I hope that every gay professional would just say, "Enough!," come forward and tell everybody, wear a sign, let the world know. Maybe that will help. These are my strong requests, knowing that it could happen, hoping it doesn't...and if it does, I think I've already achieved something. I think it's been worth it. If a bullet should enter my brain, let that bullet destroy every closet door.

—Harvey Milk[2]

I am not going to be forced out of San Francisco by...social deviates...

—Dan White[3]

VICTIM: Harvey Milk

BORN: May 22, 1930

DIED: November 27, 1978

AGE WHEN ATTACKED: 48

OCCUPATION: City Supervisor of San Francisco, first openly gay public official in the city

ASSASSIN: Daniel James White (1946–1985), 32,[4] former San Francisco fireman, police officer, and member of the Board of Supervisors

DATE & TIME OF ATTACK: Monday, November 27, 1978, approximately 11 a.m.

LOCATION OF ATTACK: In Milk's office in the San Francisco City Hall

WEAPON: A .38-caliber revolver

ASSASSINATION OUTCOME: Milk died after being shot five times by White. Two of the bullets hit Milk in the brain. White also assassinated San Francisco Mayor George Moscone.

JUDICIAL OUTCOME: White turned himself in 35 minutes after the shootings and was charged with two counts of voluntary manslaughter. His defense team put forth the now-infamous "Twinkie Defense," trying to convince the jury that White was not in his right mind when he killed Moscone and Milk due to an excessive consumption of junk food. It worked. The jury found White not guilty of murder but guilty of voluntary manslaughter. He was sentenced to seven years and eight months, served five years and one month, and committed suicide on October 21, 1985.

Back in the Precambrian Seventies, anyone who was openly gay—that is, anyone who was honest about their sexual orientation and unconcerned about who knew—was referred to in the media as an "avowed homosexual." The use of the word *avowed* in that construct is reflective of the times: one of the definitions of avow is "confess," and "avow guilt" is commonly used to describe someone who has admitted committing a crime.

Harvey Milk was an avowed homosexual who contradicted this sense of the word *avow* by refusing to consider his gayness something about which he needed to feel guilty. He championed gay rights and was instrumental in getting a Gay Rights Ordinance passed in San Francisco in 1978, much to the chagrin and disgust of avowed homophobe and fellow City Supervisor Daniel White.

Milk and White had each been elected to one of the 11 city supervisor positions, and they were radical opposites when it came to gay rights. White was a hard-nosed conservative who viewed homosexuality as a sin and a threat to traditional family values; Milk considered homosexuals a minority that needed help and legislative protection against bigotry, discrimination, and violence.

Ten months after his election, White resigned his position, claiming he could not afford to support his family on the $800-a-month salary the part-time city supervisor position paid. He said he had to devote more time to a food concession owned and operated by his family in the San Francisco Wharf area. Within a few days of his resignation, however, White changed his mind and decided he wanted his job back. Harvey Milk advised San Francisco Mayor George Moscone against accepting White back, reminding him of the many times White had tried to get gay rights legislation (which were Moscone-supported) defeated. White found out about Milk's efforts and decided to do something about it.

Monday morning, November 28, 1978, around 10:00, Dan White sneaked into San Francisco City Hall through an open basement window. Why didn't he walk through the front door? Because the front door has metal detectors and Dan White was carrying a .38-caliber revolver in his pocket that morning.

He asked to see Mayor Moscone and was granted an interview. As soon as they were alone in a small room, White shot Moscone in the chest and then in the head, killing him.

He then walked down the hall to Harvey Milk's office, where he puts five bullets into the city supervisor, two in the brain.

Dan White then left City Hall and called his wife from a pay phone. He asked her to meet him, and together they walked to a nearby police station, where he turned himself in.

White's defense team successfully convinced a jury that White was not of his right mind because of an abnormal consumption of junk food and that what was actually premeditated, first-degree murder was really only voluntary manslaughter. White's ridiculously light sentence outraged the gay community and thousands rioted in protest.

Today, Harvey Milk is looked to as a martyr and a hero to the gay community for his ceaseless efforts as a proponent of equal treatment and protections for all minorities.

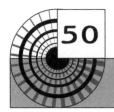

50

Sal Mineo

ASSASSINATED   ✓

SURVIVED   —

I'll never be mistaken for Pat Boone.

—Sal Mineo[1]

VICTIM: Salvatore "Sal" Mineo, Jr.

BORN: January 19, 1939[2]

DIED: February 13, 1976

AGE WHEN ATTACKED: 37

OCCUPATION: Actor, best known for role of Plato in *Rebel Without a Cause*

ASSASSIN: Lionel Ray Williams, 19, drug addict

DATE & TIME OF ATTACK: Friday, February 13, 1976, at approximately 10 p.m.

LOCATION OF ATTACK: The rear carport area of Mineo's West Hollywood, California, apartment

WEAPON: Knife (never found)

ASSASSINATION OUTCOME: Mineo died almost immediately from a large stab wound to the heart.

JUDICIAL OUTCOME: The case was unsolved for three years until Lionel Williams bragged about the murder to a cellmate while in jail in Michigan for forging checks. (A guard overheard the conversation and reported it.) Prison authorities bugged Williams's cell and, instead of being released after serving his 10 months on the forgery charge, he was then indicted for Mineo's slaying and ultimately convicted of second-degree murder. On February 14, 1979, he was sentenced to life in prison for the murder of Sal Mineo.

It was late and Sal Mineo was tired.

He had been at rehearsal all day for *P.S. Your Cat is Dead*, a new play in which he was starring with Keir Dullea. As the time neared 10:00, Mineo pulled his car into the carport behind his apartment and wearily shut off the engine. He got out of the car and shut the door, and, as he was walking towards his back door, a man with long hair and dark clothes leaped out of the shadows and raised a heavy knife above his head. The attacker planned to stab Mineo to death and rob him for drug money. The man plunged the knife into Mineo's chest with great force and struck him in the heart. As Mineo's life's blood pumped from the hole in his chest, the young actor screamed "Help! Help! Oh, my God!" loud enough for his neighbors to hear him. The drug addict panicked and fled, leaving Mineo's wallet untouched.

Mineo's neighbors called the police but it was too late. Mineo was found face-down in a pool of his own blood. He had bled to death. The coroner's report stated that Mineo "died of a massive hemorrhage due to stab wounds of the chest penetrating the heart."[3]

Was Sal Mineo targeted by someone because of his celebrity status? A cursory review of his filmography (see the end of this chapter) shows that from 1955 through 1976, the year of his death, he was quite active in movies and on TV. It is not far-fetched to imagine a stalking scenario in which Mineo was specifically singled out as likely having money and also as being an easy target. (He was slender and had a slight build.) If Mineo hadn't screamed, his killer probably would have made off with his wallet.

Police investigations following Mineo's murder went nowhere. The case was officially open and unsolved until Lionel Williams admitted his crime to a cellmate. Williams is in prison today serving a life sentence for Mineo's murder.

Sal Mineo, the son of a Sicilian coffin-maker, was thrown out of parochial school when he was 8 years old. When he was 10, his mother enrolled him in dancing class, hoping that his involvement with the arts would have a stabilizing effect on her son, who today would be described as an "at-risk child." Mineo was shortly thereafter arrested for robbery and was lucky enough to get a far-sighted judge who recognized the boy's potential. At his sentencing, he was given a choice: incarceration in a juvenile detention hall or enrollment in a professional acting school. Wisely (and no doubt with the urging of his parents), Mineo enrolled in acting school and was soon appearing on stage in a variety of productions.

His breakthrough role was in 1955 as Plato, the psychotic juvenile delinquent with a switchblade in *Rebel Without a Cause*. Up until his death, he worked steadily in motion pictures and on television.

When Mineo was 18, after having already appeared in a half-dozen movies, including *Giant* and *Rebel Without a Cause*, he decided to branch out into a career in music by recording and releasing two rock-and-roll singles. The first, "Start Movin' (In My Direction)," reached number nine in the American top 40 and stayed on the charts for 13 weeks. His second single, "Lasting Love," lasted three weeks and peaked at number 27. Mineo's music career was short-lived, however, and he decided to focus on movies and stage work from that point on.

Sal Mineo Filmography[4]	
Rebel Without a Cause (1955)	*The Dangerous Days of Kiowa Jones* (1966) (TV)
The Private War of Major Benson (1955)	*Stranger on the Run* (1967) (TV)
Six Bridges to Cross (1955)	*LSD: Insight or Insanity?* (1967) (voice)
Crime in the Streets (1956)	*Krakatoa, East of Java* (1969)
Giant (1956)	*80 Steps to Jonah* (1969)
Somebody Up There Likes Me (1956)	*The Challengers* (1970) (TV)
Rock, Pretty Baby (1956)	*In Search of America* (1970) (TV)
Dino (1957)	*Escape from the Planet of the Apes* (1971)
The Young Don't Cry (1957)	*How to Steal an Airplane* (1971) (TV)
Tonka (1958)	*The Family Rico* (1972) (TV)
Aladdin (1958) (TV)	*Such Dust As Dreams Are Made On* (1973)
A Private's Affair (1959)	*Sonic Boom* (1974)
The Gene Krupa Story (1959)	*Columbo: A Case of Immunity* (1975) (TV)
Insight or Insanity? (1960) (voice)	*James Dean, the First American Teenager* (1975)
Exodus (1960)	*Death Scenes 2* (1992)
The Longest Day (1962)	
Escape from Zahrain (1962)	
Cheyenne Autumn (1964)	
The Greatest Story Ever Told (1965)	
Who Killed Teddy Bear (1965)	

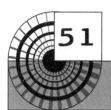

51

Lord Mountbatten

ASSASSINATED   ✓

SURVIVED   ___

*They that go down to the sea in ships, that do business in
great waters;*
These see the works of the Lord, and his wonders in the deep
*For he commandeth, and raiseth the stormy wind, which
lifteth up the waves thereof.*
*They mount up to the heaven, they go down again to the
depths: their soul is melted because of trouble.*

—Psalm 107: 23-26[1]

VICTIM: Louis Francis Albert Victor Nicholas Earl Mountbatten of Burma

BORN: June 25, 1900

DIED: August 27, 1979

AGE WHEN ATTACKED: 79

OCCUPATION: Royal Prince of Battenburg, English naval officer, statesman, World War II hero, last Viceroy of India (March 1947–August 1947), uncle of Prince Phillip, cousin of Queen Elizabeth,
great-grandson of Queen Victoria.

ASSASSIN: Thomas McMahon (b. 1948) of the Irish Republican Army. The
provisional wing of the IRA immediately issued a statement calling
the explosion an "execution" and vowing to continue the "noble
struggle to drive the British intruders out of our land."[2] The IRA
also described Mountbatten as a "symbolic" target selected for

his importance to "sentimental" Britain."[3] They also said, "This operation is one of the discriminate ways we can bring to the attention of the English people the continuing occupation of our country."[4] The IRA also claimed responsibility for a bombing in Northern Ireland in which 18 British soldiers were killed. McMahon was in custody when the bomb exploded but was later identified as the IRA terrorist who built the bomb that killed Mountbatten. Ironically, Mountbatten had willingly worked with people many considered to be blatant terrorists, and he personally did more to de-imperialize the British than anyone else. The IRA terrorists responsible for his death obviously never read their history books.

DATE & TIME OF ATTACK: Monday, August 27, 1979, around noon

LOCATION OF ATTACK: Aboard Mountbatten's 27-foot green and white fishing boat, the *Shadow V,* in the small harbor of Mullaghmore in County Sligo off the northwestern coast of Ireland. Mountbatten's boat was checked from time to time while berthed, but there was no full-time guard watching the vessel, and Mountbatten had not received any death threats.

WEAPON: A 50-pound bomb detonated by remote control

ASSASSINATION OUTCOME: The party consisted of Lord Mountbatten; his twin 14-year-old grandsons Timothy and Nicholas Knatchbull; family friend and boathand, 15-year-old Paul Maxwell; Mountbatten's daughter, Lady Patricia Brabourne; Patricia's husband, Lord Brabourne; and Lord Brabourne's mother, the dowager Lady Brabourne. Lord Mountbatten, Nicholas, and Paul Maxwell were killed instantly. Lord Brabourne was hospitalized in serious condition. Patricia, Lady Brabourne, and Timothy were all hospitalized in critical condition. Dowager Lady Brabourne died later from her injuries in Sligo General Hospital. Mountbatten's funeral was held in Westminster Cathedral and he was buried at Romsey Abbey in Hampshire near his royal mansion.

JUDICIAL OUTCOME: This was a terrorist attack for which the IRA took full responsibility. IRA member Thomas McMahon, 31, was convicted of building and planting the bomb on Mountbatten's boat after evidence of nitroglycerine was found on his clothing and dirt from the launch at Mullaghmore was found on his shoes. He was sentenced to life in prison with no appeal. McMahon was freed on

August 1, 1998, as part of the Britain/Ireland Good Friday Peace Agreement. Another man, Frances McGirl, suspected of being an accomplice to McMahon, was acquitted for lack of evidence.

Witnesses said the *Shadow V* lifted completely up out of the water when the bomb in its engine room detonated, and, within seconds, it was a floating pile of flaming tinder. The boat exploded 10 minutes or so after Lord Mount-batten and his six passengers had departed from a berth at Mullaghmore to check some lobster pots Mountbatten had set the previous week. It was a Monday, around noon, the sky was clear, and the weather was warm.

Everyone on board was thrown into the water, and fishing vessels in nearby waters immediately headed to the site of the explosion.

Amazingly, Lord Mountbatten was still alive, and he was quickly pulled out of the water onto one of the fishing boats. His legs, however, were almost completely severed from his body, and he died on the deck of a fishing boat within minutes. The fishermen pulled the living and the dead onto their boats and headed for shore. By the time they arrived, ambulances were waiting, and two doctors had set up a triage station in hopes of providing emergency aid to the most critically injured. Old doors were used as stretchers; broomsticks became makeshift splints. After attempts to stabilize the injured, they were brought to Sligo General Hospital.

British Lord Mountbatten pays a visit to a U.S. carrier during World War II

Ultimately, there was nothing the doctors at the hospital could do for Dowager Lady Brabourne, such was the severity of her injuries. After several hours of surgery, she died the following morning.

The IRA assassination of Lord Mountbatten was the result of competition and rivalry between two splinter divisions of the Provos (Provisional

Army) faction of the organization. Global outrage against the assassination was quick and vehement. A London newspaper filled their front page with the headline "THOSE EVIL BASTARDS." U.S. President Jimmy Carter said he was "profoundly shocked and saddened" by Mountbatten's murder. Pope Paul II described the seemingly pointless slaughter as "an insult to human dignity" and ultimately canceled a planned trip to Ireland.

Lord Mountbatten never saw himself as a target. He eschewed personal protection and was at ease in public situations. His assassination was the first time the IRA had specifically targeted a member of the British royal family. Mountbatten himself was probably the most surprised by the attack. As he was famous for saying when asked if he was afraid of the IRA, "What would they want with an old man like me?"[5]

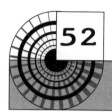

52

Hosni Mubarak

ASSASSINATED	
SURVIVED	✓

On behalf of the American people, I wish to express my outrage at the attempt made today by terrorists to assassinate President Mubarak of Egypt. I am relieved that President Mubarak was not harmed and has now returned safely to Cairo. The United States stands by Egypt—our partner for peace and prosperity in the Middle East and around the world at this moment. The enemies of peace will not be allowed to thwart the peaceful hopes of the people of the region, and the efforts of President Mubarak and the peacemakers to make those hopes a reality.

—Bill Clinton[1]

VICTIM: Mohamed Hosni Mubarak

BORN: May 4, 1928

DIED: n/a

OCCUPATION: President of the Arab Republic of Egypt (1981–present), successor of Anwar el-Sadat (Chapter 65), recipient of Bachelor of Military Sciences (1948), recipient of B.A. in Aviation Sciences (1950) recipient of honorary doctorate from George Washington University (1999), father of two sons, husband, grandfather

There have been many assassination attempts on the life of Egyptian President Hosni Mubarak. Here are three of the more conspicuous attempts.

The Bomb Plot Betrayal

INTENDED ASSASSINS: A group of Egyptian Air Force officers

DATE & TIME OF PLANNED ATTACK: Sometime in 1994

LOCATION OF ATTACK: Undetermined

WEAPONS: Bombs

ASSASSINATION OUTCOME: The Egyptian officers conspired to blow up Mubarak, and the plot was uncovered before they could carry out their plan.

JUDICIAL OUTCOME: All the officers involved were executed. Little else is known about this assassination attempt.

The Airport Ambush

UNSUCCESFUL ASSASSINS: Egyptian Muslim extremists, led by Muhammad Seraj, and trained and sponsored by the National Islamic Front (the government of Sudan), which was responsible for the plot against Mubarak. Diplomatic accommodations were utilized to smuggle the weapons and ammunition into Egypt. Osama bin Laden was believed to have been involved in the planning of this attempt also.

DATE & TIME OF ATTACK: Monday, June 26, 1995, 8:15 a.m.

LOCATION OF ATTACK: In a motorcade exiting the Addis Ababa airport in Ethiopia

WEAPONS: AK-47 assault rifles, explosives, rocket-propelled grenades[2]

ASSASSINATION OUTCOME: Mubarak was uninjured; two police officers guarding his motorcade were shot and killed by the assassins.

JUDICIAL OUTCOME: On September 20, 1995, three Egyptian militants (of the 11 people who reportedly took part in the attack) were convicted and sentenced to death in Addis Ababa, Ethiopia, for the attempted assassination of Mubarak.

A Knife in the Crowd

UNSUCCESSFUL ASSASSIN: Said Hassan Suleiman (1959–1999), 40, street vendor, known to the police, criminal record for assault and theft, according to a statement from the Egyptian Interior Ministry "He is known for his foolish acts."[3]

DATE & TIME OF ATTACK: Monday, September 6, 1999, midday

LOCATION OF ATTACK: A parade in Port Said, Egypt

WEAPON: A small, sharp weapon, probably a knife or a tool of some kind

ASSASSINATION OUTCOME: Mubarak was cut on his arm but was otherwise uninjured. Mubarak went on to deliver a speech at the Governorate Building.

JUDICIAL OUTCOME: Suleiman was shot to death on the spot by Mubarak's guards.

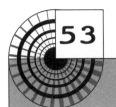

53

Haing S. Ngor

ASSASSINATED   ✓

SURVIVED   ___

He never bought anything for himself. The major mission of his life was to save Cambodia.

—Reverend Jack Ong[1]

VICTIM: Haing S. Ngor

BORN: 1951? 1961?

DIED: February 25, 1996

AGE WHEN ATTACKED: 45? 55?[2]

OCCUPATION: Cambodian physician, best known for winning a Best Supporting Actor Academy Award in 1984 for his performance as Dith Pran (a Cambodian interpreter who saves the life of several journalists) in the movie *The Killing Fields*

ASSASSINS: Tak Sun Tan, 19, Indra Lim, 18, and Jason Chan, 18; three Asian members of the Oriental Lazyboyz street gang

DATE & TIME OF ATTACK: Sunday, February 25, 1996, 8:45 p.m.

LOCATION OF ATTACK: In the open parking garage outside his apartment building in the Chinatown section of Los Angeles, California

WEAPON: A .38-caliber handgun (never recovered)

ASSASSINATION OUTCOME: Two bullets struck and instantly killed Ngor after he was shot when he refused to turn over to his muggers a gold pocketwatch that held a picture of his dead wife. His assailants subsequently fled; Ngor's car and wallet, containing $3,000 in cash, were not taken.

JUDICIAL OUTCOME: In April 1996, three gang members were arrested and charged with Ngor's murder. In an extraordinary trial involving an unprecedented three juries in one courtroom (three juries for three defendants), all three men were convicted of Ngor's murder in July 1999, although the actual shooter was never determined. Chan was sentenced to life without parole; Tan was sentenced to 56 years to life; Lim was sentenced to 26 years to life. After passing sentence, Judge J.D. Smith said, "Just a message for those people who go commit these kinds of crimes...You put people in eternity. Someone has to pay."[3]

Cambodian dictator Pol Pot's Khmer Rouge torture squads crucified Dr. Haing Ngor and suspended the cross he was on over a smoldering fire for four days to force him to confess to being college-educated.

The Khmer Rouge also put Dr. Ngor's head in a vise, tightened it until it caused excruciating pain (stopping just before it killed him), and then left him there for hours.

The Khmer Rouge also cut off part of his little finger, whipped him until his skin came off in bloody strips, and starved him almost to death. Ngor also endured water torture and having an ankle bone hacked at with an axe; the Khmer Rouge also placed a heavy leather yoke around his neck and made him pull a plow like an ox, flogging him mercilessly if he did not move fast enough or if he collapsed.

These horrible abuses fully inspired his performance in *The Killing Fields*, but he dismissed his abilities as an actor. "After all," he would often say with sadness, "I spent four years in the Khmer Rouge school of acting."[4]

Under orders from the ruthless dictator Pol Pot, the Khmer Rouge set out to eliminate the "cultural elite" from Cambodia. In a misguided, idiotic attempt at forcing communist equality, the educated members of Cambodia society were to be put to work in the fields. Everyone would be equal. This did not work when Mao Zedong tried it during the Cultural Revolution in China in the mid-Sixties, and it did not work in Cambodia. Martin Gilman Wolcott, writing in *The Evil 100*, noted, "In an attempt to paint all of Chinese society with the brush of communist ideology, it somehow actually made sense to Mao to 'abolish the distinction between mental and manual labor,' and put professors to work in the fields and peasants in the schools to learn and teach. Resistance was considered counterrevolutionary and proponents were imprisoned, tortured, and killed."[5] Mao had his cruel and almost completely autonomous Red Guard; Pol Pot had his equally brutal Khmer Rouge.

This was not a safe environment for Ngor, an obstetrician and gynecologist, nor his wife, a university professor. For four years, Ngor survived by telling anyone in authority who confronted him that he was a taxi driver. He also hid his eyeglasses, because the Khmer Rouge apparently associated the need for corrected vision with the intelligentsia. His story was regularly challenged, he was tortured for the truth, and yet he managed to survive and make it to America. His wife was not so fortunate. She went into premature labor and desperately needed a Caesarian section but, in a case of tragic irony, her husband, a gynecologist, did not have the surgical tools he needed to save her, and both she and her unborn child died.

Ngor escaped to the United States in 1979 and shortly thereafter answered a casting call for the movie *The Killing Fields*, which was about Cambodia's Khmer Rouge. Out of 7,000 auditioners, Ngor got the role of Dith Pran, a Cambodian interpreter.

Ngor went on to other film and TV roles but spent almost all of his earnings on helping Cambodian refugees.

Haing Ngor, who managed to survive the atrocities of the Khmer Rouge, could not survive the mean streets of Los Angeles, California.

54

Richard Nixon

ASSASSINATED	___
SURVIVED	✓

I will try to get the plane aloft and fly it toward the target area, which will be Washington, D.C., the capital of the most powerful, wealthiest nation in the world. By guise, threats or trickery, I hope to force the pilot to buzz the White House—I mean, sort of dive towards the White House. When the plane is in this position, I will shoot the pilot and then in the last few minutes try to steer the plane into the target, which is the White House.

—Samuel Byck[1]

VICTIM: Richard Nixon

BORN: January 9, 1913

DIED: April 22, 1994

AGE WHEN ATTACKED: 61

OCCUPATION: 37th president of the United States (1969–1974)

INTENDED ASSASSIN: Samuel J. Byck (1930–1974), 44, tire salesman

DATE & TIME OF ATTACK: Friday, February 22, 1974, approximately 7 a.m.

LOCATION OF ATTACK: Byck's target was the White House; the assassin died in a plane on the runway at Baltimore-Washington International Airport.

WEAPONS: A .22-caliber revolver and a homemade gasoline bomb

— 182 —

ASSASSINATION OUTCOME: President Nixon was never in any danger, because the plane never took off.

JUDICIAL OUTCOME: The would-be assassin committed suicide in the airplane cockpit while under siege in a barrage of gunfire by security agents.

The 1972–73 winter season in Washington, D.C., holds the record as having the least snowfall in history: 0.1 inches for the entire season. Thus, there was nothing on the sidewalks surrounding the White House on Monday, December 24 of that year. Nothing to impede Samuel Byck's protest march; nothing to muddy his black boots or to dirty his red trousers.

On Christmas Eve, 1973, Samuel Joseph Byck, dressed in a complete Santa Claus suit, marched back and forth on the sidewalk outside the White House carrying a sign. The front of the sign read (in all caps): "Santa sez, all I want for Christmas is my constitutional right to peaceably petition my government for a redress of my grievances." The back of the sign had only two words on it: "Impeach Nixon." In order to dissuade the D.C. cops or the White House Security detail from arresting him, Byck would every so often take a break from his protesting and invite the children of passersby to sit on his lap and tell him what they wanted for Christmas.

Exactly 60 days later, Byck would be dead, an airport security guard and airplane co-pilot would be dead, an airplane pilot would be seriously wounded, a 21-year-old stewardess would have a broken vertebra, and history would record a failed assassination attempt against President Richard Nixon. Aspiring presidential assassin Samuel Byck made a crucial mistake: he forgot to wait until the plane was off the ground before attempting to hijack it.

Byck hated Nixon and his administration, and it seems as though his rancor was spawned by the most prosaic of events: Byck was turned down for a loan by the Small Business Administration during Nixon's time in the White House. This seemingly innocuous trigger sent the father-of-four tire salesman into an anti-Nixon rage that would ultimately attract the attention of the United States Secret Service. He threatened Nixon's life in 1972 and he began sending bizarre tapes to public figures like scientist Jonas Salk and conductor Leonard Bernstein.

Byck served in the U.S. Army, where he learned about weapons and explosives. When he got out of the service, he began to work as a tire salesman. After coming up with the idea of opening his own tire store, he applied for a $20,000 loan from the Small Business Administration and, while waiting for a response, checked himself into a psychiatric hospital to be treated for manic depression. It was while undergoing treatment that Byck learned that his loan request had been rejected. This marked the beginning of a downward spiraling cycle that would culminate in Byck's suicide in an airplane cockpit.

Early on the morning of Friday, February 22, 1974, Samuel Byck drove to the Baltimore-Washington International Airport carrying a .22-caliber pistol and a gasoline bomb that was designed to explode on impact. His plan was to hijack a plane and force the pilot to fly it into the White House, where the plane's fuel and the gasoline bomb would detonate and kill President Nixon and destroy the building.

Upon his arrival at the airport, Byck shot and killed an airport security guard. He then stormed his way onto Delta Flight 523, which was scheduled to take off for Atlanta, burst into the cockpit, and shot and killed the co-pilot. He then ordered the pilot to take off, but he refused. Byck then grabbed a female passenger and forced her into the cockpit at gunpoint, telling her to help the pilot fly the plane.

By this time, security personnel had been alerted to the hijacking, and armed agents surrounded the plane. They immediately began firing furiously into the cockpit, and Byck was quickly hit in the chest and the stomach. Unable to stand, he fell to the cockpit floor and committed suicide by shooting himself in the head.

Byck was deranged and, after his death, it was learned that he had sent a tape to *Washington Post* columnist Jack Anderson before the hijacking on which he detailed his plans to use a plane as a guided missile to kill President Nixon. In these post–September 11th days, there has been much criticism of both the FBI and CIA for their failure to conceive of terrorists (Byck called himself a terrorist, by the way) using a loaded plane as a weapon. It seems no one had ever thought of it.

Well, Samuel Byck thought of it, and it is not at all far-fetched to imagine Al-Qaeda operatives perusing recent American history and coming upon Byck's story. Byck's attempt was also chronicled in the 1991 Stephen Sondheim musical *Assassins* and it would be the ultimate dark irony if the worst terrorist attack in American history was prompted by the act of a deranged tire salesman who couldn't get a loan.

Note: Arthur Bremer, the assassin who shot and paralyzed Alabama Governor George Wallace (page 247), also considered assassinating Richard Nixon. His plot was revealed when excerpts from Bremer's diary were read at his trial in August 1972. Bremer also wrote that he briefly considered assassinating George McGovern.

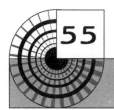

55

Lee Harvey Oswald

ASSASSINATED ✓

SURVIVED ___

The loss to the United States and to the world is incalculable. Those who come after Mr. Kennedy must strive the more to achieve the ideals of world peace and human happiness and dignity to which his Presidency was dedicated.

—Winston Churchill[1]

VICTIM: Lee Harvey Oswald

BORN: October 18, 1939

DIED: November 24, 1963

AGE WHEN ATTACKED: 24

OCCUPATION: Assassin of President John F. Kennedy

ASSASSIN: Jack Ruby, nee Jack Rubenstein, nickname "Sparky" (1911–1967), 52, owner of the Carousel Club, a Dallas nightclub and strip joint

DATE & TIME OF ATTACK: Sunday, November 24, 1963, 11:20 a.m.

LOCATION OF ATTACK: On a basement garage ramp exiting from the municipal City Hall building where the police department was located in Dallas, Texas. Oswald was on his way to an armored van for transport to the county jail.

WEAPON: A .38-caliber Colt Cobra snub-nose revolver. Ruby had purchased the gun in Dallas for $62.50.

ASSASSINATION OUTCOME: Oswald was shot once in the abdomen (Ruby placed the barrel of the gun directly against Oswald's stomach), and the bullet did massive damage. It went through Oswald's diaphragm, spleen, and stomach and cut off his main intestinal artery, as well as his aorta. It also did serious damage to his right kidney. Oswald lost consciousness almost immediately and was rushed to Parkland Memorial Hospital by ambulance within minutes. Doctors performed surgery and gave him blood transfusions, but the damage was too great. Oswald died at 1:07 p.m.

JUDICIAL OUTCOME: Ruby was indicted for Oswald's murder on November 26, 1963. His lawyer pled not guilty by reason of insanity. The prosecution sought the death penalty. In 1964, Ruby was convicted after very brief jury deliberations and sentenced to die in the electric chair. This verdict was overturned due to problems with the trial, including the facts that Ruby had been questioned by Dallas police without a lawyer after the shooting and that he should have been granted a change of venue, because it had been patently impossible for him to obtain a fair trial in Dallas. Ruby was granted a new trial in Wichita Falls, Texas, in December 1966. By this time he was very sick with liver, brain, and lung cancer, and he died in Dallas on January 3, 1967 of a blood clot.

In 1960, Lee Harvey Oswald visited the American embassy in Moscow, where he freely signed an affidavit that said, "I affirm that my allegiance is to the Soviet Socialist Republic." At the time, Oswald was a U.S. Marine on inactive reserve duty, and when the Marines learned that he had sworn allegiance to a nation that, at the time, was considered an enemy, they immediately convened a special board and gave Oswald a Dishonorable Discharge from the Marine Corps.

Surprisingly, Oswald was furious about his discharge. He wrote an angry letter to John Connally, who was then running for Governor of Texas that states, "I shall employ all means to right this gross mistake or injustice to a bona fide U.S. citizen and ex-serviceman."

His fidelity oath notwithstanding, the Russian government rejected Oswald's citizenship application and agreed only to allow him to stay in the Soviet Union as a resident alien.

Oswald eventually returned to the United States, and he ultimately became immortalized in the annals of assassins for killing President John F. Kennedy.

Why did Jack Ruby kill Lee Harvey Oswald?

There have been a number of conspiracy theories surrounding Oswald's death, and most of them involve Ruby being "in on" the Kennedy assassination plot and being charged with the task of eliminating the trigger man.

After Ruby was arrested, he explained his actions in the simplest of terms. Oswald shot his president, so he shot Oswald. "You killed my President, you rat!" he is reported to have shouted after shooting Oswald. This may ultimately be the unvarnished truth, for Ruby was mentally deranged and seems an unlikely candidate for recruitment for a complicated assassination plot.

Ruby gave the following account of his crime to his defense lawyer, and it was reprinted in the *New York Times*:[2]

I left Western Union and walked up Main Street toward the City Hall not knowing the time they were about to transfer the man.

I walked past them and I guess they didn't notice me. They were talking. I walked on down into the area where Oswald was being led out.

I saw Captain Fritz. Then the others came on and I saw Oswald. I remember lunging at him.

He was smirking and so cocky and acted so proud of what he had done I could not get it out of my mind.

I could not forget that Communists had sent Oswald to kill our President. I couldn't forget how Jackie had suffered and that Caroline and John wouldn't have a daddy anymore.

Oswald's body was claimed by the Miller Funeral Home on behalf of the family and the total cost of his funeral, $710, was paid by Oswald's brother, Robert Oswald.

He was buried in an isolated section of the Rose Hill Cemetery in Fort Worth, Texas, in a plain, cloth-covered wooden box. His wife, Marina, kissed his body when the coffin was opened briefly and, immediately following the burial, the family was whisked away by U.S. Secret Service agents back into protective custody.

At the brief ceremony, the Reverend Louis Saunders said, "We are not here to judge. We are here to lay him before an understanding God."[3]

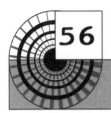

56

Pope John Paul II

| ASSASSINATED | ___ |
| SURVIVED | ✓ |

John Paul was struck in the abdomen and fell backward into the arms of his secretary, Monsignor Dziwisz. The image of the inert Pope, flashed around the world later that day, instantly reminded millions of people of artistic renderings of Christ being taken from the cross.

—George Weigel[1]

VICTIM: Pope John Paul II (Karol Wojtyla)

BORN: May 18, 1920

DIED: n/a

AGE WHEN ATTACKED: 60

OCCUPATION: Roman Catholic pontiff

UNSUCCESSFUL ASSASSIN: Mehmet Ali Agca (b. 1958), 23, convicted Turkish murderer

DATE & TIME OF ATTACK: Wednesday, May 13, 1981, 5:19 p.m.

LOCATION OF ATTACK: Inside the Popemobile (a specially outfitted Jeep) in St. Peter's Square, Vatican City, Rome, Italy

Pope John Paul II

WEAPON: A 9-millimeter Browning semi-automatic pistol

ASSASSINATION OUTCOME: The Pope was hit by two bullets. One penetrated his abdomen, and one hit his right arm and left hand. He was rushed to Gemelli Hospital in Rome and was in the operating room by 6 p.m. The emergency surgery lasted 5 hours and 25 minutes. Twenty-two inches of his intestines had to be removed, and he was fitted with a temporary colostomy. The Pope needed a great deal of blood during the surgery and ultimately received 6 pints, both from the blood bank and blood that had been freshly donated. The freshly donated blood harbored a cytomegalovirus, which made the Pope extremely sick. His body ultimately fought off the virus and the Pope managed to recuperate fully. One of the bullets had missed the Pope's spinal column by inches and also missed his main abdominal artery by a fraction of inch. If the bullet had hit the artery, he would have bled to death before arriving at the hospital; if it had hit his spinal column, he would have been paralyzed for life. The Pope later said, "One hand fired, and another guided the bullet."[2] Two bystanders attending the Pope's general audience in St. Peter's Square were also struck by the assassin's bullets. Ann Odre, 60, of Buffalo, New York, was struck in the chest. Rose Hill, 21, of Jamaica, was wounded in the arm. Both survived.

JUDICIAL OUTCOME: Agca was swarmed and restrained by the crowd (especially a rather large nun named Suor Letizia) in St. Peter's Square after shooting the Pope and was then taken into custody by Italian police. Although Agca was eligible to be tried by the autonomous Vatican courts, the Vatican authorities turned him over to Italian law enforcement, ceding to the Italian government their right to try Agca. Agca was sentenced to life in prison in Italy for attempting to kill the Pope and served 19 years of the sentence before being pardoned (at the Pope's request) by the Italian government. In 2000, he was extradited to Turkey to finish serving a 10-year sentence for killing a Turkish newspaper editor in 1979. It is quite possible that Agca will be freed in 2008 after serving the eight years remaining on his sentence in Turkey.

"How is it that I could not kill you?" Mehmet Ali Agca said to Pope John Paul II when the Pontiff visited him in his cell and forgave him for trying to assassinate him. The two men then spoke in Italian for 20 minutes, after which Agca kissed the Pope's hand and told a reporter, "The Pope knows everything."

Agca had previously threatened the Pope's life in the name of Islam, and security had been tightened around the Pope at the Vatican. But it obviously had not been tightened enough. Agca managed to smuggle a gun into Italy (with the help of four confederates, only one of whom was caught), and he was able to get within 10 feet of the Pope in St. Peter's Square. This proximity in and of itself would not have put the Pope in jeopardy if not for the fact that his Popemobile was an open vehicle. Yes, even after the assassination of John F. Kennedy, in 1981 the Pope was still making appearances in his open, specially outfitted Jeep. (Since Dallas, American presidents have never again been allowed to be exposed to the public in an open vehicle. And, it is said, the presidential limousine is now designed to be able to withstand a direct missile hit and still protect its occupants.)[3]

During the Pope's third circuit around St. Peter's Square, Agca waited until he was in close range and then fired four bullets at the Pope. The Pope was hit by two; two pilgrims were hit by the other two.

The Pope was immediately placed in the ambulance that was always present at papal audiences and other Vatican events, and he was rushed to Gemelli Hospital, where a special suite of surgical rooms and hospital rooms are always kept open for the Pope. Surgeons were called in and, after a lengthy surgery and two months of recuperation, the Pope recovered fully, only to shortly thereafter be afflicted with Parkinson's disease, a progressive neurological disease that has taken a toll (albeit relatively minor) on the Pontiff's ability to fulfill his demanding schedule.

The Pope, speaking from his hospital bed, forgave his assassin three days after he was shot. Also, years after the assassination attempt on his life, the Pope revealed the last of the three Fatima secrets. The first two were common knowledge, but the Church had never revealed the third, which stated that an attack would be made on "a bishop clothed in white." John Paul II was clad all in white when he was shot. When Agca the shooter heard this, he believed that he had fulfilled a prophecy and that he was part of a larger design. He has said that he hopes he is released at the end of his sentence so he can retire to a rural Turkish village.

This, from the man who shouted in court, "I am Jesus Christ. In the name of the omnipotent God, I announce the end of the world. No one, neither the Americans nor the Soviets, will be saved. There will be destruction."[4]

The Popemobile is now covered with a bulletproof dome.

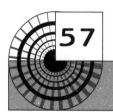

57

Pope Paul VI

ASSASSINATED	__
SURVIVED	✓

I feel disappointed for failing to kill the Pope and would do it again if given another chance.

—Benjamin Mendoza[1]

VICTIM: Pope Paul VI (Giovanni Battista Montini)

BORN: September 26, 1897

DIED: August 6, 1978

AGE WHEN ATTACKED: 73

OCCUPATION: Italian-born Roman Catholic Pontiff (June 21, 1963–August 6, 1978), ordained priest in 1920, named Archbishop of Milan in 1953, named Cardinal in 1958

UNSUCCESSFUL ASSASSINS: Benjamin Mendoza y Amor Flores (b. 1935), 35, Bolivian surrealist artist

DATE & TIME OF ATTACK: Friday, November 27, 1970, early afternoon

LOCATION OF ATTACK: The Manila International Airport in the Philippines

WEAPONS: A long Malay knife hidden inside a crucifix

ASSASSINATION OUTCOME: Mendoza, disguised as a priest, approached the Pope as he walked through the Manila Airport with Ferdinand and Imelda Marcos (page 156), several clerics from around the world, and his papal security guards. Mendoza withdrew a foot-long dagger that had been concealed in a crucifix and moved aggressively towards the Pope with the knife in his hand. Mendoza managed to strike the Pope in the chest with the double-edged, wavy-bladed knife, and the Pope suffered a minor chest wound (which was not revealed until later) but survived the attempt. He continued with his visit, making little public acknowledgment of the assassination attempt. Eight years later, Pope Paul VI suffered a massive heart attack during a Mass that was being said for him in his chapel at Castel Gandolfo. He lapsed into semiconsciousness after managing to receive Communion and died a few hours later, two months short of his 81st birthday.

JUDICIAL OUTCOME: Mendoza was quickly apprehended by Anthony Galvin, the bishop of Singapore (a former professional rugby player), after a papal security guard gave Mendoza a karate chop and pushed him into Galvin's arms. Galvin wrapped his arms around the assassin and held him until he could be taken into custody. Mendoza, who some psychiatrists believed suffered from "delusions of grandeur,"[2] was ultimately deemed fit to stand trial and was charged with attempted murder, illegal possession of a weapon, perpetrating a grave threat, and causing a public scandal. (During his trial, Mendoza burned a Bible in the courtroom.) He was sentenced to 28 months in prison. He was eventually deported to Bolivia in August 1974, and little is known of his whereabouts or situation.

Pope Paul VI is the Catholic pontiff known for issuing the encyclical *Humanae Vitae* (*Of Human Life*), which stated the Roman Catholic Church's unequivocal and *nonnegotiable* opposition to any artificial means of birth control, including condoms, the birth control pill, the diaphragm, and sterilization. Catholic doctrine also prohibits masturbation, premarital sex, pornography, and homosexuality, defining them as "gravely contrary"[3] to chastity, which the Church mandates for all its members. *Humanae Vitae* was roundly rejected by American Catholics and was directly responsible for an exodus of younger Catholics to other religions that were not so harshly judgmental of their way of life.

Pope Paul VI survived an assassination attempt, yet his legacy is one of alienating many of his previously faithful with a harshly dogmatic, inflexible declaration that did not respect, nor even acknowledge, the desperate financial straits many Catholics were in at the time. Reportedly, the Pope was deeply hurt by the passionate rejection of his teachings.[4]

At the time of his assassination attempt, Benjamin Mendoza's paintings were being shown and sold in New York art galleries. One of his works, "Jesus Christ and the Ire," was priced at $5,000 the day of the attack. One gallery owner, Louis Ruocco, told *The New York Times* that he considered Mendoza "more of a contrived personality than crazy. He knew exactly what he was doing. He was a very cunning fellow."[5] Ruocco believed Mendoza might have attacked the Pope to make a worldwide name for him and inflate the values of his paintings. Macabre collectability aside, Mr. Ruocco, noting Mendoza's arrogation of the style and characteristics of the work of the great 20th-century Spanish surrealist Salvador Dali, also considered Mendoza's *work* contrived. "My opinion is and was that if he had concentrated less on contrivance and shock and more on his natural talent he could be a great painter."[6]

The Pope did not allow the attempt on his life to deter him from his reason for visiting the Philippines, which was to speak out for reform and persuade the Philippine hierarchy to initiate social programs that fulfilled the mandates of the Catholic Church. The Pope said Mass, addressed an assembly of Catholic bishops from Asia, addressed a huge gathering of students, and even watched a pig being roasted on a spit. While the Pope was still in the Philippines, the Vatican issued a statement that the Pope had forgiven his assailant and had even blessed the crucifix Mendoza had used to conceal his dagger.

58

Yitzhak Rabin

ASSASSINATED ✓

SURVIVED ___

I want to tell you we found a partner for peace among the Palestinians—the PLO, which used to be an enemy...without partners for peace, there is no peace.

—Yitzhak Rabin[1]

VICTIM: Yitzhak Rabin

BORN: March 1, 1922

DIED: November 4, 1995

AGE WHEN ATTACKED: 73

OCCUPATION: Prime Minister of Israel (1974–1977, 1992–1995), ambassador to the United States (1968–1973), ordered the 1976 raid on the Entebbe Airport in Uganda to rescue Jewish hostages held by Palestinian terrorists

ASSASSINS: Yigal Amir (b. 1970), 25, law student, member of the extreme right-wing group, Eyal; Hagai Amir, Yigal's brother, helped prepare the bullets (Hagai Amir admitted fashioning the bullet but swore he did not know that his brother was planning to use it to kill Rabin.)

DATE & TIME OF ATTACK: Saturday, November 4, 1995, 9:30 p.m.

LOCATION OF ATTACK: At a peace rally in Kings of Israel Square in Tel Aviv, Israel, the slogan of which was "Yes to Peace, No to Violence"

WEAPON: A 9-millimeter Beretta pistol (which Amir was licensed to carry) loaded with fragmenting dumdum bullets

ASSASSINATION OUTCOME: Rabin was struck in the back with two of the three bullets fired. He was placed in a car and rushed to Ichilov Hospital, where he was immediately taken to the operating room. Rabin had no blood pressure and his heart had already stopped by the time he arrived at the hospital, a trip that took longer than it should have because of the crowds blocking the streets, making it difficult for the car carrying Rabin to move quickly. Medical personnel gave the prime minister 22 units of blood and managed to resuscitate him for a brief time, but one of the dumdum bullets had entered one of Rabin's lungs and tore it to pieces. He died during surgery at 11:10 p.m.

JUDICIAL OUTCOME: Yigal Amir was sentenced on March 27, 1996 to life imprisonment for the murder of Rabin (Israel only imposes the death penalty on Nazis), plus an additional 11 years for wounding Rabin's bodyguard. His brother, Hagai Amir, was sentenced to 12 years in prison for conspiracy, specifically for cutting the holes in the top of the bullets so that that would break apart on impact.

The Arabs do not believe that Israel has the right to exist. In 1948, three years after the end of World War II, the United Nations decreed that a part of Palestine would become the state of Israel, a new Jewish homeland. There has been bloodshed and violent conflict ever since, the recent rash of Palestinian suicide bombings being the latest volleys in this seemingly never-ending war.

So was Israeli Prime Minister Yitzhak Rabin gunned down, as might be expected, by a Palestinian? Rabin himself once downplayed the possibility of a Jewish plot against him, telling a French reporter, "I don't believe a Jew will kill a Jew."[2]

Rabin *was* killed by a Jew, one of his own countrymen, who claimed orders from God as his justification. "I acted alone on God's orders and I have no regrets," he told police after being arrested. "I did it to save the state. He who endangers the Jewish people, his end is death. He deserved to die, and I did the job for the Jewish people." Amir also told police that he had expected to be shot at the scene. "I came to the scene fully recognizing that I would have to give up my life for the success of the holy mission. I had no escape plans."[3]

This alleged willingness to martyr himself may have been a bit disingenuous, because Amir had somehow learned that there was to be a phony assassination attempt against Rabin to test security procedures. So he repeatedly shouted that the bullets he was firing were blanks. Perhaps he believed that he would be able to get away before anyone realized that Rabin had, indeed, been hit with real bullets.

After news of the assassination was broadcast around the world, leaders from almost every nation expressed their sorrow, including the avowed enemy of Israel, Yasser Arafat, Chairman of the Palestine Liberation Organization (PLO). "I am very sad and very shocked for this awful and terrible crime," he said in a statement after the news of Rabin's death. "He is one of the brave leaders of Israel and the peacemakers. I hope that we will have the ability, the Israelis and Palestinians, to overcome this tragedy. I offer my condolences to his wife, his family, the Israeli government, and the Israeli people."[4] Israel invited Arafat to Rabin's funeral, but he stayed away, concerned about further inflaming tensions by his presence. Several other Arab leaders did attend, however, including Egyptian president Hosni Mubarak (chapter 52) and Jordan's King Hussein. Later, it was revealed that Arafat made a secret, late-night visit to Rabin's widow, Leah, to express his condolences. This was believed to have been the first time the Palestinian leader had set foot in the Jewish state.

Rabin's death greatly affected the Arab-Israeli peace process. Rabin's successor, Shimon Peres, did almost nothing in the subsequent years to advance negotiations, and it is believed the current volatile state of affairs in the Middle East is partly due to the loss of the man many called a great man of peace.

59

Rasputin

ASSASSINATED	✓
SURVIVED	—

It is a curious phenomenon and in keeping with Russian tradition. For the peasants Rasputin has become a martyr. He was from the people; he made the voice of the people known to the tsar; he defended the people against the court, and so courtiers killed him! That is what is being said in all the izbas.[1]

VICTIM: Grigorii Efimovich Rasputin

BORN: 1871?

DIED: December 30, 1916

AGE WHEN ATTACKED: 45?

OCCUPATION: Healer, adviser to Empress Alexandra Romanov

ASSASSINS: Prince Felix Yusupov, main conspirator in the assassination; Grand Duke Dmitri Pavlovich Romanov, the Tsar's cousin and fiance of the Tsar's oldest daughter; Dr. Lazovert, physician to Purishkevich and driver of the car they used to transport Rasputin to the river; Vladimir Purishkevich, member of the Russian parliament; and Sukhotin, officer in the Russian Army

DATE & TIME OF ATTACK: Friday night–Saturday morning, December 16–17, 1916

LOCATION OF ATTACK: In the wine cellar of Yusupov's Moika Palace in a room decorated specially for the assassination to mimic a den;

then in the yard of the palace; then in an automobile; and finally in the frozen-over Neva River

WEAPONS: Potassium cyanide crystals crushed into cakes and dissolved into wine, a Browning revolver, brass finger-knuckles (or some other heavy steel object), and the Neva River

ASSASSINATION OUTCOME: Rasputin managed to survive being poisoned, being shot in the chest, back, and head, and then being beaten, but he couldn't prevent his drowning when he was thrown bound, but alive, into a hole in the frozen Neva River.

JUDICIAL OUTCOME: The Russian people were so thrilled that Rasputin had been killed that Tsar Nicholas Romanov was warned by powerful people not to punish the assassins in any way or try to do anything to them legally. Nicholas reluctantly acceded to the will of the people.

Rasputin, which means "debauched one" in Russian, is one of the more bizarre characters from history, and the supremely strange circumstances of his assassination contribute to his legend.

Rasputin needed to be poisoned, shot, thrashed, and drowned before he would die; thus, his epithet, "The Man Who Would Not Die."

Rasputin was a monk, a mystic healer, a prophet, and a sexual glutton who was able to seduce people of both genders into perceiving him as a holy and magical man—a supernatural being of some sort. He had piercing eyes that seemed to see into a person's very soul, and he knew how to wield his gaze to manipulate, seduce, and, it is believed, hypnotize whomever he chose. (One of my research interns jotted, "Look at those eyes!" on a print-out of a photo of Rasputin included with her notes. His power survives, eh?) Rasputin was drunk almost all the time, ate with his fingers, never bathed, and reportedly could sexually service 30 women in one night. He reeked of bad breath, body odor, and worse, yet he mesmerized all with whom he came in contact.

He was a personal favorite of the Russian czarina Alexandra because of his healing of her hemophiliac son, Alexis.

News of Rasputin's legendary reputation as a healer had reached the royal palace and he was thus summoned by the czarina to help her son, who lay suffering from swellings, internal bleeding, and pain. It is believed that Rasputin's personal charisma relaxed the boy enough that his body was thus able to improve on its own. Placebo effect? Probably. But to Empress

Alexandra, the monk with the unwashed hair and dirty fingernails was a miracle worker. He began to come and go as he pleased and is reputed to have manipulated his way into acting as the unofficial ruler of Russia. Rasputin began to influence royal decisions, and he became so powerful that the political, military, and religious leaders who saw what a threat he was to their control decided he must be eliminated.

On the night of the assassination, Rasputin was invited to Prince Yusupov's palace on the pretext of a late-night meeting with the prince's wife, Irina. (Rasputin had always lusted after the comely brunette.) While Rasputin waited downstairs, Yusupov persuaded him to eat some cakes that Dr. Lazovert had baked with cyanide—enough cyanide, in fact, to kill 10 men. But Rasputin did not die. He reportedly became a little drowsy, but he did not expire. It is believed that Rasputin suffered from dyspepsia and that his stomach did not produce hydrochloric acid, which was necessary to activate the cyanide.

When Yusupov came back downstairs and discovered the monk still breathing, he asked him to look upon a crucifix (believing he was demonic and that the image of Christ would harm him in some way), and as his back was turned he shot Rasputin in the back. Rasputin screamed and fell to the floor.

Rasputin (in center with beard) surrounded by some of the Russian society men and women drawn to him by his claims of paranormal predictive and healing powers.

The other conspirators came running downstairs when they heard the shot, and Dr. Lazovert examined Rasputin and declared him dead. Everyone was delighted with this news, and they all went upstairs to celebrate. Yusupov remained downstairs and, after glaring at the dead monk's body, he began to kick and punch the corpse in a drunken rage.

It was then that Yusupov was surprised for the second time that evening. Rasputin was still alive, and he began to lash out at the prince, who fled the room in panic. Rasputin crawled up the stairs behind him, ending up outside the palace on the snow-covered ground. When the others learned what had happened from a panicking Prince Yusupov, Vladimir Purishkevich rushed out to the courtyard and fired four shots at Rasputin. One hit him in the back and one hit him in the head.

Now he *must* be dead, they told themselves. Purishkevich ordered two soldiers to bring the body back to the cellar. When Rasputin's body was again downstairs, Purishkevich beat him about the head, face, and chest with either a steel bar, some kind of brass knuckles, or a blackjack, brutally disfiguring the monk's face.

The body was then wrapped in a curtain (some sources say a length of canvas), tied up, and Rasputin was transported to the Neva River. A hole had been cut into the ice and the body was thrown into the water.

When Rasputin's body was discovered, an autopsy revealed water in his lungs, meaning that he had still been alive when he was dumped in the river. In fact, one of his arms was loose, indicating he had tried to escape while underwater.

Rasputin was buried on December 22, 1916[2] in Tsarkow Selo in the center aisle of a church that was being built with royal funds. After the czar fell, Rasputin's casket was dug up in March 1917 by Russian revolutionaries and pried open, and his remains were placed on a huge log pyre on the side of a road. His corpse was then soaked with kerosene and set on fire.

Perhaps only the Mad Monk's ashes convinced his enemies that he was truly dead. Perhaps.

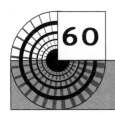

60

Ronald Reagan

ASSASSINATED _____

SURVIVED ✓

I didn't know I was shot. I heard a noise, when we came out of the hotel and headed for the limousine, and I heard some noise, and I thought it was firecrackers. And the next thing I knew, one of the Secret Service agents behind me just seized me here by the waist and plunged me head first into the limo. I landed on the seat, and the seat divider was down, and then he dived in on top of me, which is part of their procedure to make sure that I'm covered. As it turned out later, the shot that got me careened off the side of the limousine and hit me while I was diving into the car. And it hit me back here, under the arm, and then hit a rib, and that's what caused extreme pain, and then it tumbled and turned—instead of edgewise, it went tumbling down to within an inch of my heart.

—President Ronald Reagan[1]

VICTIM: Ronald Reagan

BORN: February 6, 1911

DIED: n/a

AGE WHEN ATTACKED: 70

OCCUPATION: 40th president of the United States (1981–1989), former governor of California, former actor

— 201 —

UNSUCCESSFUL ASSASSIN: John Hinckley (b. 1955), 25, obsessed Jodie Foster fan

DATE & TIME OF ATTACK: Monday, March 30, 1981, shortly before 2:30 p.m.

LOCATION OF ATTACK: Outside the Hilton Hotel in Washington, D.C.

WEAPON: A .22-caliber Rohm R6-14 revolver loaded with exploding Devastator bullets

ASSASSINATION OUTCOME: President Reagan was hit by a bullet that ricocheted off the limousine and entered his body under his left armpit. The bullet lodged in his lung, an inch away from his heart. Emergency surgery was performed to remove the bullet, and the president survived and recovered. Press Secretary James Brady was hit in the left temple. Officer Thomas Delehanty was hit in the neck. Secret Service Agent Timothy J. McCarthy was hit in the stomach.

JUDICIAL OUTCOME: John W. Hinckley, Jr., was found not guilty by reason of insanity on May 4, 1982 by a jury comprised of 11 blacks and one white. (An ABC poll, taken on May 5, 1982, showed that 83 percent of the American people polled believed that "justice was not done" when Hinckley was acquitted.) He was sentenced to indefinite confinement in St. Elizabeth's Psychiatric Hospital in Washington, D.C. He has left the premises of the hospital several times in the last two decades on supervised trips to malls, restaurants, and the beach. The Secret Service tails him wherever he goes, and agents also drop in on him at the hospital unannounced to observe him. Hinckley's parents have repeatedly petitioned the court to allow their son short-term unsupervised releases, none of which have been approved.

John Hinckley fired six bullets at President Reagan as he was walking out of the Washington Hilton, and he didn't hit him once. The bullet that did all the damage to the president ricocheted off the limousine door and, because Reagan's left arm was in the air to wave to people across the street, the bullet had a clear path into his chest. If Reagan's arm had been by his side, it is likely the bullet would have only pierced his upper arm.

Inside the limo, Secret Service agent Jerry Parr gave Reagan a once-over and concluded that Reagan probably had a broken rib from being manhandled into the car. When the president began spitting up frothy blood, both he and Parr deduced that the fractured rib had probably punctured a lung.

Wrong on all counts.

We now know that Reagan was minutes away from death, had no appreciable blood pressure, and had lost a tremendous amount of blood. He managed to walk into the emergency room at George Washington Hospital, but then collapsed once inside the door. Jerry Parr's instantaneous decision to go to the hospital instead of the White House saved Reagan's life.

The assassination attempt threw the White House and its senior staff into turmoil. Reagan's presidency was only 70 days old when he was shot, and many protocols, procedures, and emergency-contingency plans were not yet in place. Also, it didn't help matters that Vice President George Bush was in the air on his way to Texas when the shooting occurred. His absence led to the now infamous gaffe by secretary of State Alexander Haig, who told the White House Press Corps (and, thus, the world) that he was in charge.

Haig's statement in response to a reporter's question about who was making the decisions for the government was:

Constitutionally, gentlemen, you have the president, the vice president, and the secretary of state in that order. And should the president decide he wants to transfer the helm to the vice president, he will do so. As of now, I am in control here in the White House, pending return of the vice president and in close touch with him. If something came up, I would check with him, of course.[2]

It was revealed at Hinckley's trial that the delusional young man shot the president to impress actress Jodie Foster, whom he had become obsessed with after seeing her in the movie *Taxi Driver* and watching it a reported 15 times. Hinckley described his assassination attempt as "the greatest love offering in the history of the world."[3]

For what it's worth, and with no armchair psychoanalysis included, we offer this Hinckley factoid: Until 1981, John Hinckley's mother's Jo Ann's nickname was "Jodie."

It took the president many months to fully recover and, during this period, his wife, Nancy, and his staff made certain that the United States and the world were shown a competent, energetic, healthy president.

After leaving office, Reagan announced he had been diagnosed with Alzheimer's disease and, today, the disease has destroyed the memory and personality of the man who had such an engaging, natural wit, he joked with his doctors before they put him under anesthesia. They were all, indeed, Republicans that day.

John Hinckley's Letter to Jodie Foster[4]

3/30/81

12:45 p.m.

Dear Jodie,

There is a definite possibility that I will be killed in my attempt to get Reagan. It is for this very reason that I am writing you this letter now.

As you well know by now I love you very much. Over the past seven months I've left you dozens of poems, letters and love messages in the faint hope that you could develop an interest in me. Although we talked on the phone a couple of times I never had the nerve to simply approach you and introduce myself. Besides my shyness, I honestly did not wish to bother you with my constant presence. I know the many messages left at your door and in your mailbox were a nuisance, but I felt that it was the most painless way for me to express my love for you.

I feel very good about the fact that you at least know my name and know how I feel about you. And by hanging around your dormitory, I've come to realize that I'm the topic of more than a little conversation, however full of ridicule it may be. At least you know that I'll always love you.

Jodie, I would abandon this idea of getting Reagan in a second if I could only win your heart and live out the rest of my life with you, whether it be in total obscurity or whatever.

I will admit to you that the reason I'm going ahead with this attempt now is because I just cannot wait any longer to impress you. I've got to do something now to make you understand, in no uncertain terms, that I am doing all of this for your sake! By sacrificing my freedom and possibly my life, I hope to change your mind about me. This letter is being written only an hour before I leave for the Hilton Hotel. Jodie, I'm asking you to please look into your heart and at least give me the chance, with this historical deed, to gain your respect and love.

I love you forever,

John Hinckley

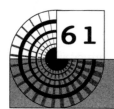

61

George Lincoln Rockwell

ASSASSINATED   ✓

SURVIVED   ___

I worshipped Rockwell and I loved him dearly. There seemed to be nothing I would not do for him. To me, he was every-thing. I loved him like a father and he loved me like his son.

—John Patler, 1972[1]

VICTIM: George Lincoln Rockwell

BORN: March 19, 1918

DIED: August 25, 1967

AGE WHEN ATTACKED: 49

OCCUPATION: Founder and leader of the American Nazi Party (ANP), white supremacist, former United States Navy pilot, gifted illustrator and graphic artist

ASSASSINS: John Patler (original name, John Patsalos, b. 1938), 29, former member of the American Nazi Party; tried and convicted killer of Rockwell[2]

DATE & TIME OF ATTACK: Friday, August 25, 1967, around noon

LOCATION OF ATTACK: In a small shopping plaza in Arlington, Virginia, across the street from Rockwell's American Nazi Party headquarters, which was known as Hatemonger's Hill

WEAPON: A Mauser semi-automatic rifle

— 205 —

ASSASSINATION OUTCOME: Two shots were fired at Rockwell through the windshield as he backed his car out of a parking space in a small shopping center. He had just come out of a coin-operated laundry. The shots were fired from a sniper's lair on top of the strip building from a distance of about 15 yards. One bullet hit Rockwell in the head; one hit him in the chest. Rockwell crawled out of his car on the passenger's side and died almost immediately, bleeding on the pavement. The bullet that struck him in the chest devastated the major arteries to his heart and he bled out before he could receive medical attention. The owner of the laundry, J.W. Hancock, rushed to Rockwell as soon as he saw him fall out of his car, but he could do nothing. "There was never any question in my mind that he was dead," Hancock later told a reporter.[3]

JUDICIAL OUTCOME: John Patler was spotted at about 12:45 p.m. at a bus stop near the site of the shooting by police officers who recognized him as a member of the American Nazi Party and an associate of Rockwell. When police officers approached Patler, he fled, was pursued, was caught, and was arrested. He offered no resistance, and he was unarmed. He was held on $50,000 bail at the Arlington County jail. Patler was charged with Rockwell's murder and was convicted on December 16, 1967, after three hours of jury deliberation. He was sentenced to 20 years in prison, which was the minimum sentence for a first-degree murder conviction. The prosecution had asked for the death penalty (which had caused Patler's wife, Alice, to scream "No, no, no!" in the courtroom and faint[4]). Patler was a model prisoner and was paroled on August 22, 1975, after serving less than eight years of his sentence. He is still alive, but his present whereabouts are unknown. It is also not known if he continues to use the name John Patler.

George Lincoln Rockwell was born in 1918, the son of a vaudeville comedian. After graduating high school, attending Brown University, and serving in the United States Navy, he married, had children, and, in 1945, began living what seemed like a normal family life. He was a talented commercial artist and found work in the field. He seemed like a typical post-war vet making his way in a post-war America.

In 1951, Rockwell became interested in the notion of General Douglas MacArthur running for president, and he got involved in politics at the local level. Someone introduced him to some anti-Semitic literature that proposed a Jewish-communist nexus, and it was then a short stroll to reading and endorsing Adolf Hitler's *Mein Kampf.* "I learned Hitler was right on the Jews,"[5] he said at the time. *"Mein Kampf* was like finding part of me. In *Mein Kampf* I found abundant mental sunshine...I was transfixed, hypnotized... Slowly, bit by bit I began to understand. I realized that National Socialism, the iconoclastic world-view of Adolf Hitler was the doctrine of scientific racial-idealism, actually a new religion for our times...[Hitler was] the greatest mind in 2,000 years."[6]

In 1958, Rockwell formed the American Nazi Party and began staging confrontational demonstrations that garnered him national attention. He was even mentioned in a Bob Dylan song, "John Birch Blues." He began publicly calling for the extermination of all Jews and the deportation of all blacks to Africa. His new ideology got him kicked out of the Navy reserves in 1960, but this did not stop him from running for governor of Virginia in 1965.

John Patler was an eager member of Rockwell's ANP but was ultimately expelled from the party for starting trouble between the light-skinned Nazis and the dark-skinned Nazis. Those who believe Patler acted alone when he shot Rockwell blame his ouster as the likely reason for the assassination.

Members of Rockwell's party (he had changed the name to the Nationalist Socialist White People's Party to focus more on white power than anti-Semitism) tried to get him buried in Arlington National Cemetery. As a veteran, he was entitled, but the new leaders of the party wanted to bury him in full Nazi regalia, they wanted to cover the coffin with a Nazi flag, and they wanted to attend the burial wearing swastikas. Arlington refused to allow the burial, as did another national cemetery, Culpeper, and Rockwell's body was returned to the funeral home, where it was quietly cremated after it was obvious that the U.S. government would never allow a Nazi to be buried next to soldiers who had died at the hands of Nazis.

Reportedly, Rockwell's ashes were returned to ANP headquarters, where they were placed under constant armed guard.

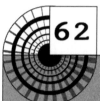

62 Franklin Delano Roosevelt

ASSASSINATED ___

SURVIVED ✓

You give me electric chair. I no afraid of that chair! You're one of capitalists. You is crook man too. Put me in electric chair. I no care!

—Giuseppe Zangara[1]

VICTIM: President-elect (his inauguration was March 4, 1933) Franklin Delano Roosevelt

BORN: January 30, 1882

DIED: April 12, 1945

AGE WHEN ATTACKED: 51

OCCUPATION: 32nd president of the United States (1933–1945)

UNSUCCESSFUL ASSASSIN: Giuseppe Zangara (1900–1933), 32, Italian-born immigrant bricklayer; hater of capitalists, presidents, and kings

DATE & TIME OF ATTACK: Wednesday, February 15, 1933, around 9 p.m.

FDR

LOCATION OF ATTACK: In Bay Front Park in Miami, Florida

WEAPON: A .32-caliber revolver bought at a pawnshop for $8

ASSASSINATION OUTCOME: President-elect Roosevelt was uninjured; four people in the crowd were wounded and later recovered; Chicago Mayor Anton Cermak was shot and died later from his injuries.

JUDICIAL OUTCOME: Zangara pleaded guilty to four counts of assault and the attempted assassination of the president and was quickly sentenced to four 20-year sentences, to run consecutively. Upon hearing of his 80-year sentence, Zangara accused the judge of being stingy and dared him to sentence him to a 100-year sentence. The judge replied that maybe Zangara would get more later. And he did. After Mayor Anton Cermak died from the gunshot wound inflicted by Zangara, the Italian immigrant was brought back to court, where he pled guilty to murder. This time the sentence was execution, and Zangara died in the Florida electric chair on March 20, 1933.

A tiny article in *The New York Times* two days after the assassination attempt on President-elect Roosevelt was headlined, "Says Mayor Cermak Ordered Four Bullet-Proof Vests." According to the story, a bulletproof vest manufacturer in Chicago told reporters that Mayor Cermak, who was critically wounded in the attempt on Roosevelt's life, had ordered four bulletproof vests from him the day before he started his trip to Florida. The Mayor's secretary said he had no knowledge of such an order.[2]

Cermak's foresight, if acted on earlier, might have saved his life.

Giuseppe Zangara wanted to kill a U.S. president and, during his short life in America, he took a shot at a president-elect, considered killing another (Herbert Hoover, Chapter 29), and did manage to assassinate a mayor. (He also told police he had wanted to kill the king of Italy before he came to America, but never got around to it.)

President-elect Roosevelt had just enjoyed a 12-day vacation on his friend Vincent Astor's yacht, the *Nourmahal*, off the coast of Miami, Florida. (FDR claimed to have caught a great many fish and also to have gained 10 pounds during his vacation.) Upon his arrival onshore in Miami, he planned to give a brief outdoor speech at Bay Front Park. The speech had been announced to the press, and more then 10,000 people filled the park to see and hear the soon-to-be president.

The speech, which many expected to be longer, consisted of two brief paragraphs of fluff, yet he was cheered and warmly received by the crowd.

Immediately after he finished speaking, the five-foot-short Giuseppe Zangara stood on a bench, pointed his .32-caliber revolver at FDR, and fired five rounds. He did not hit Roosevelt, but he did strike Mayor Anton Cermak in the chest; a woman from Newark, New Jersey was shot through the hand; the wife of the president of the Florida Power and Light Company was shot in the abdomen; a New York City cop was shot in the head; and a young man from Miami was shot in the head. Four people who were wounded survived; Mayor Cermak died 19 days following the attack.

FDR later told *The New York Times* about his efforts to keep Mayor Cermak alive:

I saw Mayor Cermak being carried. I motioned to have him put in the back of [my] car, which would be the first out. He was alive, but I didn't think he was going to last. I put my left arm around him and my hand on his pulse, but I couldn't find any pulse. He slumped forward.

On the left of Cermak, and leaning over him, was the Miami chief of detectives. He was sitting on the rear mudguard. He said after we had gone two blocks, "I don't think he is going to last."

I said, "I am afraid he isn't."

After we had gone another block, Mayor Cermak straightened up and I got his pulse. It was surprising. For three blocks I believed his heart had stopped. I held him all the way to the hospital and his pulse constantly improved.

That trip to the hospital seemed 30 miles long. I talked to Mayor Cermak nearly all the way. I remember I said "Tony, keep quiet— don't move. It won't hurt you if you keep quiet."[3]

The sad, pathetic life of Giuseppe Zangara is a classic example of how easily things can go wrong and short-circuit an otherwise well-intentioned person. Zangara's father took Giuseppe out of school when he was still a child and put him to work doing hard, physical labor. The young boy was also not fed properly and this combination, according to Zangara, led to stomach troubles and a bitter resentment of people who sent their children to school and fed them well. Short circuit. He thus grew up hating capitalists, and he made the tragic leap from vitriol to violence.

If Zangara had been allowed to stay in school and had been fed properly, would he have still tried to kill a president when he grew up? We'll never know.

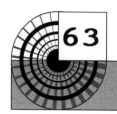

63

Theodore Roosevelt

ASSASSINATED   ___

SURVIVED   ✓

Friends, I shall have to ask you to be as quiet as possible. I do not know whether you fully understand that I have just been shot; but it takes more than that to kill a Bull Moose...The bullet is in me now, so that I cannot make a very long speech, but I will try my best...I have altogether too important things to think of to pay any heed or feel any concern over my own death. Now I would not speak to you insincerely within five minutes of being shot...I can tell you with absolute truthfulness that I am very much uninterested in whether I am shot or not.

—Theodore Roosevelt[1]

Roosevelt

Death had to take him sleeping. For if Roosevelt had been awake, there would have been a fight.

—Thomas Marshall[2]

VICTIM: Theodore Roosevelt

BORN: October 27, 1858

DIED: January 6, 1919

— 211 —

AGE WHEN ATTACKED: 53

OCCUPATION: 26th president of the United States (1901–1909), prolific author,[3] founder of the volunteer Calvary regiment—the Rough Riders, famous for his motto: "Speak softly and carry a big stick."

UNSUCCESSFUL ASSASSIN: John N. Schrank (1876–1943), 36, former saloon owner and tenement landlord

DATE & TIME OF ATTACK: Monday, October 14, 1912, early evening

LOCATION OF ATTACK: Outside a hotel in Milwaukee, Wisconsin as Roosevelt was getting into a car

WEAPON: A .38-caliber Colt revolver

ASSASSINATION OUTCOME: Schrank managed to fire only one shot at Roosevelt before he was tackled by aides and police while attempting a second shot. (As did William McKinley [Chapter 48] when he was shot, Roosevelt implored the police and the crowd not to hurt his assailant.) The bullet struck Roosevelt in the chest but was slowed by a folded 50-page speech and a steel spectacles case the Colonel was carrying in his coat. Nevertheless, the bullet lodged in his chest wall near his heart. When his aide, Henry Cochems, asked him if he had been hit, Roosevelt replied, "He pinked me, Henry."[4] Although Roosevelt was bleeding profusely (the blood was pooling on the floor between his feet), he refused to go to the hospital and instead insisted that he be driven to the Milwaukee Auditorium where he delivered a dramatic and powerful 50-minute campaign speech. (He was on the campaign trail as a third-party candidate with the Bull Moose Party, running for his third term as president, against incumbent President Taft.) After the speech, Roosevelt was examined by doctors and they concluded that the folded speech and the metal case had saved his life. He was hospitalized for six days at Mercy Hospital in Chicago, and then he continued his campaign trip. The bullet was never removed, Roosevelt claimed he never gave it a moment's thought, and he died in his sleep six years later from a coronary embolism.

JUDICIAL OUTCOME: After his arrest, John Schrank told the authorities that he shot Theodore Roosevelt because the ghost of William McKinley had appeared to him in a dream and had told him to. He also believed that anyone running for a third term as president (as was Theodore Roosevelt) was a traitor and needed to be eliminated.

In writings found on his person following his arrest, Schrank had written, "In a dream I saw President McKinley set up in a Monk's attire in whom I recognized Theodore Roosevelt. The President said: 'This is my murderer; avenge my death.'"[5] Schrank was found to be insane and was sentenced to confinement in a mental institution. He died while institutionalized in Wisconsin in 1943.

During his presidency, Teddy Roosevelt was enormously popular and a very visible presence on the American scene. Mail addressed with nothing but a pair of wire-rimmed glasses drawn on the envelope would be delivered to the White House without delay.

Thus, his challenge of incumbent President Taft for the Republican nomination in the 1912 election made sense (at least to Roosevelt and his staunch supporters) politically. He lost the nomination, however, and bolted the Republican Party to start his own Progressive Party, also known as the Bull Moose Party. He and Taft ultimately split the Republican vote, thereby handing the election to Democrat Woodrow Wilson.

After the 1912 election, he mostly retired from politics and spent his final years writing books and going on safaris.

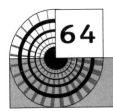

64

Anwar el-Sadat

ASSASSINATED   ✓

SURVIVED   ___

Where were his bodyguards? I asked myself—those huge men who were supposed to throw themselves between my father and any danger? What were they doing with the stun guns they had been given, weapons that could hurl a spark of electricity that would virtually paralyze an attacker fifteen feet or more away? Later, I would hear that Father's bodyguards had been distracted by an air-force jet precision flying team at the moment of the attack. I wondered whether the bodyguards themselves might have been the assassins since at the moment no one knew who had shot my father. Later, India's Indira Gandhi was to lose her life to a personal guard turned assassin.

—Camelia Sadat[1]

VICTIM: Anwar el-Sadat

BORN: December 25, 1918

DIED: October 6, 1981

AGE WHEN ATTACKED: 62

OCCUPATION: Egyptian politician, president of Egypt (1970–1981), co-recipient of the Nobel Peace Prize with Israeli Prime Minister Menachem Begin (1978); *Time*'s Man of the Year (1977)

ASSASSINS: Khalid Islambouli (1957–1982), 24, Muslim fundamentalist against Sadat's peace efforts with Israel; Mohamed Abdel-Salam Faraq Attiya; Hussein Mohamed Abbas; Abboud Zumr, Farag Fodo; and many others

DATE & TIME OF ATTACK: Wednesday, October 6, 1981, around 12:40 p.m.

LOCATION OF ATTACK: On a parade-reviewing stand in Nasr City, near Cairo, Egypt

WEAPONS: AK-47 assault rifles, submachine guns, and hand grenades

ASSASSINATION OUTCOME: Sadat was shot many times, but it is likely that the first bullet through his neck was immediately fatal. When he arrived at the hospital at approximately 1:20 p.m., he was in a state of complete coma and had no pulse or recordable blood pressure. The hospital report listed two entrance wounds beneath his left nipple and several gunshot wounds in his right arm, chest, neck, and around his left eye. As is often the case, great effort was made to resuscitate the president, but to no avail. There was no heart or brain activity, and he was pronounced dead at 2:40 p.m. Twenty-one doctors signed the report.[2] Ten others on the reviewing stand (including a prince from Oman) were killed; close to 40 more were wounded.

JUDICIAL OUTCOME: Two of the gunmen were killed at the scene; two others were arrested. Later, more than 800 people were arrested during an investigation into the assassination. Ultimately, 24 radical Muslim fundamentalists were indicted for murder and conspiracy. Islambouli was adjudged the ringleader of the conspiracy, and he and four others were executed. Additionally, 17 others ended up in prison. Two were acquitted. Abbas is currently free. Zumr is serving a life sentence in Egypt. Fodo was shot and killed by two masked Muslim fundamentalists in 1992. Sadat was succeeded by Egyptian Vice President Hosni Mubarak (Chapter 52).

The truck looked like an ordinary military vehicle, and it pulled a flatbed platform on which was mounted a field gun. It was just one of a long line of military vehicles participating in the parade to commemorate the Egyptian victory in the 1973 Egypt-Israeli war.

It was a Russian-built Zil-151 truck and, when it pulled out of line and stopped in front of the parade reviewing stand, most of those watching assumed it was having mechanical trouble and needed to get out of the line of slow-moving vehicles.

Suddenly, Khalid Islambouli and three other men jumped out of the truck and began moving quickly towards the elevated platform where Sadat and other dignitaries sat watching the parade. As they approached, Sadat stood up, but not out of fear or in an attempt to flee. It is believed he was standing to salute the approaching soldiers.

Islambouli then tossed a hand grenade into the stands. It was a dud and rolled harmlessly away. He took another one out of his pocket, pulled the pin, and tossed it. Nothing. Islambouli threw a third grenade, which did explode. At the same time, his coconspirators opened fire on the viewing stand with AK-47 assault rifles. As all this was going on, a group of jet fighters was flying overhead, adding to the confusion. For approximately 40 seconds, no one in Sadat's security team made any response. In fact, Islambouli and his men were able to use up all their ammunition before guards returned fire. (Note: Sadat's assassination was an enormous embarrassment for the United States. Earlier, the United States had agreed to take over security for Sadat and had spent $20 million of American taxpayers' money to protect him. Many Americans, while recognizing the importance of open ties with Egypt and the need to protect our critical allies, did not consider the money well-spent.)

Literally hundreds of bullets had been fired at the exposed crowd in the viewing stand, and Sadat was shot many times.

Why wasn't Sadat wearing a bulletproof vest? As in the assassinations of Indira Gandhi (page 76), and George Wallace (page 247), the decision not to wear a protective vest was personally made by Sadat. (Gandhi did not wear hers because it would not have looked good under her sari on television; Wallace did not wear his because it was an extremely hot and humid day.) Sadat did not wear his because he felt it would have made him look fat beneath his new London-made, specially tailored uniform. Although the killshot went through his neck, at least the vest would have offered some modicum of protection. Whether or not he would have survived is debatable, but it couldn't have hurt to have been wearing one while standing in a barrage of gunfire.

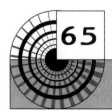

65

Theresa Saldana

ASSASSINATED	___
SURVIVED	✓

That man is going to kill me if somebody doesn't help. That is the truth.

—Theresa Saldana[1]

VICTIM: Theresa Saldana

BORN: August 20, 1954

DIED: n/a

AGE WHEN ATTACKED: 27

OCCUPATION: Actress best known for her role as Lenore, the sister of fighter Jake LaMotta (played by Robert De Niro) in the 1980 Martin Scorsese film *Raging Bull*

UNSUCCESSFUL ASSASSIN: Arthur Jackson (b. 1935), 47, mentally insane Aberdeen, Scotland, murderer and drifter

DATE & TIME OF ATTACK: Monday, March 15, 1982, morning

LOCATION OF ATTACK: Outside her West Hollywood apartment in Los Angeles, California

WEAPON: A $5 hunting knife

ASSASSINATION OUTCOME: Saldana was stabbed 10 times, but her life was saved when a bottled-water deliveryman named Jeffrey Fenn came to her rescue. He subdued and restrained her assailant until police arrived.

JUDICIAL OUTCOME: In November 1982, Arthur Jackson was sentenced to 12 years in prison for his attempted murder of Saldana. In 1989, after serving only seven years, Jackson was scheduled to be released for good behavior, but, in 1990, his sentence was extended for five years in response to a request from Saldana. Jackson sent threatening letters to Saldana the entire time he was in prison, and she told the court she feared for her life if he was released. Jackson was tried on the felony counts of sending threatening letters, convicted, and sentenced to five more years. In 1996, Jackson was released and immediately extradited to London, where he faced a murder charge. In January 1997, in the Old Bailey Criminal Court, Jackson was found guilty of the 1967 murder of a bank guard. He was sentenced to confinement in a psychiatric hospital for an indefinite amount of time, which is where he remains today.

When Arthur Jackson was 17, he asked a doctor to castrate him and then open up his head so that the dirt on his brain could be removed.

As an adult, Arthur Jackson once went to a doctor in Scotland to request that certain blood vessels be surgically removed from his eyelids. Why? Because, he told the doctor, the veins were disfiguring his soul.

Jackson also sought treatment to remove a mole that he believed was supernaturally draining his strength, and he once attempted to sue a neighbor whom he insisted was "possessed with a demon compulsion to cause distractions."[2]

Before his attack on Theresa Saldana, Jackson, a diagnosed schizophrenic, lived with his mother. She was also schizophrenic, and they reportedly never touched each other under any circumstances.

When working in New York as a resident alien, Jackson was drafted into the U.S. Army. He was quickly declared to be insane and given a Section 8 discharge. Shortly thereafter, in 1961, Jackson threatened the life of President John F. Kennedy and was deported. He managed to return to America, where he was arrested for breaking into an office building. He was again deported. In 1982, he again came back to America, had no problem getting through customs, and in March, tried to kill Theresa Saldana.

Theresa Saldana's ordeal at the hands of an insanely obsessed fan was the ultimate celebrity nightmare. Arthur Jackson decided to kill Saldana after seeing her in *Raging Bull* and two other movies. He entered the United States illegally and tracked down where she lived by hiring a private detective who used motor-vehicle records to come up with the actress's address.

The morning of March 15, 1982, Jackson waited outside Saldana's apartment and, when she came out of her home to get into a waiting car, he approached her and said, "Are you Theresa Saldana?" When she turned towards him to reply "yes," he began to ferociously stab her over and over, at one point with such force that the knife blade bent.

Jeffrey Fenn, who was delivering water nearby, saw the attack and immediately ran to Saldana's aid. He successfully subdued Jackson and restrained him until the police arrived. Reportedly, 27 people witnessed Jackson's attack on Saldana. Five major operations, a 16-pint blood transfusion, 10 stab wounds, 1,000 stitches, and a three-and-a-half-month hospitalization.

Not to mention the scars.

From that day in March 1982 until Jackson was committed to a mental hospital in England in 1997, the stabbing dominated Saldana's life. She reports that it was the cause of her divorce (she has since remarried and had a child) and that it hurt her career and damaged her financially.

Psychologically, Saldana managed to overcome the terror that can consume victims when they relive a traumatic attack. In 1984, Saldana played herself in *Victims for Victims: The Theresa Saldana Story,* a TV movie that graphically re-created the attack on her life. "Working on the film released a lot of tension for me," she said in 1984. "As we shot, I felt elated and creative. I felt that I was capable of anything. How many people are offered the opportunity to go back in time and re-live a traumatic experience, but without any of the physical or emotional pain that they felt the first time?"[3]

Saldana also helped form Victims for Victims, a support group to help victims of violent crimes.

Saldana continues to work in TV and movies and is of mixed emotions about still working in the business that was the catalyst for the near-fatal attack on her life. "It's just very sad," she said in 1989. "You pick a profession where what you want to do is entertain people and bring them creativity and joy, and a horrible aberration is going on."[4]

Theresa Saldana Filmography[5]	
I Wanna Hold Your Hand (1978)	*Of Men and Angels* (1989)
Home Movies (1979)	*Angel Town* (1990)
Sophia Loren: Her Own Story (1980) (TV)	*Double Revenge* (1990)
Raging Bull (1980)	*The Commish* (1991) TV Series
Defiance (1980)	*Shameful Secrets* (1993) (TV)
Miss Lonelyhearts (1983)	*The Commish: In the Shadow of the Gallows* (1995) (TV)
The Evil That Men Do (1984)	*She Woke Up Pregnant* (1996) (TV)
Victims for Victims: The Theresa Saldana Story (1984) (TV)	*All My Children* (1997) TV Series
The Highwayman (1987) (TV)	*The Time Shifters* (1999) (TV)
The Night Before (1988)	*Carlo's Wake* (1999)
	Ready to Run (2000) (TV)

66

Rebecca Schaeffer

ASSASSINATED   ✓

SURVIVED   —

I have an obsession with the unattainable. I have to eliminate what I cannot attain...I don't lose. Period.

—Robert John Bardo[1]

VICTIM: Rebecca Schaeffer

BORN: November 6, 1967

DIED: July 18, 1989

AGE WHEN ATTACKED: 21

OCCUPATION: Television and movie actress, best-known for her starring role on the 1986 sitcom *My Sister Sam*

ASSASSIN: Robert John Bardo (b. 1970), 19, Jack-in the-Box janitor from Tucson, Arizona

DATE & TIME OF ATTACK: Tuesday, July 18, 1989, shortly before 10:15 a.m.

LOCATION OF ATTACK: Outside the front door of her West Hollywood, California apartment

WEAPON: A .357 Magnum revolver loaded with expanding hollow point bullets

ASSASSINATION OUTCOME: Schaeffer was shot once in the chest and was pronounced dead at Cedars-Sinai Medical Center approximately 30 minutes after being shot.

JUDICIAL OUTCOME: Bardo was convicted of first-degree murder in October 1991 and is currently serving a sentence of life in prison without the possibility of parole.

There once was a time when it was perfectly legal to pay a detective to find out home addresses and other personal information about anyone at all, including celebrities. The state departments of motor vehicles would release information to anyone requesting it, and this is precisely how Rebecca Schaeffer's assassin found out where she lived. Schaeffer's murder prompted anti-stalking legislation to prevent this type of broad access, but we are now entering a new age of privacy problems as more and more information becomes available online, easily accessible on the Internet.

Robert John Bardo's profile is that of the quintessential stalker obsessed with a celebrity. Bardo rejects accusations, however, that he is insane, and he told a reporter in 1992, "I'm just emotional. If it wasn't for my obsession, I'd be law-abiding."[2]

Coming from a pathological, highly dysfunctional family (alcoholic father, paranoid mother, physically abusive brother, and so forth), Bardo began to show signs of serious problems in junior high school. He began to write threatening letters to his teachers and talk about suicide, and it was an easy jump from there to shifting his attention to someone more high profile and more visible—such as an actress whose pictures were readily available to Bardo in magazines and newspapers and who could be seen all the time on TV.

On the morning of Rebecca Schaeffer's death, Bardo visited her twice. The first time he rang her bell, she had to answer the door in person because the intercom system in her new apartment was not working properly. Schaeffer opened the door and Bardo handed her a note he had written to her, which she accepted. (There is conflicting information regarding this particular encounter. Some sources state that Bardo handed her a photograph that he had sent to her and that she had signed to him and returned.)

Whether Schaeffer intuitively sensed danger during this encounter is not known, although she may have written it off as just an overly devoted fan who had happened to locate where she lived. Bardo later told police that Schaeffer had said, "Take care" to him as she closed her front door. The killer then went to a Los Angeles diner, where he ate a breakfast of onion rings and cheesecake. He finished eating and then went into the men's room, where he loaded one hollow point bullet into his .357 Magnum revolver, a gun, which his of-age brother had purchased for him. This single bullet was all that was needed for the weapon to be completely loaded, and Bardo placed it back into a plastic grocery bag, which also contained a copy of the favorite novel of American assassins, J.D. Salinger's *The Catcher in the Rye*, a U2 tape, and a note Bardo had written to Schaeffer.

About an hour after his first visit, Bardo returned to Schaeffer's apartment and again rang the bell. According to Bardo, he hid out of sight when she slightly opened the door, forcing her to open it fully and step out onto the front step.

Bardo then leaped out, pushed her back into her apartment hallway, and shot her once in the chest with his .357 Magnum. He had specifically chosen expanding hollow point bullets because of their ability to do maximum damage. Bardo told police that Schaeffer screamed, "Why? Why?" as she fell to the floor.

Bardo then ran from the scene. Later that day, he took a bus back to Tucson, Arizona, and when he arrived in town he started walking back and forth on a highway exit ramp, dodging cars, and attracting the attention of a Tucson police officer. When confronted by the cop, Bardo told him he had killed Rebecca Schaeffer and that the California police were looking for him. Bardo was immediately arrested and, after the police confirmed his story, sent back to California, where he was indicted for Schaeffer's murder. After waiving his right to a jury trial (thereby eliminating the possibility of receiving the death penalty), Bardo was convicted of first-degree murder in October 1991 and sentenced to life without parole.

Rebecca Schaeffer Filmography[3]	
One Life to Live (1968) TV Series	*Scenes from the Class Struggle in Beverly Hills* (1989)[4]
My Sister Sam (1986–1988) TV Series	*Voyage of Terror: The Achille Lauro Affair* (1990) (TV)
Radio Days (1987)	*The End of Innocence* (1990)
Out of Time (1988) (TV)	**Notable TV guest appearances** *Amazing Stories* (1985)

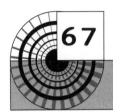

67

Monica Seles

ASSASSINATED   ___

SURVIVED   ✓

To me what was bad was that he used a knife. If he would've hit me, or...but why did he put something in me as sharp as a knife, take it out, and want to do it again. This person, you don't know if he's evil or angel: It doesn't matter. And from the back...

—Monica Seles[1]

He was thinking of giving me flowers and, I guess, cutting my hands off. But he felt that would've been too risky.

—Monica Seles[2]

VICTIM: Monica Seles

BORN: February 2, 1973

DIED: n/a

AGE WHEN ATTACKED: 19

OCCUPATION: World's top-ranked female tennis player (at the time of the attack)

UNSUCCESSFUL ASSASSIN: Günther Parche (b. 1954), 38, deranged German Steffi Graf fan and unemployed lathe operator

DATE & TIME OF ATTACK: Friday, April 30, 1993, approximately 7 p.m.

LOCATION OF ATTACK: On a tennis court at the Rothenbaum Tennis Club in Hamburg, Germany

WEAPON: A 9-inch curved, serrated boning knife. (Parche had previously used it to cut sausages in his aunt's kitchen.)

ASSASSINATION OUTCOME: Seles suffered a 1/2-inch-deep puncture wound and a torn muscle just to the left of her spinal cord below her left shoulder. The muscle healed and, with physical therapy, she recovered fully with no permanent damage. Seles says her scar tingles before it rains.

JUDICIAL OUTCOME: Parche was charged with causing grievous bodily harm and, on October 14, 1993, he received a two-year suspended sentence. (Parche himself said that he expected to serve 15 years for his crime.[3]) The prosecution appealed the verdict and requested that Seles testify at the trial. Because victims testify with their back to the defendant in German courts, Seles refused to appear, nor did she release her medical records to the court in a timely manner, all of which, if she had complied, may have resulted in a harsher penalty for Parche. The second trial resulted in the same verdict and punishment.

Monica Seles vomited the first time she watched a tape of herself being stabbed on a tennis court in Hamburg, Germany. She watched the tape in January 1995, almost two years after being attacked, and she was still not able to handle it. The physical damage done by Günther Parche's knife was relatively minor; the psychological damage probably still lingers. In July 1995, Monica Seles told *Sports Illustrated*, "My scream is what stayed with me for a long time."[4]

Seles was competing in the Hamburg Open on April 30, 1993, and she was ahead 4–3 in her second set against Bulgarian Magdalena Maleeva. After the set, there was a scheduled break, and Seles and Maleeva sat down on individual chairs, their backs to the audience. Two security guards stood behind each player. (It has never been explained how Parche got through the two security guards standing behind Monica Seles.)

As the two women rested, Günther Parche, a "balding man of medium height in a plaid shirt and jeans"[5] made his way through the crowd, moving slowly towards the waist-high barrier that separated the audience from the tennis court. As soon as he was standing behind Seles, Parche pulled out a nine-inch boning knife from a plastic bag, raised it high in both hands, and plunged it downwards into Monica Seles's back. He then withdrew the knife and raised it to stab her a second time, but he was quickly grabbed by security guards and restrained. During the scuffle, security personnel broke Parche's left arm while restraining him, and he dropped the knife onto the court, where it lay in full view of the spectators. Seles's blood could clearly be seen on the blade.

As soon as Seles was stabbed, she leaped up out of her chair, grabbed her back and began screaming. Within seconds, she was surrounded by people, including chair umpire Stefan Voss; World Tennis Association tour director Lisa Grattan; Seles's trainer, Madeleine Van Zoelen; and Seles's brother, Zoltan Seles. She was taken by ambulance to the Eppendorf University Hospital and remained there until May 2, after which she returned to the United States by private jet.

The location of Seles's stab wound was not in an extremely dangerous spot, but it was an extremely painful injury. It could, however, easily have been much worst. The moment Parche pulled the knife out of his plastic bag and raised it high, a woman in the stands saw what he was doing and screamed. On hearing the scream, Seles turned to her left to see what was happening. This slight shift of her body probably saved her from a life of total paralysis. Parche's knife entered her back only centimeters away from her spinal cord and it is likely that if she had been facing front, he would have hit her spinal cord dead-center.

Why did Günther Parche stab the world's top-ranked, number-one female tennis player? So that the world's number-two female player, Steffi Graf, could ascend to the top slot.

Parche was utterly obsessed with Steffi Graf, and he was determined to do anything he could to take Seles out of the running. Reportedly, Parche became giddily ecstatic when Graf won a match, and, likewise, he became inordinately depressed when she lost. His attic room in the house where he lived with his aunt was elaborately decorated with photos and posters of Steffi Graf, and he even went so far as to send the tennis star money on her birthday.

Parche claimed that he was not trying to kill Seles; that he only wanted to damage her ability to play tennis. In that respect, he was somewhat successful, because it was 27 months before Monica Seles returned to playing professional tennis.

On July 29, 1995, Seles played against Martina Navratilova in a "Return of the Champions" exhibition match. Seles won handily. In the years since her return to professional tennis, Seles has played Steffi Graf again and has won and lost matches against the player with whom she will be forever linked in the annals of assassination attempts.

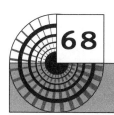

William Henry Seward

ASSASSINATED   ___

SURVIVED   ✓

I know and all the world knows, that revolutions never go backwards.

—William H. Seward[1]

VICTIM: William Henry Seward

BORN: May 16, 1801

DIED: October 10, 1872

AGE WHEN ATTACKED: 63

OCCUPATION: Lawyer, former U.S. Senator from New York, Secretary of State for presidents Abraham Lincoln and Andrew Johnson, known for arranging the purchase of Alaska from Russia for $7 million ("Seward's Folly")

Seward

UNSUCCESSFUL ASSASSIN: Lewis Paine (a.k.a. Lewis Powell; 1844–1865), 20, a conspirator in the Lincoln assassination plot (page 142)

DATE & TIME OF ATTACK: Friday, April 14, 1865, shortly after 10 p.m.

LOCATION OF ATTACK: In Seward's third-floor bedroom in his house at Lafayette Park in Washington, D.C.

WEAPON: A Bowie Knife. It was described at Paine's trial as "a heavy, horn-handled affair with a double edge at the point and a blade about 10 inches long."[2]

ASSASSINATION OUTCOME: Paine broke into Seward's dimly lit room and made immediately for the bed on the right side of the room. Seward, however, was on the far side of the bed, near the wall, in order to allow him room to rest his injured left shoulder and arm. Paine managed to stab Seward about the face and neck. The Secretary of State was seriously wounded, but his wounds were not fatal. He ultimately recovered, but complicating his recovery (and adding to his misery) was the fact that he had been recuperating from being seriously injured in a carriage accident when the assassination attempt occurred. The most seriously injured during this attempt was Seward's son, Frederick. After his pistol failed to fire, Paine struck the younger Seward in the head with the gun, fracturing his skull and exposing his brain in two places. Remarkably, Frederick Seward also recovered from his injuries. Frederick was conscious for approximately one hour after Paine struck him, but then he lapsed into a coma and remained insensible for several days. It was a solid month before his doctors judged that he was out of danger.

JUDICIAL OUTCOME: As he fled William Seward's home following his unsuccessful assassination attempt on Good Friday, 1865, Lewis Paine shouted, "I'm mad! I'm mad!"[3] Paine showed up at Mrs. Surratt's boarding house three days after the attacks on President Lincoln and Secretary of State Seward and was immediately arrested on suspicion of being involved in the assassination plot. When his identity and actions were confirmed, he was charged and ordered tried by a military commission. His self-proclaimed insanity did nothing to change the guilty verdict. At trial, Paine was detached and seemingly uninterested at the proceedings, and he denied nothing. In fact, one of the judges was overheard to say, "Paine seems to want to be hung, so I guess we might as well hang him."[4] And hang him they did, along with his co-conspirators George Atzerodt (pages 115 and 142), David Herold, and Mary Surratt. Paine was executed on July 7, 1865.

Shortly after 10:00 on Good Friday, Lewis Paine, dressed in a long overcoat, knocked on the door of Secretary of State William Seward's home opposite Lafayette Park in Washington, D.C. The door was answered by a 19-year-old black servant named William Bell. Paine told Bell that he had medicine for Mr. Seward and that he had strict orders from Dr. Verdi to deliver it to him personally. Bell resisted and told him that Mr. Seward was in bed, recuperating from injuries sustained in a carriage accident, and that no one was allowed in the chamber.

Paine insisted that his mission was critical and demanded that he be escorted upstairs to deliver Dr. Verdi's medicine to Mr. Seward.

Considering his age and station in life, Bell was probably intimidated by this tall, white gentleman, and he reluctantly agreed to lead the way upstairs.

When they reached the third-floor landing, they came upon Seward's son, Frederick. Bell was probably relieved that someone in authority could now deal with this high-handed stranger, and he deferred responsibility to Frederick. Paine told his story again, only this time, Frederick refused to allow him access to his father's bedroom and told him that he would personally see to it that Dr. Verdi did not blame him for not fulfilling his obligation. Paine pressed on, insisting on seeing Mr. Seward, and Frederick grew angry and impatient, ultimately telling Paine he would not allow him in the bedroom and to give the medicine to him.

Paine mumbled something inaudible and turned away as if to leave, but then he pulled a revolver out of his coat and fired at Frederick. The gun did not fire, however, and Paine then attacked the younger Seward with the butt of the gun, fracturing his skull in two places.

William Bell, in the meantime, ran downstairs and out the front door shouting, "Murder! Murder!" He ran next door to an Army headquarters seeking help.

Seward's soldier-nurse, George Robinson, heard the commotion from inside the bedroom and opened the door to investigate. Paine stabbed at Robinson, inflicting a minor wound, and pushed him out of the way. He then went for Seward. Robinson later recalled the scene:

> *I saw him strike Mr. Seward with the same knife with which he cut my forehead. It was a large knife, and he held it with the blade down below his hand. I saw him cut Mr. Seward twice that I am sure of; the first time he struck him on the right cheek, and then he seemed to be cutting around his neck.* [5]

Robinson and Seward's other son, Augustus, attacked Paine and pulled him off Seward. Paine then fled the house, stabbed a messenger entering the house on his way out, and fled on horseback.

Less than three months later, Paine would be swinging from a rope for his dastardly attack against the Secretary of State.

From *The New York Times*, April 15, 1865:

MR. SEWARD AND SON.

Secretary Seward will Recover—Frederick Seward Still Very Low.

Special Dispatch to the New-York Times.

WASHINGTON, Saturday, April 15.

MR. SEWARD will recover.

FREDERICK SEWARD is still unconscious. He breaths calmly and has an easy pulse. His head is dreadfully contused and lacerated.

An invalid soldier saved MR. SEWARD's life.

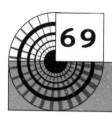

69

Alexander Solzhenitsyn

ASSASSINATED	—
SURVIVED	✓

You only have power over people as long as you don't take everything from them. But when you've robbed a man of everything he's no longer in your power—he's free again.

—Alexander Solzhenitsyn[1]

Freedom's just another word for nothin' left to lose.

—Kris Kristofferson[2]

VICTIM: Alexander (Aleksandr) Solzhenitsyn

BORN: December 11, 1918

DIED: n/a

AGE WHEN ATTACKED: 53

OCCUPATION: Russian dissident writer; author of *One Day in the Life of Ivan Denisovich* (1962), *Cancer Ward*, (1968), *The Gulag Archipelago* (1974), and others; winner of the 1970 Nobel Prize for Literature

UNSUCCESSFUL ASSASSINS: The Russian KGB

DATE & TIME OF ATTACK: 1971

LOCATION OF ATTACK: A department store counter in Rostov-on-Don, Soviet Union

WEAPON: A poisoned needle

ASSASSINATION OUTCOME: A KGB agent stabbed Solzhenitsyn as he stood at the department store counter, but the Russian writer did not feel the puncture, nor did he know he had been stabbed when he left the store. For some unknown reason, however, the poison failed to kill Solzhenitsyn, instead causing terrible burns on his body. Solzhenitsyn saw his physicians, who were unable to explain the burns, although they did treat him successfully. The official medical finding was that the burns had been caused by some kind of severe allergic reaction or by an unknown disease that was, obviously, not fatal.

JUDICIAL OUTCOME: None. Solzhenitsyn did not find out until 1992 that he had been targeted for assassination and, three years after the attack, in 1974, the writer was exiled from the Soviet Union on charges of treason. His writings, which exposed the harsh brutality of the Soviet political prison camp system known as the "Gulag," were considered treasonous to the Soviet government, and he was deported. He took up residence in Vermont, where he lived until 1994. That year, under the new regime of Mikhail Gorbachev, Solzhenitsyn returned to Russia and settled in Moscow. The treason charges against him were officially dropped and his Russian citizenship was restored.

Alexander Solzhenitsyn became a thorn in the side of the Soviet Union at an early age.

In 1945, after World War II had ended victoriously for Russia, Solzhenitsyn, who had served as captain of artillery in the Soviet Army during the war, wrote a letter severely criticizing then-Premier of the Soviet Union, Joseph Stalin.

In the post–World War II communist Soviet Union, proud citizens of Mother Russia did not write letters criticizing the premier. At the age of 27, after serving bravely in the War, Solzhenitsyn paid a dear price for his fearless candor. He was arrested, charged with treason, convicted, and sentenced to eight years in Russian prisons and labor camps. After he was released in 1953, he was further punished with three years of forced exile.

In 1956, Solzhenitsyn was considered "rehabilitated" and allowed to settle in Ryazan in central Russia, and it was there that he began to write fiction.

In 1962, he published in the Russia literary magazine *Novy Mir* and his novella *One Day in the Life of Ivan Denisovich*, which was brutally honest about his experiences in the Russian labor camps. Russia was going through Kruschev's de-Stalinization program at the time, and the novella was released without Soviet censorship. This openness was short-lived, however, and, after Solzhenitsyn published a collection of short stories (some equally critical of the Gulag years and repressive Soviet polices) in 1963, he was denied the right to publish his work in Russia. He continued to write, however, and his novels *The First Circle, Cancer Ward,* and *August 1914,* initially published outside of Russia, garnered him an international literary reputation. The Soviet government was definitely not pleased with Solzhenitsyn, however, and when he was awarded the 1970 Nobel Prize for literature, he did not attend the awards ceremony because he was afraid he would not be allowed back into Russia when he returned from Stockholm.

It was in 1971, shortly after winning the Nobel, that the Soviet secret police, the KGB, decided to assassinate Solzhenitsyn.

They tailed him on his daily movements until, one day, an agent passed by the writer as he stood at a counter in a department store and stabbed him with a needle loaded with poison. Solzhenitsyn did not even feel the prick and was surprised when he shortly thereafter broke out in severe burns on his body. The burns were a non-fatal (but toxic) reaction to the poison and his doctors were only able to treat the symptoms. He recovered and did not learn about the assassination attempt until 1992. Solzhenitsyn was living in Vermont at that time, having been permanently exiled from Russia in 1974 for his writings, particularly the damning *The Gulag Archipelago.*

It is not known if the KGB abandoned the idea of killing Solzhenitsyn after the failed attempt in 1971. It would seem so, however, since shortly thereafter the government turned to the less violent, and more blatant, method of "eliminating" the outspoken, malcontented writer from Mother Russia: exile.

Today, Solzhenitsyn lives in Russia where he seems to be treated as something of an elder statesman and is allowed to write and say whatever he likes. His later works include *November 1916,* a continuation of his *Red Wheel* series begun with *August 1914.*

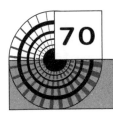

Margaret Thatcher

ASSASSINATED ___

SURVIVED

The bomb attack...was an attempt not only to disrupt and terminate our conference. It was an attempt to cripple Her Majesty's democratically elected government. That is the scale of the outrage in which we have all shared. And the fact that we are gathered here now, shocked but composed and determined, is a sign not only that this attack has failed, but that all attempts to destroy democracy by terrorism will fail.

—Margaret Thatcher[1]

VICTIM: Margaret Roberts Thatcher

BORN: October 13, 1925

DIED: n/a

AGE WHEN ATTACKED: 59

OCCUPATION: Prime minister of Great Britain (1979–1990), first female British prime minister after 700 years of men, known as "Attila the Hun" and "The Iron Lady," proponent of the economic policy of "Popular Capitalism"

UNSUCCESSFUL ASSASSIN: Patrick Magee (b. 1951), 33, a.k.a. "The Brighton Bomber," member of the anti-British terrorist organization the Irish Republican Army

DATE & TIME OF ATTACK: Friday, October 12, 1984, 2:54 a.m.

LOCATION OF ATTACK: The Grand Hotel, Brighton, England

— 234 —

WEAPON: A 100-pound gelginite bomb planted inside a bathroom wall

ASSASSINATION OUTCOME: The bomb exploded on the sixth floor of the hotel, five floors above Thatcher's bathroom on the first floor. It collapsed the five floors below it and would have crushed Thatcher, who would normally have been preparing for bed in her room's bathroom at that time if she had not earlier been handed a document to read. Thatcher escaped the hotel unscathed. Five members of her party were killed, one was seriously injured and paralyzed below the neck, and one sustained severe crush injuries to his legs.

JUDICIAL OUTCOME: After surveying the damage and determining that the placement of the bomb had taken a great deal of time, the police investigated 800 guests of the hotel who had stayed at the Grand in the month before the bombing. The only one they could not find was "Roy Walsh." Prints from Walsh's hotel registration card matched prints of Patrick Magee, a known IRA member. Magee was arrested and given eight life sentences, with a chance for parole after 35 years. Magee was released in January 1999 after serving 14 years of his sentences.

Irish Republican Army assassin Patrick Magee was diligent, and he was patient.

On September 19, 1984, Magee checked into room 629 in the Grand Hotel in Brighton, England. He used the name Roy Walsh, and he was undoubtedly very discrete and low-key as he carried his tools and supplies through the lobby over the next 24 days. His carpenter's tools and bomb-making supplies were likely transported to his room concealed in suitcases, and he certainly took precautions not to make too much noise or allow the hotel staff into Room 629's bathroom.

For 24 days, Magee assiduously worked to tear down one entire wall in his room's bathroom, load approximately 100 pounds of the explosive gelginite into the space, rig the explosive to a timer, and then carefully and meticulously rebuild the bathroom wall so that not a trace of his efforts could be seen.

The bomb exploded shortly before 3:00 in the morning. Mrs. Thatcher described the moment of the explosion in her autobiography:

At 2:54 a.m. a loud thud shook the room. There was a few seconds' silence and then there was a second slightly different noise, in fact created by falling masonry. I knew immediately that it was a bomb—

perhaps two bombs, a large followed by a smaller device—but at this stage I did not know that the explosion had taken place inside the hotel. Glass from the windows of my sitting-room was strewn across the carpet. But I thought that it might be a car bomb outside.[2]

Margaret Thatcher was born Margaret Roberts in Grantham, England, in 1925, the daughter of a grocer and city alderman. Her family was not poor, but she later did claim a "disadvantaged" background, using the terms "aggressive thrift" and "a pervading sense of poverty, if not the painful fact of it."[3]

She graduated from Somerville College at Oxford with two degrees, chemistry and law, and worked first as a research chemist and then as a tax attorney. In 1951, she married Dennis Thatcher and, for two years, she devoted herself full-time to politics. She ran unsuccessfully for Parliament in 1951. In 1953, she gave birth to twins, Mark and Carol, and continued her political work (with the help of a nanny) during the children's early years. Thatcher ran again for Parliament in 1959 and was finally elected.

She worked for Conservative Edward Heath for several years and became education secretary in 1970.

Thatcher was installed as prime minister in 1979 and immediately made enemies. Her personal style was perceived to be abrasive and cold, and she fired several Cabinet members whom she considered inadequate for their jobs. At the time, Britain's economy was in terrible shape, and millions were on welfare. She set as her goal reducing inflation, unemployment, and public spending, and, even though her programs eventually worked, she was almost universally despised by the British people for her harsh tactics.

Thatcher also had to contend with the Argentine invasion of the British Falkland Islands (she got them back, with help from the United States), improving relations with the Soviet Union, and publicly disagreeing with her friend Ronald Reagan over the Strategic Defense Initiative.

Thatcher resigned in November 1990 and was made a member of the House of Lords after John Major was elected prime minister.

Margaret Thatcher was utterly unflappable after the bomb explosion that claimed the lives of five of her friends and that could have killed her. Thatcher was scheduled to give a critically important speech to the Conservative Party the day after the bombing, and the attempt on her life did not sway her from her mission. She quickly rewrote several passages of the speech and went ahead with her appearance.

Iron Lady, indeed.

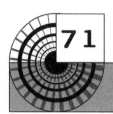

71

Leon Trotsky

ASSASSINATED   ✓

SURVIVED   ___

I put my raincoat on the table on purpose so that I could take out the ice axe which I had in the pocket...I took the piolet out of my raincoat, took it in my fist and, closing my eyes, I gave him a tremendous blow on the head...The man screamed in such a way that I will never forget as long as I live. His scream was...very long infinitely long, and it still seems to me as if that scream were piercing my brains.

—Ramon Mercader[1]

VICTIM: Leon Trotsky (real name, Lev Davidovich Bronstein)

BORN: October 26, 1879

DIED: August 20, 1940

AGE WHEN ATTACKED: 61

OCCUPATION: Russian Jewish revolutionary theoretician, leader of the Russian Bolshevik Revolution, creator and organizer of the Red Army, author

Trotsky

— 237 —

Assassination Attempt No. 1: Stalin's Long Arm

ASSASSINS: Twenty-one agents of Joseph Stalin, disguised as Mexican police officers; four members of the Mexican Communist party also implicated as organizing the assassination attempt

DATE & TIME OF ATTACK: Friday, May 24, 1940, shortly before 4 a.m.

LOCATION OF ATTACK: In the bedroom of his home in Mexico City, Mexico

WEAPONS: Thompson submachine guns, an incendiary bomb

ASSASSINATION OUTCOME: According to reports, the gunmen shot up Trotsky's bedroom for five full minutes, firing more than 300 rounds. Mr. and Mrs. Trotsky remained flat on the floor of the bedroom and were uninjured, except for some facial lacerations Trotsky sustained from flying glass. Trotsky's grandson, Segei Sedoff, was wounded in the foot by a bullet as he slept in another room. As they fled, the assassins then threw a Molotov cocktail-type bomb into Trotsky's house in an attempt to burn it down with Trotsky and his family inside, but that, too, failed when Mrs. Trotsky smothered the bomb with a blanket before it could do any harm.

JUDICIAL OUTCOME: On June 18, 1940, according to General José Manuel Nunez, head of the Mexico City police, 21 men were arrested and charged with the attempt on Trotsky's life. Nunez also said that day that "complete light has been shed on the attack on Leon Trotsky's house" and that they were also looking for the four masterminds of the assassination attempt.[2] However, three months later, in an article in *The New York Times* reporting Trotsky's murder, the *Times*, when referring to the May attempt on his life, stated "Mexican police were unable to find the machine-gunners...."[3] Little else is known regarding the result of the June 18th arrest, nor does there seem to be any documented explanation for the apparent contradiction by the Mexico City police.

Assassination Attempt No. 2: Death by Friend

ASSASSIN: Ramon Mercader, a.k.a. Jacques Mornard van den Dreschd, a.k.a. Frank Jacson, 26, Spanish-born, son of a Spanish father and Cuban mother, close friend of Trotsky and his family. Mercader's accomplice, Sylvia Ageloff, introduced the assassin to Trotsky and was charged as a conspirator in the crime. (Although Mercader is the one who wielded the axe, Trotsky's murder was actually an execution ordered by Joseph Stalin. Stalin knew that Trotsky was an ongoing threat to his supremacy and considered his elimination a necessity.)

DATE & TIME OF ATTACK: Tuesday, August 20, 1940, 5:30p.m.; died 26 hours later on August 21, 1940, at 7:25 p.m.

LOCATION OF ATTACK: In Trotsky's study in his home in Mexico City, Mexico (the same house where the first assassination attempt took place)

WEAPON: An ice axe

ASSASSINATION OUTCOME: Mercader lured Trotsky into his study by asking him to look at an article he had written. When Trotsky sat down at his desk, Mercader pulled out an ice axe he had concealed in a coat he had lain on the table, raised it, closed his eyes, and buried it deep in the middle of Trotsky's head. He immediately withdrew the axe and raised it for a second blow, but this was not to be. Mercader had expected Trotsky to be rendered immediately unconscious by the first plunge of the pick, but instead Trotsky stood up, let out a scream, and began fighting with his assassin. He grabbed Mercader's arm and bit his hand to prevent him from striking him again. Trotsky then staggered out of the room, blood running down his face, calling for his guards. They quickly responded and took Mercader into custody, after giving him a quintessentially brutal beating. (While awaiting the ambulance, Trotsky shouted "Let him live! Let him live!" to his guards, knowing that if they killed Mercader, no one would ever know who was responsible for the attack against him.) Trotsky's wounds were fatal (although he maintained lucidity in the hospital and made several statements), and he died the following day. His wife never left his side from the moment he was attacked until the time he died.

JUDICIAL OUTCOME: Mercader was immediately arrested by Mexican police and, after a perfunctory judicial hearing in which Mercader claimed several defenses, including killing Trotsky because he was in love with Trotsky's wife, he was found guilty of premeditated murder and sentenced to 20 years in a Mexican prison. The preponderance of evidence as well as Mercader's confession made his guilt a foregone conclusion. Mercader served his sentence and, after he was released in 1960, changed his name and traveled around, ultimately returning to Havana in his mother's homeland of Cuba, where he died in 1978.

When Leon Trotsky lost the struggle for control of the Soviet Union to Joseph Stalin after Lenin's death in 1924, his death warrant was, for all intents and purposes, already written. Trotsky repeatedly challenged Stalin's authority and in 1924 in his autobiography, *My Life*, he wrote, "It was the supreme expression of the mediocrity of the apparatus that Stalin himself rose to his position."[4]

Stalin kicked Trotsky out of the Communist Party in 1927 and out of the Soviet Union in 1929. Even in exile, however, Trotsky continued to rail against Stalin, resulting in his being tried and convicted as a "heretic" *in abstentia* and, ultimately, sentenced to death.

At the time of his assassination, Trotsky was working on an enormous biography of Stalin he described as an "antibiography" called *Stalin*.

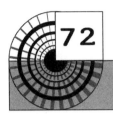

72

Harry S Truman

ASSASSINATED ____

SURVIVED ✓

A President has to expect such things.

—Harry S Truman[1]

VICTIM: Harry S Truman

BORN: May 8, 1884

DIED: December 27, 1972

AGE WHEN ATTACKED: 66

OCCUPATION: 33rd president of the United States (1945–1953)

UNSUCCESSFUL ASSASSINS: Griselio Torresola (1925–1950), 25; Oscar Collazo (1915–1994), 36; both members of the Puerto Rican Nationalist Party, a terrorist organization fighting for the independence of Puerto Rico

DATE & TIME OF ATTACK: Wednesday, November 1, 1950, approximately 2:20 p.m.

Truman

— 241 —

LOCATION OF ATTACK: Outside of Blair House on Pennsylvania Avenue in Washington, D.C., President Truman's residence while the White House was being renovated

WEAPONS: A German Luger (Torresola); a German Walther P-38 automatic pistol (Collazo)

ASSASSINATION OUTCOME: Truman was not injured. White House police officer Private Donald Birdzell, 41, was shot in both legs. Private Joseph Downs, 44, was shot three times. Private Leslie Coffelt, 40, was killed. Torresola was shot in the head and killed instantly; Collazo was shot three times. Agents Birdzell and Downs survived their wounds, as did the assassin Collazo. All told, 27 rounds were fired in less than three minutes. Torresola and Collazo had come to Blair House with a total of 69 rounds of ammunition between them.

JUDICIAL OUTCOME: Collazo survived to stand trial and was convicted on four counts, including one of murder. He was sentenced to death. President Truman commuted his sentence to life in prison. President Jimmy Carter freed Collazo in 1979. Upon his return to Puerto Rico, Collazo was hailed as a hero by the few Puerto Rican Nationalists still alive. He died in Puerto Rico in 1994 at the age of 80.

Griselio Torresola and Oscar Collazo's assassination attempt on the life of President Harry Truman was the only presidential assassination attempt solely for political reasons, and it was one of the more botched tries at killing a president.

Their motivation was freedom for Puerto Rico. Somehow, the two Puerto Rican Nationalists had concluded that the United States was oppressing their homeland and that Puerto Ricans in both Puerto Rico and America were being economically exploited and systematically discriminated against by Americans and the U.S. government.

It did not seem to matter to Torresola and Collazo that the United States had granted self-government to Puerto Rico in the 1940s, had worked diligently to eradicate diseases from the island, and even paid Puerto Ricans Social Security benefits. They felt oppressed, and they wholeheartedly believed that by assassinating Truman they would initiate a revolution in America in which the American people would rally behind the Nationalists return to power in Puerto Rico.

Misguided is too small a word to describe this idiotic ideology. They did not realize that the majority of Americans at that time quite simply did not care about Puerto Rico or the difficulties of Puerto Rican immigrants in America. Many Americans were immigrants themselves, or the descendants of immigrants, and they had worked their way up out of the slums on their own and become prosperous citizens living the American dream. Americans in 1950 would have found it ludicrous that Puerto Rican immigrants expected special treatment that would have allowed them to skip over the hardships that everyone else coming to America from a foreign land had to endure.

Nonetheless, Torresola and Collazo decided that they would kill President Truman and that this would bring liberty to their beloved island. All of the progress made in Puerto Rico with the help of the American government somehow did not seem to register with the two revolutionary zealots.

Torresola and Collazo arrived in Washington around 7:30 p.m. on October 31, 1950, and checked into the Hotel Harris separately. They pretended they did not know each other, and they both appeared well-dressed and polite.

The following morning they walked by Blair House and studied the layout. Blair House was guarded by White House Police and Secret Service agents, but its front door was only a few feet away from a highly trafficked sidewalk. Never before, nor since, has an American president been so vulnerable in his residence.

That afternoon they returned to Blair House, heavily armed, and opened fire almost immediately. After Collazo's pistol misfired on his first shot, a gun battle ensued that resembled a shoot-out in a frontier town—yet it took place on a Washington, D.C. avenue in the middle of the day.

President Truman, who was upstairs taking a nap at the time (he had a scheduled 2:50 departure for a statue dedication), was awakened by the gunfire and stood in a window looking down on the commotion. Secret Service agent Floyd Boring saw the president and shouted at him to get away from the window, and Truman obeyed. It was all over in three minutes and the president left for his afternoon appointments through the back door of Blair House as White House employees washed the mingled blood of his guards and his assassins off the sidewalk.

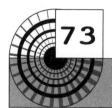

73

Gianni Versace

| ASSASSINATED | ✓ |
| SURVIVED | ___ |

Gianni Versace will be remembered, first and foremost, as a talented designer. But his legacy is greater than that: He was the first person to create a synergy between fashion and pop culture, especially Hollywood and rock-and-roll...He understood that there were no boundaries. Gianni Versace was the most unafraid person I ever met.

—Liz Tilberis[1]

VICTIM: Gianni Versace

BORN: February 2, 1946

DIED: July 15, 1997

AGE WHEN ATTACKED: 51

OCCUPATION: World-renowned fashion designer

ASSASSIN: Andrew Cunanan (1969–1997), 27, homosexual prostitute, serial killer responsible for four murders in addition to Versace's

DATE & TIME OF ATTACK: Tuesday, July 15, 1997, 8:46 a.m.

Location of Attack: On the front steps of Versace's mansion in Miami Beach, Florida

WEAPON: A .40-caliber handgun

ASSASSINATION OUTCOME: Versace was shot twice in the head and died immediately.

JUDICIAL OUTCOME: After a massive nationwide police manhunt and the placing of Cunanan on the FBI's Ten Most Wanted list, Cunanan was located on a houseboat moored two and a half miles from Versace's home. After a four-hour standoff during which Cunanan was neither heard from nor seen, police fired tear gas into the boat and then six police SWAT team members stormed the boat and found Cunanan dead from a single gunshot to the side of the head. A .40-caliber handgun similar to the one used to kill Versace was found on the boat.

Andrew Cunanan is best known for assassinating Gianni Versace, but the famous fashion designer was the fifth of the serial killer's victims. After coldly shooting two "friends" point-blank (and leaving one corpse wrapped up in a rug behind a sofa for two days), Cunanan then moved on to stranger murder, but he added torture to the mix.

Cunanan's first two slayings were for expediency, and both victims were known to him. He had had an affair with one, and the second was a witness to the initial murder.

Cunanan's third victim, however, 72-year-old realtor Lee Miglin, was just in the wrong place at the wrong time, and he paid for this happenstance with his life.

Miglin was standing in front of his townhouse in Chicago, and Cunanan zeroed in on him as his next victim—simply because he happened to be the first person the serial killer saw as he drove around town.

He forced Miglin into his garage at gunpoint, and then bound him and covered his face with duct tape, leaving only his nose exposed. Cunanan then indulged his sickest, darkest fantasies on the helpless Miglin, many of which he culled from a favorite "snuff" film called *Target for Torture.*

Cunanan then spent the night in Miglin's townhouse (his wife was away), slept in Miglin's bed, ate his food, and stole some gold coins he found.

The following morning he left in Miglin's green Lexus. The tires were probably still bloodstained for the first couple of miles.

Cunanan's fourth and final victim before Versace was a 45-year-old cemetery caretaker whom he shot in cold blood—*after* the man had willingly surrendered the keys to his truck to Cunanan.

So why did Cunanan assassinate Gianni Versace?

Cunanan did not leave a note or any other writings that would have revealed his reason or reasons, but theories about the murder abound.

One FBI theory is that Versace once turned down Cunanan for a modeling job. Cunanan was a bar-hopper, a drug-user (possibly including steroids and rage-inducing testosterone), and he often sold himself to older, wealthy men. It is now believed that Cunanan and Versace were never involved sexually, but it is known that the two men had met at least once.

Miami Beach Police documents released after Versace's death revealed that the fashion designer and his lover, Antonio D'Amico, regularly hired male prostitutes for orgies. Because Cunanan was often involved in these kinds of "sex for hire" parties with affluent older men, it was thought at first that he may have been scorned by Versace for one reason or another and sought to exact revenge by killing him.

An unnamed Versace employee, quoted in the gay newspaper *The Advocate*, admitted that he often hired hookers for his boss and D'Amico but insisted that Cunanan had never been considered because "he wasn't their type."[2]

It is known that Cunanan stalked Versace before he killed him, often walking the same routes, sometimes following him.

The morning of the shooting, Versace left his house to walk to the News Café on Ocean Drive, where he had his favorite gourmet coffee and picked up several newspapers and magazines. When he arrived back at his home on 11th Street, Cunanan walked up behind him and fired two shots into the back of Versace's head, killing him instantly.

He then fled, and the case wasn't closed until Cunanan's dead body was found eight days later on a houseboat owned by a friend of Cunanan's who was in Germany at the time.

The outpouring of grief following Versace's murder spanned the globe. Elton John, one of Versace's closest friends, was seen openly weeping at his funeral and being comforted by Princess Diana. Sales of Versace suits, dresses, and accessories jumped around the world. Bloomingdales in New York reported daily increases of 200 to 300 percent in Versace apparel and other items.

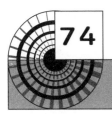

74

George Wallace

ASSASSINATED   ___

SURVIVED   ✓

Somebody's going to get me one of these days. I can just see a little guy out there that nobody's paying any attention to. He reaches into his pocket and out comes the little gun, like that Sirhan guy that got Kennedy.

—George Wallace[1]

VICTIM: George Wallace

BORN: August 25, 1919

DIED: September 13, 1998

AGE WHEN ATTACKED: 52

OCCUPATION: Governor of Alabama, vying for the Democratic presidential nomination at the time of the shooting, racial segregationist, notorious for denying two black students access to the University of Alabama until President Kennedy called in the National Guard

UNSUCCESSFUL ASSASSIN: Arthur Herman Bremer (b. 1950), 21

DATE & TIME OF ATTACK: Monday, May 15, 1972, 4 p.m.

LOCATION OF ATTACK: In a shopping center in Laurel, Maryland, between a drive-in bank and a variety store during a political rally. Wallace was shaking hands at a rope line when Bremer pushed through the crowd and fired point-blank at him.

WEAPON: A .38-caliber Charter Arms snub-nose revolver. Bremer had paid $80 for the gun at Casanova Guns on January 13, 1972.

ASSASSINATION OUTCOME: George Wallace usually wore a bulletproof vest when he was in public, but the hot and humid weather of May 15, 1972, convinced him to forego the vest—just this one time. Wallace was struck by four of Bremer's .38-caliber bullets. One of the bullets lodged "within the spinal canal, between the bony structure of the spinal column and the spinal cord."[2] Wallace's 12th thoracic intercostal nerve, the nerve that controls feeling and movement on the right side of the body below the waist, was damaged. Tests of Wallace's spinal fluid—which is supposed to be perfectly clear—revealed blood. This injury resulted in Wallace losing all control of his legs, his bowel, his bladder, and his sexual functioning for the rest of his life. He would also suffer intractable pain that would not be alleviated by drugs or surgery. Another of Bremer's bullets struck Wallace in the abdomen, perforating his stomach and large intestine; this bullet was surgically removed. Much of Wallace's still-undigested lunch spilled into his abdominal cavity, however, and later caused several infections. Bullet wounds to his right arm, right shoulder, and left shoulder blade were surgically repaired. Three others were also wounded by Bremer's bullets: Secret Service Agent Nicholas Zarvos suffered a throat wound; a local Wallace volunteer named Dorothy Thompson was shot in the right leg; and Alabama State Trooper Eldred C. Dothard was shot in the stomach. All survived their injuries.

JUDICIAL OUTCOME: Bremer was immediately apprehended by the crowd and the police, and shouts of "Get him!" and "Get that bastard!" were heard. According to an article in *The New York Times,* "[S]ome pummeling ensued."[3] Bremer was taken to Hyattsville jail and then to Leland Hospital for treatment of head lacerations sustained while he was being restrained. He was held on $200,000 bond. Bremer requested and was granted a lawyer from the American Civil Liberties Union. He was charged with four counts of assault with intent to murder, four counts of assault and battery, four counts of using a gun in a felony, and one count of illegally transporting a gun into Maryland. On August 4, 1972, a jury found him guilty after deliberating only 90 minutes, and he was sentenced to 63 years in prison. He is currently incarcerated at the Maryland Correctional Institute and, if he serves his full sentence, he will be a very old man when he is released.

In 1971, Arthur Bremer was demoted from being a busboy to working in the kitchen at the Milwaukee Athletic Club because the patrons complained that he talked to himself.

In 1972, he almost shot himself in a hotel room when the gun he was planning to use to shoot Richard Nixon accidentally discharged.

While constructing his plot to assassinate George Wallace, Bremer decided he needed a "cute phrase" to shout out after he emptied his gun into the Alabama governor, something with the gravitas of "Sic semper tyrannis!" ("Thus be it ever to tyrants!"), which had been shouted by John Wilkes Booth after he shot Abraham Lincoln (page 142.) Bremer's choice? "A penny for your thoughts." He never managed to shout it after the shooting, however.

Bremer had a troubled, alienated childhood, and he seems to have been the textbook definition of a loner. He had no friends in school, he felt isolated, he believed he was always being laughed at, and his attempt to lose his virginity to a prostitute before shooting Wallace never happened.

After deciding to kill Wallace, he followed him from rally to rally until May 15, 1972. Wallace finished a political speech from behind a bulletproof podium in a shopping center and then stepped down off the stage. He decided to shake some hands and sign some autographs, and he removed his suit coat and began to move down the rope line. As he smiled and greeted his supporters, a young man with blonde hair and a pasty complexion repeatedly shouted, "George! Over here! Over here!"

Wallace obeyed the shouted request and walked over to where Arthur Bremer stood in the crowd, wearing red, white, and blue clothing and a George Wallace pin on his shirt.

Within seconds, Wallace was on his back on the asphalt and Bremer was being restrained by the police and the crowd.

George Wallace died in 1998 after enduring a quarter-decade of immobility and excruciating pain, thanks to Arthur Bremer.

After hundreds of days in the hospital and dozens of surgeries, Wallace re-entered the political world, but he had lost any hope of every winning the presidency. In his later years Wallace denounced his earlier racist, segregationist views and became a born-again Christian. Ironically, after his redemption, the black vote played an enormous role in getting him re-elected governor of Alabama four times.

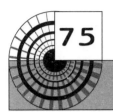

75

Andy Warhol

Assassinated	___
Survived	✓

No, no, Valerie! Don't do it!
—Andy Warhol[1]

I guess it was just being in the wrong place at the right time. That's what assassination is all about.

—Andy Warhol[2]

VICTIM: Andy Warhol, born Andrew Warhola

BORN: April 6, 1928[3]

DIED: February 22, 1987

AGE WHEN ATTACKED: 40

OCCUPATION: Artist, filmmaker

UNSUCCESSFUL ASSASSIN: Valerie Solanas (April 9, 1936–April 26, 1988), 32, actress and writer

DATE & TIME OF ATTACK: Monday, June 3, 1968, 4:20 p.m.

LOCATION OF ATTACK: Warhol's film studio, The Factory, 33 Union Square West in New York City

WEAPONS: A .32-caliber automatic; .22 revolver (not used)

ASSASSINATION OUTCOME: Warhol was seriously wounded and hospitalized for close to a month, but he survived. It took him almost a year to fully recuperate.

JUDICIAL OUTCOME: Solanas surrendered to police, expressed no remorse ("I was right in what I did! I have nothing to regret!"), refused legal counsel, and, after a comprehensive psychiatric examination, was committed to Bellevue Hospital in New York on August 16, 1968. She never stood trial for shooting Andy Warhol.

The ambulance driver that transported Andy Warhol to the emergency room charged him 15 dollars to turn on the siren.

Minutes later, at Columbus Hospital, Andy was declared dead.

Valerie Solanas hated men. Many who have studied her life look to the sexual and physical abuse inflicted upon her as a child by male relatives as the reasons *why* she hated men: She was sexually molested by her father and repeatedly beaten by her grandfather, and this, indeed, can be considered a valid rationalization of her male loathing. But Valerie Solanas was also mentally unstable. Her 1967 *SCUM Manifesto* (SCUM was an acronym for the fictitious group, the Society for Cutting Up Men—Solanas was apparently its only member) is a vivid example of her bizarre and irrational thought processes. In the following excerpt from *The SCUM Manifesto*, note how easily her first paragraph can be interpreted as deliberately satirical, which is often a sign of someone seriously out of touch with reality:

Life in this society being, at best, an utter bore and no aspect of society being at all relevant to women, there remains to civic-minded, responsible, thrill-seeking females only to overthrow the government, eliminate the money system, institute complete automation, and destroy the male sex.

After rooting for the complete elimination of men, Solanas goes on to verbally decimate the species:

[T]he male is an incomplete female, a walking abortion...[t]o be male is to be deficient, emotionally limited; maleness is a deficiency disease and males are emotional cripples...The male is completely egocentric, trapped inside himself, incapable of empathizing or identifying with others, or love, friendship, affection of tenderness. He is a completely isolated unit, incapable of rapport with anyone. His responses are entirely visceral, not cerebral; his intelligence is a mere tool in the services of his drives and needs; he is incapable of mental passion, mental interaction; he can't relate to anything other than

his own physical sensations. He is a half-dead, unresponsive lump, incapable of giving or receiving pleasure or happiness; consequently, he is at best an utter bore, an inoffensive blob, since only those capable of absorption in others can be charming.

Such nonsense can easily be written off as one of the unfortunate side effects of the First Amendment, but, as do many psychopaths, Solanas took her paranoid ranting to the next level and acted on her misguided hatred.

Late in the afternoon on Monday, June 6, 1968, Andy Warhol and his boyfriend, Jed Johnson, arrived at Warhol's film studio, The Factory, to find Valerie Solanas, an actress who had appeared in Warhol's 1967 movie, *I, a Man*, waiting for him outside. Solanas had been hanging around outside the front of the building all day, and the two men thought nothing of her following them into the building and taking the elevator upstairs to Warhol's offices. Later, Warhol and others who were in the office on the day of the shooting recalled little things about Solanas that might have triggered some suspicion, but that, unfortunately, did not. Solanas bounced nervously on her feet in the elevator; she wore a heavy sweater and a coat in warm weather; she had put on makeup and combed her hair (genuinely odd behavior for Solanas, who never bought into society's view of what was feminine and attractive on a woman); and, most ominously, she carried a brown paper bag.

Shortly after they entered the offices, Solanas pulled a .32-caliber automatic pistol out of the bag and began shooting. She shot at Warhol three times, hitting him once; she shot at art curator Mario Amaya twice, hitting him once; and she shot once at Warhol employee Fred Hughes, but the gun jammed. She then fled, leaving Warhol bleeding and in agony on the floor beneath his desk. It took 15 minutes for emergency medical personnel to arrive, and it was 23 minutes from the time Warhol was shot until he got to the hospital.

Solanas's third bullet had entered Warhol's right side, passed through his right lung, and then tore through his esophagus, gall bladder, liver, spleen, and intestines. The bullet exited his body on his left side, and he was in surgery almost six hours to repair the damage. At 4:51 p.m., 29 minutes after the shooting, while lying on a table in the operating room, Andy Warhol was pronounced clinically dead, but the doctors did not stop working on him, and, even though he was dead for one and a half minutes, they managed to pull him through.

At 8:00 that evening, as doctors worked desperately to repair the terrible damage Valerie Solanas had done to Andy Warhol's body, the man-hating feminist walked up to a 22-year-old rookie cop in Times Square and surrendered. "The police are looking for me and want me," she told him as she pulled the two handguns out of her pockets.

Solanas was arrested and booked on charges of felonious assault and possession of a deadly weapon. The police waited through the night for word of Warhol's survival—or death. They would charge Solanas with murder if Warhol died, but he did not, and she showed up for arraignment the following day defiant and insisting on representing herself. The judge ordered a psychiatric examination, and Solanas was ultimately found to be incapable of standing trial and was committed to a mental institution.

Upon her release, she moved to California, turned tricks to survive, and died in a homeless shelter of pneumonia and emphysema in 1988.

Warhol returned home on June 28 and, after a lengthy recovery, returned to creating art. He died in 1987 of a heart attack following successful gallbladder surgery.

Warhol's art is now neatly ordered into two schools, pre-shooting and post-shooting. He was enormously affected by dying and being brought back to life, and many art critics see profound thematic changes in his works from 1968 until his death in 1987.

Afterword

Death by Design

"Assassin" is an umbrella term for an individual, a group, or a government that uses murder to advance its agenda. This agenda can be blatantly insane (obsession, delusion), sociological (racial, religious, ethnic), or purely political (regime change).

It has been rumored that almost every government on earth has, at one time or another, conducted clandestine assassinations. These "terminations with great prejudice" (intelligence code for killings) don't usually make the papers. The assassinations and assassination attempts that do make the news and get wall-to-wall coverage on CNN are the highly visible, public attempts in which a celebrity or a political figure is targeted during an event in which he or she is visible and accessible.

What conclusions can we draw from a review of the 75 assassinations or attempts covered in *In the Crosshairs*? Only one: There is no way to predict or prevent as assassination if the assassin is committed to the act. American presidents have long known—and often admitted publicly—that if someone wants to get them, he or she will. Thus, the often rabid attention to security for high-profile people.

Assassination is unlike other types of murder, many of which occur in a moment of passion or during the commission of a crime. Assassinations are *planned*. They are thought through and, in many cases, they are successful. This simple fact leads inexorably to the fatalistic view held by American presidents—and explains why the Pope now rides with a bulletproof bubble over his vehicle and why no American president has ridden in an open vehicle since 1962.

Appendix

Weapons of Choice

In parentheses following the weapon is the name of the victim. Almost all assassins turn to a firearm of some sort for their nefarious acts, although knives do make an appearance now and then, usually when a killer sees their mission as personal. (Note: If a caliber is not given for a gun, it is because this detail was not found in any of the literature or media reports about the assassination or the attempt).

Handguns

.22-caliber Iver Johnson Cadet revolver (Robert F. Kennedy)

.22-caliber revolver (Andy Warhol)

.22-caliber revolver (Richard Nixon)

.22-caliber Rohm R6-14 revolver loaded with exploding Devastator bullets (Ronald Reagan)

.32-caliber automatic pistol (Andy Warhol)

.32-caliber Browning semi-automatic pistol (Huey Long)

.32-caliber Iver Johnson Revolver (William McKinley)

.32-caliber revolver (Franklin Delano Roosevelt)

.357 Magnum revolver loaded with expanding hollow-point bullets (Rebecca Schaeffer)

.36-caliber 1851 Colt Navy cap and ball plack powder single action pistol (Wild Bill Hickok)

.38-caliber Charter Arms snub-nose revolver (George Wallace)

.38-caliber Colt Cobra snub-nose revolver (Lee Harvey Oswald)

.38-caliber Colt revolver (Theodore Roosevelt)

.38-caliber handgun (Haing Ngor)

.38-caliber revolver (Harvey Milk)

.38-caliber Smith and Wesson revolver (Gerald Ford)

.40-caliber handgun (Gianni Versace)

.44-caliber British Bulldog revolver (James Garfield)

.44-caliber Bulldog revolver (John Lennon)

.44-caliber Derringer (Abraham Lincoln)

.44-caliber Smith & Wesson No. 3 nickel-plated revolver with a 6 1/2-inch (Jesse James)

.45-caliber automatic pistol (Malcolm X)

.45-caliber Colt semi-automatic pistol (Gerald Ford)

9-millimeter Beretta pistol loaded with fragmenting dumdum bullets (Yitzhak Rabin)

9-millimeter Browning semi-automatic pistol (Pope John Paul II)

Beretta 7-chamber automatic pistol (Mohandas Gandhi)

Browning automatic pistol (Archduke Franz Ferdinand)

Browning pistol (Vladimir Lenin)

Browning revolver (Rasputin)

Derringer single-shot dueling pistols (2) (Andrew Jackson)

German Luger pistol (Harry S Truman)

German Luger pistol (Malcolm X)

German Walther P-38 automatic pistol (Harry S Truman)

Handgun (Jimmy Carter)

Pistol (Henry Clay Frick)

Pistol (Herbert Hoover)

Pistol with a silencer (Thomas Dewey)

Revolver (Indira Gandhi)

Smith & Wesson revolver (Phil Hartman)

Rifles · Shotguns · Machine Guns

.22-caliber hunting rifle (Jacques Chirac)

.30-06-caliber Enfield rifle with telescopic sight (Medgar Evers)

.30-06-caliber Remington 700 rifle (Vernon Jordan)

.30-06-caliber Remington 760 Gamemaster pump rifle with a Redfield 2 x 7 telescopic sight (Martin Luther King, Jr.)

.44-caliber rifle (Larry Flynt)

.45-caliber semi-automatic machine gun (Alan Berg)

12-gauge double-barreled shotgun (Malcolm X)

6.5-mm bolt-action Mannlicher-Carcano carbine (John F. Kennedy)

6.5-mm bolt-action Mannlicher-Carcano carbine (John Connally)

Aircraft-mounted artillery (Winston Churchill)

AK-47 assault rifles (Anwar el-Sadat)

AK-47 assault rifles (Hosni Mubarak)

AR-15 assault rifle with telescopic sight (Jesse Jackson)

Firearms (Jefferson Davis)

Machine guns (Charles De Gaulle)

Mauser semi-automatic rifle (George Lincoln Rockwell)

Mossberg pump-action shotgun (Bill Clinton)

Norinco semi-automatic rifle (Bill Clinton)

Sawed-off shotgun (Hubert Humphrey)

Sten submachine gun (Indira Gandhi)

Submachine guns (Anwar el-Sadat)

Thompson submachine guns (Leon Trotsky)

Knives

Bowie knife (Andrew Johnson)

Bowie knife, 10 inches long (William Henry Seward)

Dagger (Henry Clay Frick)

Dagger, 12 inches long (Imelda Marcos)

Daggers (Julius Caesar)

Hunting knife (Theresa Saldana)

Knife (Hosni Mubarak)

Knife (Jean-Paul Marat)

Knife, 6 inches long (George Harrison)

Knife, described as "heavy" (Sal Mineo)

Malayan kris (dagger) with a wavy, double-edged blade hidden inside a crucifix (Pope Paul VI)

Poniard dagger (Christopher Marlowe)

Serrated boning knife, 9 inches long (Monica Seles)

Miscellaneous

100-pound gelginite bomb (Margaret Thatcher)

110-pound time bomb (Adolf Hitler)

2-pound bomb (Adolf Hitler)

50-pound bomb detonated by remote control (Lord Mountbatten)

Blackjack (Rasputin)

Bombs (Hosni Mubarak)

Brass finger-knuckles (Rasputin)

Butane bombs (Charles De Gaulle)

Camera tripod (Bob Crane)

Fireplace poker (Germaine Greer)

Gasoline bomb (Richard Nixon)

Grenade loaded with nails and pieces of lead and iron (Archduke Franz Ferdinand).

Hand grenades (Anwar el-Sadat)

Ice axe (Leon Trotsky)

Incendiary, Molotov cocktail-type bomb (Leon Trotsky)

Plastic explosives (Charles De Gaulle)

Poisoned mushrooms (Claudius)

Poisoned needle (Alexander Solzhenitsyn)

Potassium cyanide (Rasputin)

Rocket-propelled grenades (Hosni Mubarak)

Swords (Thomas á Beckett)

Time bomb (Adolf Hitler)

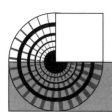

Endnotes

Sic Semper Famous
[1] *Shewing up of Blanco Posnet* (1911), "Limits to Toleration."
[2] *Time*, September 15, 1975.

1. Thomas á Beckett
[1] This description of Thomas á Beckett by Robert of Cricklade comes from the *Icelandic Saga*, circa 1145–1150. (*www.newadvent.org/cathen/14676a.htm*)
[2] After Thomas's assassination, the FitzUrse family was so mortified by the actions of their kin that they reportedly changed their name to Bearham (using the "Urse" component of the surname; "Urse" is Old English for "bear"), which was eventually shortened to Barham, which is now the name of a village near Canterbury.
[3] This comment has also been reported as "Who will rid me of this lowborn priest?!" and "Who will rid me of this turbulent priest?!"

2. Alan Berg
[1] *Chicago Sun–Times*, December 21, 1988.

3. Julius Caesar
[1] From *Julius Caesar* by William Shakespeare, Act 3, Scene 2.

4. Jimmy Carter
[1] *Newsweek*, May 24, 1982.

5. Fidel Castro
[1] BBC News: "Castro: the Great Survivor," October 19, 2000. (news.bbc.co.uk/hi/english/world/americas/newsid_244000/244974.stm)
[2] BBC News: "Country Profile: Cuba," April 25, 2002. (news.bbc.co.uk/hi/english/world/americas/country_profiles/newsid_1203000/1203299.stm)
[3] BBC News: "Castro: the Great Survivor," October 19, 2000. (news.bbc.co.uk/hi/english/world/americas/newsid_244000/244974.stm)

6. Jacques Chirac
[1] Nicolas Couteau, a spokesman for Force Ouvriere, a French police union, made this statement shortly after the gunman was taken into custody. United Press International, Sunday, July 14, 2002.
[2] BBC News, July 15, 2002.
[3] Associated Press, July 14, 2002.

7. Winston Churchill
[1] Address to the British House of Commons, June 4, 1940.

8. Claudius
[1] *Caligula*, Chapter 30.
[2] Agrippina enlisted the aid of Halotus, the Imperial Taster, and Locusta, the resident expert poisoner.
[3] Some historical accounts state that Claudius was killed when his doctor stuck a poisoned feather down his throat. Feathers were commonly used to induce vomiting back in the orgiastic days of ancient Rome, and Agrippina may have poisoned the doctor's feather when she knew Claudius would request a vomiting session. There are also accounts of Claudius being given a poisonous enema by a physician in on the plot after getting sick and summoning a doctor.

9. Bill Clinton
[1] *New York Times*, October 30, 1994. President Clinton said this at the annual dinner of the National Italian–American Federation on the evening of October 29, 1994. He had just returned from a trip to the Middle East where he had been constantly threatened by terrorists, and, as soon as he returned, a gunman fired at the White House.

10. John Connally
[1] From an interview with Connally from his hospital bed by Martin Agronsky of NBC, published in *The New York Times* on Thursday, November 28, 1963, p. 23.
[2] *The Warren Report on the Assassination of President John F. Kennedy*. Washington, D.C.: U.S. Government Printing Office, 1964.
[3] Ibid.
[4] Ibid.

11. Bob Crane
[1] The Greensboro, North Carolina *News & Record*, November 1, 1994.
[2] *People*, November 14, 1994.
[3] *Arizona Republic*, November 13, 1994.
[4] Ibid.
[5] Quoted in the *Phoenix New Times*, September 10, 1998.
[6] *People*, November 14, 1994.
[7] *Variety*, July 18, 2002.
[8] The Internet Movie Database (*www.imdb.com*).

12. Jefferson Davis
[1] Jefferson Davis's Farewell Address in the Senate Chamber in the U.S. Capitol, January 21, 1861.
[2] Ibid. Davis said, "I rise, Mr. President, for the purpose of announcing to the Senate that I have satisfactory evidence that the State of Mississippi, by a solemn ordinance of her people in convention assembled, has declared her separation from the United States... It is known to Senators who have served with me here, that I have for many years advocated, as an essential attribute of State sovereignty, the right of a State to secede from the Union. Therefore, if I had not believed there was justifiable cause; if I had thought that Mississippi was acting without sufficient provocation, or without an existing necessity, I should still, under my theory of the Government, because of my allegiance to the State of which I am a citizen, have been bound by her action. I, however, may be permitted to say that I do think she has justifiable cause, and I approve of her act."
[3] *Richmond Examiner*, March 5, 1864.

[4] Ibid.

[5] "Civil War Richmond" (*www.mdgorman.com*).

13. Charles De Gaulle

[1] From a widely reproduced 1952 speech.

[2] Henry C. Pinkham, Columbia University, quoted in the *New York Review of Books*, December 20, 1990.

[3] Don Cook, *Charles De Gaulle: A Biography*, p. 417.

[4] Ibid., pp. 417–18.

14. Thomas Dewey

[1] Schultz shouted this at mob boss Louis Lepke when Lepke tried to talk Schultz out of killing Dewey. Quoted in Jay Robert Nash, *Bloodletters and Badmen*, p. 107.

[2] Richard H. Smith, *Thomas E. Dewey and His Times*, p. 167.

[3] Smith, p. 169.

[4] Smith, p. 174.

15. Medgar Evers

[1] From a 1958 speech to the Milwaukee branch of the NAACP, reproduced in *Of Long Memory* by Adam Nossiter, p. 52.

[2] Evers said this during in an interview in his office on June 2, 1963, 10 days before he was assassinated. The quote appeared in *The New York Times* on June 13, 1963, p. 12.

[3] Jim Crow laws enforced strict segregation and legally treated blacks as inferior, second-class citizens.

[4] *The Economist*, February 12, 1994, Vol. 330, Issue 7850, p 27.

[5] *The New York Times*, June 13, 1963, p. 12.

[6] Adam Nossiter, *Of Long Memory*, p. 35.

[7] Ibid.

16. Louis Farrakhan

[1] *Meet The Press* interview, October 1998.

[2] *The Final Call*, May 15, 2000.

[3] *Philadelphia Inquirer*, March 2000.

[4] Saviours' Day speech, Chicago, February 1998.

[5] Boston speech, August 1997.

17. Archduke Franz Ferdinand

[1] Quoted in *David Wallechinsky's Twentieth Century*, p. 140.

[2] *The New York World*, June 29, 1924.

[3] *The London Daily News & Leader*, June 29, 1914, p. 1.

[4] Jevtic, *New York World*.

[5] *The London Daily News & Leader*, June 29, 1914, p. 1.

[6] *David Wallechinsky's Twentieth Century*, p. 142.

[7] Carl Sifakis, *The Encyclopedia of Assassinations*, p. 64.

18. Larry Flynt

[1] From his autobiography, *An Unseemly Man*.

[2] *New Times* (Los Angeles), October 24, 1996.

[3] *www.serialkillercentral.com*

[4] *New York Times*, February 16, 1977, pp. 40–41.

19. Gerald Ford

[1] Judith St. George, *In the Line of Fire*, p. 124.

[2] Fromme was given the nickname "Squeaky" by Manson himself because of her tiny, high-pitched voice.

[3] *American Heritage Dictionary*.

[4] Oliver Sipple was a gay man who had kept his sexual identity a secret from his family. After his courageous act, which probably saved President Ford's life, Sipple was inadvertently

"outed" by openly gay politician Harvey Milk (Chapter 49), who, when talking about Sipple to a reporter said, "It shows that *we* do good things" [emphasis added]. A few weeks after the shooting, President Ford sent Sipple a brief note, writing, "I want you to know how much I appreciated your selfless actions last Monday. The events were a shock to us all, but you acted quickly and without fear for your own safety. By doing so, you helped to avert danger to me and to others in the crowd. You have my heartfelt appreciation." By this time, though, Sipple's sexual orientation had been made public, and the exposure began to take its toll on Sipple. He slipped into alcoholism and drug use and gained a great deal of weight. Sipple was found dead in his apartment in February 1989. Although he had a pacemaker and was experiencing breathing difficulties in the month before his death, it is believed he committed suicide. President and Mrs. Ford sent a sympathy card.

5 *New York Times*, December 13, 1975.
6 *New York Times*, September 23, 1975.

20. Henry Clay Frick
1 Diary entry, quoted in Mathew Josephson, *The Robber Barons*.
2 Goldman was also questioned following the assassination of William McKinley (Chapter 48) and is notorious for expressing no remorse when she learned that he had died.
3 Harper's Weekly, July 30, 1892.

4 Alexander Berkman, *Prison Memoirs of an Anarchist*.

21. Indira Gandhi
1 Inder Malhotra, *Indira Gandhi: Personal and Political Biography*, p. 17. Indian security authorities detained Ustinov and his team because they were afraid the camera crew had filmed the assassination. They had not, and they were eventually allowed to leave.
2 No relation to Mohandas Gandhi (Chapter 22).
3 No relation to Beant Singh.
4 *The New York Times*, November 1, 1984, p. A18.
5 *Time*, November 11, 1985, Vol. 126, No. 19, p. 55.

22. Mohandas Gandhi
1 Gandhi said this on January 28, 1948, two days before his assassination. Quoted on the Official Mahatma Gandhi eArchive. (*www.mahatma.org*)
2 From a February 14, 2000 Web-only interview on Time.com. (*www.time.com/time/asia/magazine/2000/0214/india.godse.html*)
3 J.C. Jain, *The Murder of Mahatma Gandhi*.

23. James Garfield
1 From a letter Charles Guiteau wrote to Union General William Tecumseh Sherman after he was arrested for shooting James Garfield, quoted in *The Evil 100* by Martin Gilman Wolcott, p. 306.
2 Martin Gilman Wolcott, *The Evil 100*, p. 305.
3 James C. Clark, *The Murder of James A. Garfield: The President's Last Days and the Trial and Execution of His Assassin*.

[4] Theodore Clark Smith, *The Life and Letters of James Abram Garfield, Volume 2: 1877–1882*, p. 1200.

24. Germaine Greer

[1] BBC News, April 27, 2000.
[2] BBC News, July 4, 2000.
[3] Ibid.
[4] Ibid.

25. George Harrison

[1] Quoted in the *New York Times*, December 31, 1999.
[2] Quoted in "A Hard Day's Night" by Steve Dougherty in *People*, January 17, 2000.
[3] The *New York Times*, December 31, 1999.
[4] Ibid.

26. Phil Hartman

[1] From a June 1998 interview with Hooks by David Bianculli. (*www.saturday-night-live.com*) The interview originally appeared in the *New York Daily News*.
[2] Quoted on CNN.com, June 2, 1998.
[3] *The New York Times*, May 28, 1998.
[4] *Newsweek*, June 8, 1998.

27. Wild Bill Hickok

[1] Thadd Turner, "The First Trial." (*www.heartofdeadwood.com/ Interpretive/firsttrial.htm*)
[2] Joseph C. Rosa, *Wild Bill Hickok: The Man & His Myth*, p. 195.

28. Adolf Hitler

[1] Michael C. Thomsett, *The German Opposition to Hitler*, p. 3.
[2] As ranked in Martin Gilman Wolcott's *The Evil 100*.
[3] Thomsett, p. 101.

29. Herbert Hoover

[1] Carl Sifakis, *Encyclopedia of Assassinations*, p. 189.

[2] *American Spectator*, "A Date Which Should Live in Irony," February 1999, Vol. 32, Issue 2, p. 71.

30. Hubert Humphrey

[1] Quoted in *Second Choice* (1966) by Michael V. DiSalle.

31. Andrew Jackson

[1] James Parton, *Life of Jackson*, Vol. III, Ch. 35.

32. Jesse Jackson

[1] From his speech at the Democratic National Convention, July 16, 1984.
[2] Jackson's "Reverend" title is not honorary. Jesse Jackson earned his Master of Divinity degree at the Chicago Theological Seminary and is an ordained Baptist minister.

33. Jesse James

[1] Tuesday, April 18, 1882, p. 1.
[2] Sources differ on precisely what this framed picture showed. Various reports include a painting of a racehorse, the death scene of Stonewall Jackson, and a sampler that read "In God We Trust."
[3] Carl W. Breihan, *The Day Jesse James Was Killed*, p. 175.

34. Andrew Johnson

[1] *www.surratt.org*
[2] There is some disagreement in the literature about the year in which Atzerodt was born. Some sources state 1830; one source stated 1842. 1832 is the most commonly used.
[3] *www.surratt.org*
[4] Ibid.
[5] Ibid.
[6] Ibid. Doster's contention notwithstanding, John Wilkes Booth did, indeed, assign Atzerodt the duty of assassinating Johnson. Doster's

argument—that his client was such a well-known coward that no one in their right (murderous) mind would have given him a job requiring backbone—is bold, indeed. It didn't work, but it was a daring defense approach.

35. Vernon Jordan
1 *www.igc.org/laborquotes/politics.html*
2 *The New York Times*, May 30, 1980, p. 1.
3 *The New York Times*, October 30, 1980, p. 16.

36. Edward Kennedy
1 Speech to the U.S. Senate, February 17, 1971.

37. John F. Kennedy
1 This was Lyndon Johnson's first public statement after being sworn in as president following the death of President John F. Kennedy.
2 Gerald Posner, *Case Closed*, p. 292.
3 Dallas and Parkland hospital officials at first refused to allow the Presidential contingent to remove President Kennedy's body from Texas. His murder had been committed in Dallas and, thus, Dallas had jurisdiction for the autopsy and other matters concerning his corpse. This was quickly overruled by the new president, Lyndon Johnson, and one of the Dallas doctors, Dr. Charles Crenshaw, claimed in his 1992 book, *JFK: Conspiracy of Silence*, that Secret Service agents drew their weapons and physically removed the President's casket from the hospital over the protests of the Dallas officials. (Charles Crenshaw, *JFK:*

Conspiracy of Silence, pp. 118–19.)
4 *Report of the House Select Committee on Assassinations*, quoted in Posner, p. 308.

38. Robert Kennedy
1 From Edward Kennedy's eulogy for his brother, given at St. Patrick's Cathedral on June 8, 1968.
2 Jay David Andrews, *Young Kennedys: The New Generation*, p. 9.
3 *Newsweek*, June 12, 1995, Volume 125, Issue 24, p. 32.

39. Martin Luther King
1 This excerpt is from a prophetic speech given by Dr. King at the Mason Street Temple in Memphis, Tennessee, on April 3, 1968, the night before he was assassinated. Quoted in *David Wallechinsky's Twentieth Century*, p. 155.

40. Vladimir Lenin
1 Lenin's lieutenant Yakov Sverdlov issued this decree, giving de facto permission for a mass slaughter to take place.
2 Craig Sifakis, *Encyclopedia of Assassinations*, p. 124.

41. John Lennon
1 Various contemporary December 1980 news reports (newspapers, magazines, and so on) were consulted for this chapter.

42. Abraham Lincoln
1 Martin Gilman Wolcott, *The Evil 100*, p. 299.
2 From the play *Our American Cousin*, Act III, Scene 2, spoken by the character Asa Trenchard, played on April 14, 1865 by actor Harry Hawk.
3 From the doctor's 1909 account of his attempts to save the president,

quoted in *Kennedy and Lincoln: Medical and Ballistic Comparisons of Their Assassinations* by John K. Lattimer.

4 Dr. Joseph K. Barnes, Surgeon General of the United States Army, quoted in *Kennedy and Lincoln: Medical and Ballistic comparisons of Their Assassinations*, by John K. Lattimer, p. 38.

5 Ibid.

6 Witness Clara Harris, quoted in *Lincoln*, by David Herbert Donald, p. 597.

7 *Encyclopedia Americana*, Vol. 17, p. 513.

43. Huey P. Long

1 From a 1927 Huey Long speech, quoted in *Huey Long* by T. Harry Williams.

2 Long's self-proclaimed nickname, after the character on the radio show *Amos 'n' Andy,* which is now considered to be racially offensive. (Long used to answer his phone by saying, "This is the Kingfish.") It is unlikely a politician would deliberately choose such an epithet as his nickname these days.

3 *American History Illustrated*, July/ August 1993, Vol. 28, Issue 3.

4 Ibid.

44. Malcolm X

1 This is from Malcolm's X's seminal "The Ballot or the Bullet" speech, which he delivered on April 13, 1964, 10 months before his assassination. This speech has been ranked by academics, historians, and rhetoric experts as one of the 10 greatest American speeches of all time. (See *The USA Book of Lists* (Career Press, 2000) by Stephen J. Spignesi

for details on these 10 greatest speeches.)

2 Lee Davis, *Assassinations*, p. 97.

3 *www.biography.com*

45. Jean-Paul Marat

1 *Déclaration des Droits de l'homme*, April 24, 1973, Ch. 19.

46. Imelda Marcos

1 *People Weekly*, July 29, 1996, Vol. 46, p. 75.

47. Christopher Marlowe

1 This excerpt is from original court documents pertaining to Marlowe's murder, discovered by Dr. J. Leslie Hotson, and published in his book, *The Death of Christopher Marlowe.*

2 John Bakeless, in *The Tragicall History of Christopher Marlowe*, writes that "Frizer was a swindler by whose schemes Sir Thomas [Walsingham—Marlowe's patron] seems at least once to have profited. Poley was an adulterer and spy. Skeres seems to have been a jackal for both." (p. 183)

3 In a letter to author Samuel Tannebaum (*The Assassination of Christopher Marlowe (A New View)*), Professor W.G. MacCallum, head of the Pathology Department at John Hopkins University, wrote, "I should think that a wound such as you described...would hardly have gone further than through the frontal sinus and into the frontal lobe of the cerebrum and I don't see how it caused instant death. Of course, one might imagine that the force of the blow was such as to stun him and allow time for fatal hemorrhage in that position. The only other thing one could think of would be perhaps that

with extreme violence some further injury might have been produced in a more vital part of the brain, but on the whole it seems to me questionable that instant death would follow such a blow."

[4] It should also be noted that at least one source (*The Theatrical Intelligencer*, 1788, cited in Bakeless, p. 150) describes Bull's house as a "brothel." If this were true, it would explain the men's ease of access to the place, although there is no mention of prostitutes being present on the day of the assassination.

48. William McKinley

[1] *Speeches and Addresses of William McKinley*, p. 537.

[2] A comment McKinley made to some friends in Canton, Ohio, in August 1901, a few days before his assassination, quoted in *World Almanac of Presidential Quotation*, p. 16.

[3] Emma Goldman was questioned at length following McKinley's shooting and, although she defended his actions and expressed no sadness when told of the president's death, there was never any connection found between Czolgosz and Goldman. Apparently, he was a follower from a distance and, even though he had actually met Goldman at a lecture, she claimed no knowledge of him when she was brought in for questioning after Czolgosz told police he supported her policies. Two years after McKinley's death, laws were enacted that forbade avowed anarchists from living in the United States. In 1919, federal authorities used this law to deport Goldman back to Russia.

[4] Charles Olcott, *The Life of William McKinley*, pp. 265–66.

[5] It should be noted that the speed of judicial resolution of this case is a far cry from the lengthy trial and appeals processes of today. Czolgosz was tried and found guilty of assassinating the president a little more than three weeks after he pulled the trigger, and he was in his grave within eight weeks. Compare that with the case of Timothy McVeigh, who was found guilty of the 1995 Oklahoma City terrorist bombing but was not executed until 2001, six years after the crime.

[6] Murat Halstead, *The Illustrious Life of William McKinley, Our Martyred President*, p. 54.

[7] Halstead, p. 55.

[8] John Mason Potter, *Plots Against the President*, p. 184.

49. Harvey Milk

[1] San Francisco Mayor George Moscone was assassinated by Daniel White before he shot Milk. Milk's murder has retained the notoriety over the years, though, because of its blatant homophobic motivation.

[2] This is from a chillingly precognitive tape recording Harvey Milk made for his staff and friends on November 18, 1977, with instructions to play it only if he was assassinated. A year and a week later, he was.

[3] From one of Dan White's early campaign brochures, quoted in the *New York Times*, November 29, 1978.

[4] Some sources say White was 34 at the time of the shooting. On November 28, 1978, the *New York Times* said White was 32.

50. Sal Mineo
1 1975, Internet Movie Database. (www.mdb.com)
2 Some reports say January 10, 1939.
3 The *New York Times*, February 14, 1976.
4 Internet Movie Database.

51. Lord Mountbatten
1 In honor of Lord Mountbatten's naval leadership, Psalm 107 was read at Lord Mountbatten's funeral by Prince Charles, who was wearing full dress naval uniform.
2 *The New York Times*, August 28, 1979, p. 1.
3 *The Washington Post*, August 28, 1979, p. 17.
4 *Time*, September 10, 1979.
5 Quoted in Carl Sifakis, *Encyclopedia of Assassinations*, p. 151.

52. Hosni Mubarak
1 This was the statement made by President Clinton on June 26, 1995, after learning of the assassination attempt against President Mubarak. Source: *The Weekly Compilation of Presidential Documents,* July 3, 1995, Vol. 31, Issue 26, p. 1,136.
2 Only the AK-47s were actually used in the attack; the other artillery and the explosives were found later in vehicles abandoned by the assassins as they fled the scene.
3 *The New York Times*, September 7, 1999, p. A10.

53. Haing Ngor
1 *People*, March 11, 1996, Volume 45, Issue 10, p. 99.
2 There were (and still are) conflicting reports about Ngor's age. The Los Angeles Coroner reported that Ngor was 55 at the time of his death. Ngor's longtime publicist Marion Rosenberg, however, told the media that Ngor was 45 when he died.
3 *www.infobeat.com*
4 *People*, March 11, 1996, Volume 45, Issue 10, p. 99.
5 Martin Gilman Wolcott, *The Evil 100*, 12.

54. Richard Nixon
1 *The New York Times*, February 27, 1974.

55. Lee Harvey Oswald
1 From Winston Churchill's official statement on the assassination of President Kennedy.
2 *The New York Times*, November 27, 1963, p. A1.
3 *The New York Times*, November 26, 1963, p. A12.

56. Pope John Paul II
1 From *Witness to Hope* by George Weigel.
2 Ibid.
3 Quoted on *www.cnn.com*.
4 Quoted in *Encyclopedia of Assassinations*.

57. Pope Paul VI
1 Mendoza said this at a press conference on November 28, 1970. Quoted in *Mabini's Ghost* by Ambeth R. Ocampo.
2 *The New York Times*, January 13, 1971, p. 8.
3 *Catechism of the Catholic Church*, p. 635.
4 *The Top 100 Catholics of the Century. (www.dailycatholic.org/issue/archives/ 1999Dec2,vol.10,no.229txt/ dec2top.htm)*
5 *The New York Times*, November 27, 1970, p. 11.
6 Ibid.

58. Yitzhak Rabin

1 This is from the last speech Rabin gave before he was assassinated. *The New York Times*, November 5, 1995, p. A16.
2 Carl Sifakis, *The Encyclopedia of Assassinations*, p. 178.
3 Sifakis, p. 179. (*www.cnn.com/WORLD/9511/rabin/index.html*)
4 *www.cnn.com/WORLD/9511/rabin/index.html*

59. Rasputin

1 Alex De Jonge, *The Life and Times of Grigorii Rasputin*, p. 327.
2 Some sources say December 22, 1916, and some say January 2, 1917.

60. Ronald Reagan

1 January 11, 1990.
2 March 30, 1981.
3 Judith St. George, *Ronald Reagan*.
4 Entered into evidence at Hinckley's trial, making it a matter of public record and, therefore, public domain.

61. George Lincoln Rockwell

1 Frederick J. Simonelli, *American Fuehrer*, p. 131.
2 Rockwell's bodyguard and friend, Frank Smith, did not believe Patler was the killer and that his assassination was part of a conspiracy involving high level officials from the American Nazi Party. From *American Fuehrer* (p. 138): "Distrustful of the police—and fulfilling a pledge he made to Rockwell in the event of his death by assassination—Smith conducted his own investigation. It led him to conclude that [Matt] Koehl, [William L.] Pierce, and [Robert Allison] Lloyd had masterminded the assassination. Smith identified Christopher Vidnjevich, a violent and unstable ANP officer from the party's Chicago headquarters, as Rockwell's killer...Smith's investigation and subsequent accusations culminated in a gunfight between Smith and Vidnjevich in rural Maine. Both men survived. Smith declined to pursue his allegations through conventional channels."
3 *The New York Times*, August 26, 1967, p. 14.
4 *The New York Times*, December 16, 1967, p. 33.
5 George Lincoln Rockwell, *Why Nazism?*, an American Nazi party pamphlet from the early sixties.
6 George Lincoln Rockwell, *This Time the World*, p. 154–55.

62. Franklin Delano Roosevelt

1 Zangara said this after being sentenced to die in the electric chair for the death of Chicago Mayor Anton Cermak. (*www.eastlandmemorial.org/zangara.shtml*)
2 *The New York Times*, February 15, 1933, p. 2.
3 *The New York Times*, February 17, 1933, p. 1.

63. Theodore Roosevelt

1 From the 50-minute speech Theodore Roosevelt delivered immediately after being shot. He unbuttoned his vest and showed the audience his bloody shirt before continuing with his talk. From *The New York Times*, October 15, 1912, p. 2.
2 Thomas Marshall was Theodore Roosevelt's vice president (but ended up running with Woodrow Wilson in the election of 1912 after

Roosevelt started his own party). Quoted in *TR and Will: A Friendship that Split the Republican Party* by William Manners, p. 310

3 Theodore Roosevelt's books: *The Naval War of 1812* (1882); *Hunting Trip of a Ranchman* (1885); *Life of Thomas Hart Benton* (1887); *Gouverneur Morris* (1888); *Ranch Life and the Hunting Trail* (1888); *The Winning of the West 1769–1807* (4 volumes, 1889–1896); *New York* (1891); *Hero Tales from American History* (1895); *Rough Riders* (1899); *African Game Trails* (1910); *The New Nationalism* (1910); *History as Literature, and Other Essays* (1913); *Theodore Roosevelt, An Autobiography* (1913); *Through the Brazilian Wilderness* (1914); *Life Histories of African Game Animals* (1914); *America and the World War* (1915); *Fear God and Take Your Own Part* (1916); *The Foes of Our Own Household* (1917); *National Strength and International Duty* (1917).

4 *The Milwaukee Journal Sentinel,* January 27, 1998, p. 1.

5 *The New York Times,* October 15, 1912, p. 1.

64. Anwar el-Sadat

1 Camelia Sadat, *My Father and I,* p. 172.

2 Mohammed Keikal, *Autumn of Fury: The Assassination of Sadat,* pp. 260–61.

65. Theresa Saldana

1 *Los Angeles Times,* June 2, 1989.

2 *A Biographical Dictionary of World Assassins.*

3 *The New York Times,* November 6, 1984.

4 *Newsday,* July 21, 1989.

5 Internet Movie Database. (*www. imdb.com*)

66. Rebecca Schaeffer

1 Katherine Ramsland, "Stalkers: The Psychological Terrorist."

2 Mike Tharp, "In the Mind of a Stalker."

3 Internet Movie Database. (*www. imdb.com*)

4 This is the film that seems to have triggered Bardo's murder of Schaeffer. In the movie, Schaeffer is seen in bed with a man and, because he was utterly incapable of separating fantasy from reality, Bardo interpreted this scene as evidence of Schaeffer's complete abandonment of morals, and he vowed to teach her a lesson.

67. Monica Seles

1 *Sports Illustrated,* July 17, 1995.

2 Ibid.

3 *A Biographical Dictionary of the World's Assassins.*

4 *Sports Illustrated,* July 17, 1995.

5 *The New York Times,* May 1, 1993.

68. William Henry Seward

1 *Speech on the Irrepressible Conflict,* October 25, 1858.

2 John M. Taylor, *William Henry Seward: Lincoln's Right Hand,* p. 248.

3 Roy Z. Chamlee, Jr., *Lincoln's Assassins,* p. 2.

4 Taylor, p. 248.

5 Taylor, p. 244.

69. Alexander Solzhenitsyn

1 *The First Circle,* Ch. 17.

2 "Me and Bobby McGee," 1969.

70. Margaret Thatcher

1 From Margaret Thatcher's speech to the Conservative Party following the

terrorist bombing attempt on her life. Quoted in Margaret Thatcher, *The Downing Street Years*, p. 382.
[2] *The Downing Street Years,* p. 379.
[3] *www. biography.com*

71. Leon Trotsky
[1] Carl Sifakis, *The Encyclopedia of Assassinations*, p. 217.
[2] *The New York Times*, June 19, 1940, p. 8.
[3] *The New York Times*, August 22, 1940, p. 14.
[4] Leon Trotsky, *My Life*.

72. Harry S Truman
[1] A calm and collected Truman said this after the gun battle in front of the Blair House during an assassination attempt by two Puerto Rican Nationalists. Quoted in *American History*, July/August 1997, Vol. 32, Issue 3, p. 32.

73. Gianni Versace
[1] Liz Tilberis was the editor in chief of *Harper's Bazaar* at the time of Versace's death and wrote this in an Op-Ed piece in *The New York Times*, July 16, 1997, p. 19.
[2] *The Advocate*, February 17, 1998, Issue 753, p. 13.

74. George Wallace
[1] Wallace said this to the *Detroit News* and it was quoted in "Portrait of an Assassin." (*www.pbs.org*)
[2] *The New York Times*, May 16, 1972, p. 34.
[3] *The New York Times*, May 18, 1972, p. 1.

75. Andy Warhol
[1] Victor Bockris, *Warhol*.
[2] Bockris.
[3] There is some question as to the accuracy of Warhol's date of birth. The years 1927, 1929, and 1930 have also been cited. August 6, 1928 is the commonly accepted date, however, and is the date on which Warhol would celebrate his birthday. August 6, 1928 is also the date used on Warhol's tombstone.

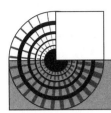

Selected Sources

Abrams, Herbert L. *"The President Has Been Shot": Confusion, Disability, and the 25th Amendment.* Stanford, Calif.: Stanford University Press, 1992.

Allen, Felicity. *Jefferson Davis: Unconquerable Heart.* Columbia, Missouri: University of Missouri Press, 1999.

American Political Leaders, 1789–2000. Washington, D.C.: Congressional Quarterly, 2000.

Andrews, Jay David. *Young Kennedys: The New Generation.* New York: Avon, 1998.

Bakeless, John. *The Tragicall History of Christopher Marlowe.* Hamden, Conn.: Archon Books, 1942.

Baldwin, James. *One Day, When I Was Lost: A Scenario Based on Alex Haley's "The Autobiography of Malcolm X."* New York: Dell, 1992.

Ballard, Michael B. *A Long Shadow: Jefferson Davis and the Final Days of the Confederacy.* Jackson, Miss.: University Press of Mississippi, 1986.

Barrett. A. A. *Agrippina: Sex, Power, and Politics in the Early Empire.* New Haven, Conn.: Yale University Press, 1996.

Basler, Roy P., editor. *The Collected Works of Abraham Lincoln.* New Brunswick, N.J.: Rutgers University Press, 1953.

Bernstein, Carl, and Marco Politi. *His Holiness: John Paul II and the Hidden History of Our Time.* New York: Doubleday, 1996.

Bishop, Jim. *The Day Kennedy Was Shot.* New York: Gramercy Books, 1984.

Bloom, Harold, editor. *Christopher Marlowe.* New York: Chelsea House Publishers, 1986.

Bobb, Dilip. *The Great Betrayal: Assassination of Indira Gandhi.* New Delhi, India: Vikas Publishing, 1985.

Bockris, Victor. *Warhol.* New York: Da Capo Press, 1997.

Bogosian, Eric. *Talk Radio.* New York: Vintage Books, 1987.

Brands, H. W. *T. R.: The Last Romantic.* New York: Basic Books, 1997.

Brant, Marley. *Jesse James: The Man and the Myth.* New York: Berkley, 1998.

Bravin, Jess. *Squeaky: The Life and Times of Lynette Alice Fromme.* New York: St. Martin's Griffin, 1998.

Breihan, Carl W. *The Day Jesse James Was Killed.* New York: Bonanza Books, 1962.

Breitman, George, and Herman Porter. *The Assassination of Malcolm X.* New York: Merit Publishers, 1969.

Breitman, George: *The Last Year of Malcolm X: The Evolution of a Revolutionary.* New York: Schocken Books, 1968.

Bremer, Arthur H. *An Assassin's Diary.* New York: Pocket Books, 1973.

Brooke, C. F. Tucker. *The Life of Marlowe and the Tragedy of Dido, Queen of Carthage.* New York: Gordian Press, 1930.

Brooks, Stewart M. *Our Murdered Presidents.* New York: Frederick Fell, 1966.

Brown, Paul Alonzo. *The Development of the Legend of Thomas Becket.* Philadelphia, Pa.: University of Pennsylvania Press, 1930.

Buchan, John. *Julius Caesar.* London: Peter Davies Limited, 1932.

Bullock, Alan. *Adolf Hitler: A Study in Tyranny.* New York: HarperCollins, 1962.

Bumgarner, John R. *The Health of the Presidents: The 41 United States Presidents Through 1993 From a Physician's Point of View.* Jefferson, N.C.: McFarland & Company, 1994.

Butler, John. *The Quest for Becket's Bones: The Mystery of the Relics of St. Thomas Becket of Canterbury.* New Haven, Conn.: Yale University Press, 1995.

Caplan, Lincoln. *The Insanity Defense and the Trial of John W. Hinckley Jr.* Boston: Mass.: Daniel R. Godine, 1984.

Catechism of the Catholic Church. New York: Image Books, 1995.

Chambers, John Whiteclay II, editor. *The Oxford Companion to American Military History.* New York: Oxford University Press, 1999.

Chamlee, Roy Z. *Lincoln's Assassins: A Complete Account of Their Capture, Trial, and Punishment.* Jefferson, N.C.: McFarland & Company, 1990.

Charnwood, Lord. *Abraham Lincoln.* Garden City, N.Y.: Garden City Publishing, 1917.

Clark, James C. *The Murder of James A. Garfield: The President's Last Days and the Trial and Execution of His Assassin.* Jefferson, N.C.: McFarland & Company, 1993.

Clark, Ronald C. *Lenin: A Biography.* New York: Harper & Row, 1988.

Clarke, James W. *American Assassins.* Princeton, NJ: Princeton University Press, 1982.

——. *On Being Mad, Or Merely Angry: John W. Hinckley Jr. and Other Dangerous People.* Princeton, N.J.: Princeton University Press, 1990.

Compton, Piers. *The Turbulent Priest: A Life of St. Thomas of Canterbury.* London: Staples Press, 1957.

Cone, James H. *Martin & Malcolm & America: A Dream or a Nightmare.* New York: Orbis Books, 1991.

Cook, Don. *Charles De Gaulle: A Biography.* New York: G.P. Putnam's Sons, 1983.

Cooper, William J. Jr. *Jefferson Davis, American.* New York: Alfred A. Knopf, 2000.

Courtois, Stéphanie, Nicolas Werth, Jean-Louis Panné, Andrzej Paczkowski, Karel Bartosek, and Jean-Louis Margolin. *The Black Book of Communism: Crimes, Terror, Repression.* Boston, Mass.: Harvard University Press, 1999.

Crenshaw, Charles. *JFK: Conspiracy of Silence.* New York: Signet, 1992.

Dale, Philip Marshall. *Medical Biographies: The Ailments of Thirty-three Famous Persons.* Norman, Okla.: University of Oklahoma Press, 1952.

Davis, Jefferson. *The Rise and Fall of the Confederate Government*, Vols. 1 & 2. New York: Da Capo, 1990.

Davis, Lee. *Assassination: Twenty Assassinations That Changed History.* North Dighton, Mass.: JG Press, 1997.

Davison, Jean. *Oswald's Game.* New York: W. W. Norton & Co., 1983.

De Jonge, Alex. *The Life and Times of Grigorii Rasputin.* New York: Dorset Press, 1982.

Degregorio, William A. *The Complete Book of U.S. Presidents.* New York: Barricade Books, 1993.

Delaney, John J. *Pocket Dictionary of Saints.* New York: Doubleday, 1983.

Deutsch, Herman B. *The Huey Long Murder Case.* Garden City, N.Y.: Doubleday, 1963.

DiSalle, Michael V. *Second Choice.* New York: Hawthorn Books, 1966.

Dodd, William Edward. *Jefferson Davis.* New York: Russell & Russell, 1966.

Doenecke, Justus D. *The Presidencies of James A. Garfield and Chester A. Arthur.* Lawrence, Kansas: The University of Kansas Press, 1981.

Donald, David Herbert. *Lincoln.* New York: Simon and Schuster, 1995.

Downie, J. A., and J. T. Parnell, editors. *Constructing Christopher Marlowe.* Cambridge: Cambridge University Press, 2000.

Duffy, James P., and Vincent L. Ricci. *Target Hitler: The Plots to Kill Adolf Hitler.* Westport, Conn.: Praeger Publishers, 1992.

Dugan, Alfred. *Julius Caesar: A Great Life in Brief.* New York: Alfred A. Knopf, 1955.

Dyson, Michael Eric. *Making Malcolm: The Myth and Meaning of Malcolm X.* New York: Oxford University Press, 1995.

Eddowes, Michael. *The Oswald File.* New York: Clarkson N. Potter, 1977.

Encyclopedia Americana. Danbury, Conn.: Grolier, 2001.

Epstein, Edward Jay. *Inquest: The Warren Commission and the Establishment of the Truth.* New York: Bantam, 1966.

Estleman, Loren D. *Billy Gashade: An American Epic.* New York: Tor Books, 1997.

Fetherling, George. *A Biographical Dictionary of the World's Assassins*. New York: Random House, 2002.

Fineran, John Kingston. *The Career of a Tinpot Napoleon: A Political Biography of Huey P. Long*. New Orleans, La.: Private Press, 1986.

Fischer, Louis. *The Life of Lenin*. New York: Harper & Row, 1964.

Flynt, Larry. *An Unseemly Man: My Life as a Pornographer, Pundit, and Social Outcast*. New York: Dove Books, 1996.

Frank, Joe. *The Death of Trotsky*. [sound recording] Washington, D.C.: National Public Radio, 1979.

Frost-Knappman, Elizabeth, editor. *The World Almanac of Presidential Quotations: Quotations from America's Presidents*. New York: Pharos Books, 1988.

Fuhrmann, Joseph T. *Rasputin: A Life*. New York: Praeger, 1990.

Gaffikin, Frank. *Northern Ireland: The Thatcher Years*. London: Zed, 1990.

Ganguly, Meenakshi. "His Principle of Peace Was Bogus," February 14, 2000. (*www.time.com/time/asia/magazine/2000/0214/india.godse.html*)

Gardiner, Joseph L. *Departing Glory: Theodore Roosevelt as Ex-President*. New York: Scribner's, 1973.

Garrison, Jim. *On the Trail of the Assassins*. New York: Warner Books, 1991.

Geary, Rick. *The Fatal Bullet: The True Account of the Assassination, Lingering Pain, Death, and Burial of James A. Garfield, Twentieth President of the United States*. New York: Nantier, Beall Minoustchine, 1999.

Giancana, Sam, and Chuck Giancana. *Double Cross*. New York: Warner Books, 1992.

Gilbert, Martin. *Churchill: A Life*. New York: Henry Holt, 1991.

Gilbert, Robert E. *The Mortal Presidency: Illness and Anguish in the White House*. New York: Basic Books, 1992.

Godse, Gopal. *Gandhi's Murder & After*. Delhi, India: S. T. Godbole, 1989.

Goldman, Peter. *The Death and Life of Malcolm X*. New York: Harper & Row, 1973.

Gottschalk, Louis R. *Jean Paul Marat: A Study in Radicalism*. New York: Benjamin Bloom, 1927.

Gould, Lewis L. *The Presidency of William McKinley*. Lawrence, Kansas: Regents Press of Kansas, 1980.

Graves, Robert. *I, Claudius: From the Autobiography of Tiberius Claudius, Born B.C. 10, Murdered and Deified A.D. 54*. New York: Time, Inc., 1965.

Hair, William Ivy. *The Kingfish and His Realm: The Life and Times of Huey P. Long*. Baton Rouge, La.: Louisiana State University Press, 1991.

Halstead, Murat. *The Illustrious Life of William McKinley, Our Martyred President*. Privately published, 1901.

Hamerow, Theodore S. *On the Road to the Wolf's Lair: German Resistance to Hitler*. Cambridge, Mass.: The Belknap Press of Harvard University Press, 1997.

Hansen, Ron. *The Assassination of Jesse James by the Coward Robert Ford*. New York: W. W. Norton & Co., 1983.

Harrison, Alexander. *Challenging De Gaulle*. New York: Praeger, 1989.

Hayes, H. G., and C. J. Hayes. *A Complete History of the Trial of Charles Julius Guiteau, Assassin of President Garfield*. Philadelphia, Pa.: National Publishing Company, 1882.

Heikal, Mohamed. *Autumn of Fury: The Assassination of Sadat*. New York: Random House, 1983.

Hennisart, Paul. *Wolves in the City: The Death of French Algeria*. New York: Simon and Schuster, 1970.

Hertz, Emanual. *Lincoln Talks: A Biography in Anecdote*. New York: Viking Press, 1939.

Hidell, Al, and Joan D'Arc, editors. *The Conspiracy Reader: From the Deaths of JFK and John Lennon to Government-Sponsored Alien Coverups*. Secaucus, N.J.: Citadel Press, 1999.

Hinckley, Jack and Jo Ann Hinckley. *Breaking Points*. Grand Rapids, Mich.: Chosen Books, 1985.

Hitler, Adolf. *Mein Kampf*. New York: Houghton Mifflin, 1971.

Hoffman, Peter. *Hitler's Personal Security*. New York: Da Capo Press, 2000.

Hoover, Herbert. *The Memoirs of Herbert Hoover: The Cabinet and the Presidency, 1920–1933*. New York: Macmillan, 1951.

Horan, James D., and Paul Sann. *Pictorial History of the Wild West*. New York: Crown, 1954.

Hotson, J. Leslie. *The Death of Christopher Marlowe*. London: Nonesuch Press, 1925.

Hunter-Gault, Charlayne. *In My Place*. New York: Vintage Books, 1992.

Indiana, Gary. *Three Month Fever: The Andrew Cunanan Story*. New York: HarperCollins, 1999.

Jain, J.C. *The Murder of Mahatma Gandhi, Prelude and Aftermath*. Bombay, India: Chetana Limited, 1961.

Jeffers, H. Paul. *Sal Mineo: His Life, Murder, and Mystery*. New York: Carroll & Graf, 2000.

Johns, A. Wesley. *The Man Who Shot McKinley*. New York: A.S. Barnes, 1970.

Jordan, Vernon E., Jr., with Annette Gordon Reed. *Vernon Can Read!* New York: PublicAffairs, 2001.

Josephson, Matthew. *The Robber Barons*. New York: Harcourt Brace and Company, 1934.

Kaiser, Robert Blair. *"R.F.K. Must Die!" A History of the Robert Kennedy Assassination and Its Aftermath*. New York: E.P. Dutton, 1970.

Kane, Joseph Nathan. *Facts About the Presidents: A Compilation of Biographical and Historical Information*, 6th edition. New York: H. W. Wilson Company, 1993.

Karpin, Michael I., and Ina Friedman. *Murder in the Name of God: The Plot to Kill Yitzhak Rabin.* New York: Metropolitan Books, 1998.

Khosla, G.D. *The Murder of the Mahatma.* London: Chatto & Windus, 1963.

Klaber, William, and Philip H. Melanson. *Shadow Play.* New York: St. Martin's Press, 1997.

Knight, Janet M., editor. *Three Assassinations: The Deaths of John & Robert Kennedy and Martin Luther King.* New York: Checkmark Books, 1978.

Knowles, David. *Thomas Becket.* Stanford, Calif.: Stanford University Press, 1991.

Kramarz, Joachim. *Stauffenberg: The Architect of the Famous July 20th Conspiracy to Assassinate Hitler.* New York: Macmillan, 1967.

Lacoutre, Jean. *Nasser: A Biography.* New York: Alfred A. Knopf, 1974.

Lane, Mark. *Rush to Judgment.* New York: Fawcett Crest, 1967.

Lattimer, John K. *Kennedy and Lincoln: Medical and Ballistic Comparisons of Their Assassinations.* New York: Harcourt Brace Jovanovich, 1980.

Lee, Spike, with Ralph Wiley. *By Any Means Necessary: The Trials and Tribulations of the Making of Malcolm X.* New York: Hyperion, 1992.

Leech, Margaret. *In the Days of McKinley.* New York: Harper, 1959.

Lenwood, Davis G. *Malcolm X: A Selected Bibliography.* Westport, Conn.: Greenwood Press, 1984.

Lesher, Stephan. *George Wallace: American Populist.* Reading, Mass.: Addison-Wesley, 1994.

LeVert, Suzanne. *Huey P. Long: The Kingfish of Louisiana.* New York: Facts on File, 1995.

Levick, Barbara. *Claudius.* New Haven, Conn.: Yale University Press, 1990.

Lewis, Wm. Draper. *The Life of Theodore Roosevelt.* New York: United Publishers, 1919.

Lifton, David. *Best Evidence: Disguise and Deception in the Assassination of John F. Kennedy.* New York: Carroll & Graf, 1988.

Lloyd, Craig. *Aggressive Introvert: A Study of Herbert Hoover and Public Relations Management, 1912–1932.* Columbus, Ohio: Ohio State University Press, 1973.

Long, Huey P. *Every Man a King: The Autobiography of Huey P. Long.* New Orleans, La.: National Book Company, 1933.

Low, Peter. *The Trial of John W. Hinckley Jr.* Mineola, N.Y.: Foundation Press, 1986.

Lyons, Herbert. *Herbert Hoover: A Biography.* Garden City, N.Y.: Doubleday & Company, 1948.

Magill, Frank N. *Great Lives from History.* Englewood Cliffs, N.J.: Salem Press, 1987.

Malgonkar, Manohan. *The Men Who Killed Gandhi.* Delhi, India: Macmillan, 1978.

Malhotra, Inder. *Indira Gandhi: Personal and Political Biography.* Boston, Mass.: Northeastern University Press, 1989.

Manchester, William. *The Death of a President*. London: Michael Joseph, 1967.

Manners, William. *TR and Will: The Friendship that Split the Republican Party*. New York: Harcourt, Brace & World, 1969.

Mansfield, Peter. *Nasser's Egypt*. New York: Penguin, 1965.

Manvell, Roger, and Heinrich Fraenkel. *The Men Who Tried To Kill Hitler*. New York: Coward-McCann, 1964.

Markham, Ronald and Ron LeBreque. *Obsessed: The Stalking of Theresa Saldana*. New York: William Morrow & Co., Inc., 1994.

Maxwell-Stuart, P. G. *Chronicle of the Popes: The Reign-by-Reign Record of the Papacy from St. Peter to the Present*. London: Thames and Hudson, 1997.

McKinley, William. *Speeches and Addresses of William McKinley*. New York: Appleton, 1893.

McMillan, Priscilla Johnson. *Marina and Lee*. New York: Harper & Row, 1977.

McPherson, James M. *"To the Best of My Ability": The American Presidents*. New York: Dorling Kindersley, 2000.

———. *Abraham Lincoln and the Second American Revolution*. New York: Oxford, 1991.

Melanson, Philip H. *Spy Saga: Lee Harvey Oswald and U.S. Intelligence*. New York: Praeger Publishers, 1990.

———. *The Murkin Conspiracy: An Investigation into the Assassination of Dr. Martin Luther King Jr*. New York: Praeger Publishers, 1989.

Miller, Nathan. *Star-Spangled Men: America's Ten Worst Presidents*. New York: Scribner, 1998.

Moldea, Dan E. *The Killing of Robert F. Kennedy: An Investigation of Motive, Means and Opportunity*. New York: W. W. Norton & Co., 1995.

Momigliano, Arnaldo D. *Claudius: The Emperor and His Achievements*. Oxford, England: Clarendon Press, 1934.

Moore, Jim. *Conspiracy of One: The Definitive Book on the Kennedy Assassination*. Fort Worth, Texas: The Summit Group, 1991.

Morgan, H. Wayne. *William McKinley and His America*. Syracuse, N.Y.: Syracuse University Press, 1963.

Morgan, Ted. *FDR: A Biography*. New York: Simon and Schuster, 1985.

Morris, Edmund. *Dutch: A Memoir of Ronald Reagan*. New York: Random House, 1999.

———. *Theodore Rex*. New York: Random House, 2001.

Nash, Jay Robert. *Bloodletters and Badmen: A Narrative Encyclopedia of American Criminals, from the Pilgrims to the Present*. New York: M. Evans & Co., 1995.

Ngor, Haing. *Haing Ngor: A Cambodian Odyssey*. New York: Macmillan, 1987.

Noguchi, Thomas T., M.D., with Joseph Di Mona. *Coroner at Large*. New York: Simon and Schuster, 1985.

Nossiter, Adam. *Of Long Memory: Mississippi and the Murder of Medgar Evers.* Reading, Mass.: Addison-Wesley, 1994.

O'Balance, Edgar. *The Algerian Insurrection, 1954–62.* Hamden, Conn.: Archon Books, 1967.

Ocampo, Ambeth R. *Mabini's Ghost.* Manila, Philippines: Anvil Publishing, 1995.

Olcott, Charles S. *The Life of William McKinley.* Boston, Mass.: Houghton, Mifflin, 1916.

Orth, Maureen. *Vulgar Favors: Andrew Cunanan, Gianni Versace, and the Largest Failed Manhunt in U.S. History.* New York: Delacorte Press, 1999.

Oswald, Robert L., with Myrick Land and Barbara Land. *Lee: A Portrait of Lee Harvey Oswald.* New York: Coward-McCann, 1967.

"The Papal Years: Charisma and Restoration." (*www.cnn.com/SPECIALS/ 1999/pope/bio/papal*)

Parton, James. *Life of Jackson.* New York: Mason Brothers, 1860.

Pavy, Donald. *Accident and Deception: The Huey Long Shooting.* New Ibeiera, La.: Cajun Publishing, 1999.

Payne, Robert. *The Life and Death of Lenin.* New York: Simon and Schuster, 1964.

———. *The Life and Death of Trotsky.* New York: McGraw-Hill, 1977.

Pedrosa, Carmen Navarro. *Imelda Marcos: The Rise and Fall of One of the World's Most Powerful Women.* New York: St. Martin's Press, 1987.

Pepper, William F. *Orders to Kill: The Truth Behind the Murder of Martin Luther King.* New York: Carroll & Graf, 1995.

Peri, Yoram, editor. *The Assassination of Yitzhak Rabin.* Stanford, Calif.: Stanford University Press, 2000.

Picchi, Blaise. *The Five Weeks of Giuseppe Zangara: The Man Who Would Assassinate FDR.* Chicago, Ill.: Academy Chicago Publishers, 1998.

Pickles, Dorothy. *Algeria and France: From Colonialism to Cooperation.* New York: Praeger Publishers, 1963.

Pinciss, Gerald. *Christopher Marlowe.* New York: Frederick Ungar Publishing, 1975.

Posner, Gerald. *Case Closed: Lee Harvey Oswald and the Assassination of JFK.* New York: Random House, 1993.

Potter, John Mason. *Plots Against the Presidents.* New York: Astor-Honor, 1968.

Radzinsky, Edvard. *The Rasputin File.* New York: Doubleday, 2000.

Ramsland, Katherine. "Stalkers: The Psychological Terrorist." *www.thecrimelibrary.com* (Courtroom Television Network, 2001)

Randall, J. G., and Richard N. Current. *Lincoln the President: Last Full Measure.* New York: Dodd, Mead & Company, 1955.

Ray, James Earl. *Who Killed Martin Luther King?* New York: Shooting Star Press, 1997.

Reader's Digest Press. *Legend: The Secret World of Lee Harvey Oswald.* New York: McGraw-Hill, 1978.

Report of the President's Commission on the Assassination of President Kennedy. Washington, D.C.: United States Government Printing Office, 1964.

Rohrs, Richard C. "Partisan Politics and the Attempted Assassination of Andrew Jackson." *Journal of the Early Republic*, 1981.

Rosa, Joseph G. *Alias Jack McCall: A Pardon or Death?* Kansas City, Kans.: University of Kansas Press, 1967.

———. *Wild Bill Hickok: The Man & His Times.* Lawrence, Kans.: University of Kansas Press, 1996.

Rosenberg, Charles E. *The Trial of the Assassin Guiteau: Psychiatry and the Law in the Gilded Age.* Chicago, Ill.: University of Chicago Press, 1995.

Ross, James. *I, Jesse James.* Thousand Oaks, Calif.: Dragon Publishing, 1988.

el-Sadat, Anwar. *In Search of Identity.* New York: Harper & Row, 1977.

Sadat, Camelia. *My Father and I.* New York: Macmillan, 1985.

Sandburg, Carl. *Abraham Lincoln: The Prairie Years and the War Years: One-Volume Edition.* New York: Harcourt, Brace and Company, 1954.

Scammell, Michael. *Solzhenitsyn: A Biography.* New York: W. W. Norton & Co., 1984.

Schoenbrun, David. *The Three Lives of Charles De Gaulle.* New York: Atheneum, 1968.

Schultz, Duane. *The Dahlgren Affair: Terror and Conspiracy in the Civil War.* New York: W.W. Norton & Co., 1999.

Segal, Ronald. *Leon Trotsky: A Biography.* New York: Pantheon Books, 1979.

Seles, Monica, and Nancy Ann Richardson. *Monica: From Fear to Victory.* New York: HarperCollins, 1996.

Service, Robert. *Lenin: A Biography.* Cambridge, Mass.: Harvard University Press, 2000.

Shearing, Joseph. *The Angel of the Assassination.* London: Heinemann, 1935.

Sheffer, Gabriel, editor. *Innovative Leaders in International Politics.* Albany, N.Y.: State University of New York Press, 1993.

Shilts, Randy. *The Mayor of Castro Street: The Life and Times of Harvey Milk.* New York: St. Martin's, 1982.

Sifakis, Carl. *Encyclopedia of Assassinations.* New York: Checkmark Books, 2001.

Simonelli, Frederick J. *American Fuehrer: George Lincoln Rockwell and the American Nazi Party.* Chicago, Ill.: University of Illinois Press, 1999.

Singh, Harbhajan. *Indira Gandhi: A Prime Minister Assassinated.* New Delhi, India: Vikas Publishing, 1985.

Singular, Stephen. *Talked to Death: The Life and Murder of Alan Berg.* New York: William Morrow and Co., 1987.

Sinkin, Stevie. *A Preface to Marlowe*. Essex, England: Pearson Education Limited, 2000.

Smith, Richard H. *Thomas E. Dewey and His Times*. New York: Simon and Schuster, 1982.

Smith, Theodore Clark. *The Life and Letters of James Abram Garfield*. Hamden, Conn.: Archon Books, 1968.

Solanas, Valerie. *The SCUM Manifesto*. New York: Olympia Press, 1968.

Spignesi, Stephen J. *JFK Jr.* Secaucus, NJ: Citadel Press, 1997.

———. *The Beatles Book of Lists*. Secaucus, N.J.: Citadel Press, 1998.

———. *The Italian 100*. Secaucus, N.J.: Citadel Press, 1997.

———. *The USA Book of Lists*. Franklin Lakes, N.J.: New Page Books, 2000.

St. George, Judith. *In the Line of Fire: Presidents' Lives at Stake*. New York: Holiday House, 1999.

Steers, Edward, Jr. *Blood on the Moon: The Assassination of Abraham Lincoln*. Lexington, Ky.: University of Kentucky Press, 2001.

Stern, Philip Van Doren. *The Man Who Killed Lincoln: The Story of John Wilkes Booth and His Part in the Assassination*. New York: Random House, 1939.

Stevens, Serita Deborah, with Anne Klarner. *Deadly Doses: A Writer's Guide to Poisons*. Cincinnati, Ohio: Writer's Digest Books, 1990.

Stryker, Susan, and James Van Buskirk. *Gay by the Bay: A History of Queer Culture in the San Francisco Bay Area*. San Francisco, Calif.: Chronicle Books, 1996.

Sullivan, George. *They Shot the President: Ten True Stories*. New York: Scholastic, 1993.

Sumner, William Graham. *Andrew Jackson as a Public Man: What He Was, What Chances He Had, and What He Did With Them*. Boston, Mass.: Houghton, Mifflin and Company, 1882.

Tannebaum, Samuel A. *The Assassination of Christopher Marlowe (A New View)*. Hamden, Conn.: The Shoe String Press, 1928.

Taylor, John M. *William Henry Seward: Lincoln's Right Hand*. New York: HarperCollins, 1991.

Tharp, Mike. "In the Mind of a Stalker." *U.S. News & World Report*. February 17, 1992 (Vol. 112, Issue 6).

Thatcher, Margaret. *The Downing Street Years*. New York: HarperCollins, 1993.

Thomas, Benjamin. *Abraham Lincoln*. New York: Alfred A. Knopf, 1952.

Thompson, Josiah. *Six Seconds in Dallas: A Microstudy of the Kennedy Assassination*. New York: Berkley, 1976.

Thomsett, Michael C. *The German Opposition to Hitler: The Resistance, the Underground, and Assassination Plots, 1938–1945*. Jefferson, N.C.: McFarland & Company, 1997.

Toland, John. *Hitler*. Garden City, N.J.: Doubleday, 1976.

Triplett, Frank. *The Life, Times & Treacherous Death of Jesse James.* Chicago, Ill.: Swallow Press, 1970.

Trotsky, Leon. *My Life.* New York: Charles Scribner's Sons, 1930.

Tucker, Robert C., editor. *The Lenin Anthology.* New York: W. W. Norton & Co., 1975.

Turner, Lowri. *Gianni Versace: Fashion's Last Emperor.* London: Essential, 1997.

Ulam, Adam B. *The Bolsheviks.* New York: Macmillan, 1965.

Vidal, Gore. *Lincoln.* New York: Random House, 1984.

Wallechinsky, David. *David Wallechinsky's Twentieth Century: History with the Boring Parts Left Out.* New York: Little, Brown and Company, 1995.

Warhol, Andy. *The Andy Warhol Diaries.* New York: Warner Books, 1989.

Warren Commission Report on the Assassination of President John F. Kennedy, The. Washington, D.C.: U.S. Government Printing Office, 1964.

Weigel, George. *Witness to Hope: The Biography of Pope John Paul II.* New York: Cliff Street Books, 1999.

Wells, H. G. *The Outline of History: Being a Plain History of Life and Mankind,* 2 volumes. Garden City, N.Y.: Garden City Books, 1961.

Wieczynski, Joseph L., editor. *The Modern Encyclopedia of Russian and Soviet History.* Gulf Breeze, Fla.: Academic International Press, 1982.

Williams, Harry T. *Huey Long.* New York: Alfred A. Knopf, 1970.

Wilson, Francis. *John Wilkes Booth: Fact and Fiction of Lincoln's Assassination.* New York: Houghton Mifflin, 1929.

Winston, Richard. *Thomas Becket.* New York: Alfred A. Knopf, 1967.

Wolcott, Martin Gilman. *The Evil 100.* New York: Kensington, 2002.

Wood, Joe, editor. *Malcolm X: In Our Own Image.* New York: St. Martin's Press, 1992.

X, Malcolm, and Bruce Perry, editor. *Malcolm X: The Last Speeches.* New York: Pathfinder, 1989.

X, Malcolm, with Alex Haley. *The Autobiography of Malcolm X.* New York: Grove Press, 1965.

Yang, Hugo. *The Iron Lady: A Biography of Margaret Thatcher.* New York: Farrar, Strauss Giroux, 1989.

Ziegler, Philip. *Mountbatten.* New York: Alfred A. Knopf, 1985.

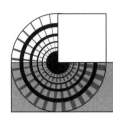

Index

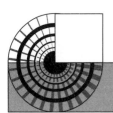

About the Author

Stephen J. Spignesi is a *New York Times*–bestselling author who writes about historical biography, popular culture, television, film, American and world history, and contemporary fiction.

Spignesi, christened "the world's leading authority on Stephen King" by *Entertainment Weekly* magazine, has written many authorized entertainment books and has worked with Stephen King, Turner Entertainment, the Margaret Mitchell Estate, Andy Griffith, Viacom, and other entertainment industry personalities and entities on a wide range of projects. Spignesi has also contributed essays, chapters, articles, and introductions to a wide range of books. Spignesi's more than 30 books have been translated into several languages, and he has also written for *Harper's, Cinefantastique, Saturday Review, TV Guide, Mystery Scene, Gauntlet,* and *Midnight Graffiti* magazines, as well as the *New York Times,* the *New York Daily News,* the *New York Post,* the *New Haven Register,* the French literary journal *Ténébres* and the Italian online literary journal, *Horror.It.* Spignesi has also appeared on CNN, MSNBC, Fox News Channel, and other TV and radio outlets, and in the 1998 E! documentary, *The Kennedys: Power, Seduction, and Hollywood,* as a Kennedy family authority, and in the A&E *Biography* of Stephen King that aired in January 2000. Spignesi's 1997 book *JFK Jr.* was a *New York Times* bestseller. Spignesi's *Complete Stephen King Encyclopedia* was a 1991 Bram Stoker Award nominee.

In addition to writing, Spignesi also lectures on a variety of popular culture and historical subjects and teaches writing in the Connecticut area. He is the founder and editor-in-chief of the small press publishing company, The Stephen John Press, which published the acclaimed feminist autobiography *Open Windows.*

Spignesi lives in New Haven, Connecticut, with his wife, Pam, and their cat, Carter, named for their favorite character on *ER.*

287